AFRO-HISPANIC POETRY

AFRO-HISPANIC POETRY
1940–1980
From Slavery to "Negritud" in South American Verse

Marvin A. Lewis

University of Missouri Press
Columbia, 1983

Copyright © 1983 by
The Curators of the University of Missouri
University of Missouri Press, Columbia, Missouri 65211
Library of Congress Catalog Card Number 82–25925
Printed and bound in the United States of America

Library of Congress Cataloging in Publication Data

Lewis, Marvin A., 1942–
    Afro-Hispanic poetry
    Bibliography: p.
    Includes index.
    1. Spanish American poetry—Black authors—
History and criticism.   2. Spanish American
poetry—20th century—History and criticism.
3. Blacks in literature.
I. Title.
PQ7552.P7L49   1983   861   82–25925
ISBN 0–8262–0405–8

For Judy, Monica, and Kevin—Latin lovers

Acknowledgments

My sincere appreciation to the families of Pilar Barrios and Virginia Brindis de Salas and to Nicomedes Santa Cruz, Adalberto Ortiz, Nelson Estupiñán Bass, Antonio Preciado, Jorge Artel, Hugo Salazar Valdés, and Juan Zapata Olivella for granting me permission to quote from their works. Thanks to the Ford Foundation Minority Fellowship Program, the Fulbright Commission, the Research Board of the University of Illinois, and the Newberry Library for providing me with financial and technical assistance. Thanks to Peggy Hills for typing the drafts and to Vera Mitchell, Stephen Fleming, and Leticia Díaz for editorial assistance.

*   *   *

A note on translations: unless otherwise indicated, all translations from Spanish into English are my own.

*,   *   *

M. A. L.
Urbana, Ill.
August 1983

Contents

We are in a free country;
And I don't find a reason
That we are oppressed
Only because of color.

—Timoteo Olivera, "To Men of Color"
Montevideo, September 1872

Introduction:
Toward a Definition of
Afro-Hispanic Poetry

Negroide, Negrista, Negro

Although my overall objective is to define and to demonstrate through specific examples and analyses precisely what Afro-Hispanic poetry is, it is imperative to begin with the essentials. In order to clarify basic terminology utilized in this study, it is useful to examine some of the labels attributed to literature written by and about authors of African descent in the Hispanic world. A sampling of the better-known critics reveals the following descriptions and classifications of the body of literature in question.

In the introductory remarks to her study *La poesía negroide en América (Blackish Poetry in America)*, Rosa E. Valdés Cruz classifies the genre under discussion as *poesía negroide* for the following reasons:

> Poetic manifestations about the life of the black man have received several denominations, such as "black poetry," "off black," "Afro-Cuban," "mulatta," "Afro-Antillean." We prefer to call it BLACKISH, without meaning any disrespectful treatment, because to us it seems more appropriate and more broad, since it embraces just as much the manifestations of Whites as of Blacks and mulattos.[1]

It is interesting that the term *blancoide* does not exist, especially when the term *negroide* carries negative connotations throughout the Americas in the sense that it suggests something less than authentic as related to blackness. Yet an all-encompassing term cannot embrace the literary production of black and nonblack writers and interpret the experiences of people of African descent in the Americas; it does not allow for the differences in perspectives presented by the authors. Sensibility, for example, is an important factor in their creative endeavors. There is a perceptible difference between writers who write about a collective personal experience and those who attempt to interpret circumstances that are foreign to them.

Oscar Fernández de la Vega and Alberto N. Pamies also offer a general definition of Afro-Hispanic poetry:

> Afroamerican poetry cannot be properly called "black poetry" but rather "mulatto poetry" being that in its verse is expressed the contrast and assimilation of cultures; expression of the sensibility of the Black, the mulatto, and the White through the sensibility of the Black in America whose psyche has been modified by the transition and by living the drama of slavery.[2]

1

The definition outlined by Fernández de la Vega and Pamies is similar to the one advanced by Valdés Cruz. These authors reflect a Caribbean attitude as demonstrated in their assimilationist thrust. The term *mulatto* is more appropriate as a biological term than as a poetic classification. In this case, Fernández de la Vega and Pamies are relying upon Fernando Ortiz's definition of *poesía mulata*, which has also provided the theoretical framework for Enrique Noble.

In an article entitled "Ethnic and Social Aspects of Negro Poetry of Latin America," Noble defines both *literatura negrista* and *poesía mulata*. First, "The name 'literatura negrista' implies two distinct concepts: one ethnic and the other esthetic. And neither of them excludes the other, because in the ethnic factor there is an implicit esthetic content. The recognition of this 'ethnic-esthetic' association is of special importance for the evaluation and understanding of this literature."[3] Regarding the second category, Noble explains:

> Let us speak now about the "poesía negra hispanoamericana," very properly called by Fernando Ortiz, the distinguished Cuban scholar, 'poesía mulata'. This mulatto poetry of Latin America presents the following characteristics:
> 1. It is essentially a social poetry.
> 2. It is poetry of contrasts and assimilation of cultures: the white, the Negro, and the mulatto cultures; or as we like to call it, a real racial *pluribum*, a *poesía mulata*.
> 3. It is a poetry in which we find the spiritual and esthetic plentitude of the poets of these areas, the accent of the poets in a unitive synthesis.
> 4. For this reason, it is an art of relation—human, cultural, and esthetic—peculiar to these cultural areas.[4]

Noble extends his definitions geographically to embrace "the Caribbean area and Venezuela, Colombia, Ecuador, and Peru."[5] While *mulata* might be acceptable in some of these regions, what about the *zambos* (those of Indian and black mixes) and *negros* of Colombia, Ecuador, and Peru whose cultural expressions form an integral part of the "ethnic-esthetic" amalgam? A broader definition is needed, however, to encompass works from beyond the Caribbean and the northern coast of South America. Concomitantly, *negrista*, just as *indigenista* (superficial interpretation of Indian culture) creates a problem because it refers to works written about Afro-Hispanic and Indian peoples by authors who do not belong to these ethnic groups and who do not possess the necessary cultural sensitivity to interpret accurately the experiences portrayed.

Two critics who have grappled with the problem and who have made progress toward a coherent definition of Afro-Hispanic poetry, from a *negrista* perspective, are José Luis González and Mónica Mansour: "The themes of Iberoamerican 'off-black' poetry are specifically of blacks, their customs, their traditions, their origins, their poverty, their pride: it is a poetry *about* blacks and *for* blacks . . . what distinguishes it is the aforementioned 'sensibility': it is a poetry *by* blacks."[6] Mansour's conception of black poetry has evolved since her early formulation in a 1973 publication.[7] If the word *negra* (written from black perspective, stressing positive qualities) were substituted for *negrista,* we would have a working definition of black poetry; *negrista* carries some of the same negative connotations as *negroide.* In a positive vein, the idea that this literature is about, for, and by blacks, with black sensitivity and sensibility, is essential in any discussion of Afro-Hispanic poetry. Afro-Hispanic poets interpret their experiences from within rather than by merely describing a set of circumstances with which they are familiar. They tend to stress positive human qualities and values from a culturalist perspective.

In Spanish America the term *poesía negra* has some of the same problems of application as *poesía mulata* due to both ethnic and ideological reasons. *Afro-Hispanic,* however, indicates a poetry by, about, and written to but not just for people of African descent in the Spanish-speaking world. The writers include *negros, mulatos,* and *zambos.* Of course none of the authors in this study concentrates entirely upon black topics, but a significant portion of their literary production interprets the experiences of blacks in the Americas based upon firsthand experiences and knowledge. *Afro-Hispanic* is therefore intended to suggest both ethnic categories and a type of literary output. Since black (*negro*) in Spanish America also carries negative connotations, my discussions center on poets who acknowledge their black African heritage as being important in their artistic and personal lives but who do not necessarily write from a racist perspective.

Negritud

Although no organized movement grew up around *negritud (negritude* in English) in Spanish-speaking South America comparable to what the French-speaking worlds of Africa and the Caribbean experienced *(négritude),* most Afro-Hispanic authors adhere to the basic tenets of *negritud* in regard to their culture and identity, Viewed in its Spanish American context, *negritud,* according to Leopoldo Zea, "is an ideological concept that has its origin in a situation that is common to the men of black Africa and Afroamerica—the situation of dependency."[8] Within the contexts of colonialism and dependency, Zea analyzes both *negritud* and *indigenismo* (the analogous movement among the indigenous populations) as ideological concepts common to African and Indian peoples in their adverse relationships with Europeans. White racism is a determining factor in their oppression and subsequent reaffirmation of positive cultural values. *Negritud* consists of a reaffirmation of black culture and a rejection of white values that are often synonymous with discrimination, economic exploitation, and racial superiority. The technological society and its excessive materialism are also points of discontent for advocates of *negritud.* White society has become estranged from itself and must regain the basic values of life through an introspective reassessment. An understanding of aspects of African culture provides this opportunity for reaffirmation among blacks.

From the South American literary perspective, *negritud* has received the attention of Adalberto Ortiz, who seeks to define this term within the continent's cultural frontiers. He points out six major factors that are crucial for black artists in interpreting Afro-Hispanic culture, especially folklore, literature, music, plastic arts, religion, and world view. These six elements, plus Bantu philosophy, mask culture, drum language, black music, dances, myths, and legends, compose a great deal of black cultural expression in South America.[9]

Ortiz is indebted to Janheinz Jahn for development and application of the aforementioned concepts surrounding neo-African cultures. In *Muntu: The New African Culture*, Jahn devotes chapters to religion, dance, African philosophy, literary creation, style, literary history, and cultural conflicts. Jahn defines *negritud* as "nothing more nor less than the conscious beginning of neo-African literature. . . . Negritude has restored the legitimacy of belonging to African culture."[10] Throughout the Americas, *negritud* had the impact of revitalizing interest in and placing positive emphasis upon the African cultural heritage in societies that quite often denied its value.

Moreover, the process of developing positive self-identity enables blacks to prepare for their cultural integration into the societies of which they form a part. The knowledge that they too are contributing to the cultural amalgam in a positive sense reinforces what René Depestre calls *cimarronaje cultural*, fleeing a dominating culture's values in order to establish personal values. Cultural maroonage serves to reconstruct a lost persona; when blacks were uprooted from Africa, cultural traditions were destroyed. According to Depestre, rejection of some of the dominant culture's values along with the capacity of collective memory and imagination allowed blacks to invent new rules governing life in a society bent upon restructuring the personality. This creative vitality is manifested in many ways, including work, marriage and the family, religion, folklore, death rituals, dance, sex, magic, popular medicine, oral literature, games, concepts of beauty, mythology, and armed resistance.[11] These are, of course, essential cultural expressions that underlie the contemporary search for identity among black people in the Americas. That the very values outlined above are what proponents of *negritud* look for when they seek to reaffirm Afro-Hispanic values is testimony that they have been present for centuries. Nevertheless, in most Spanish American societies, remnants of *negritud* can be useful only in facilitating the process of integration into the national cultures rather than in aiding a flight to the past.

From a literary point of view, marriage, family, religion, folklore, language, food, funeral rituals, dance, music, oral tradition, myths, and armed resistance are the stuff creative writers draw upon constantly. For black writers in Uruguay, Peru, Ecuador, and Colombia, these themes provide the impetus for their own sense of *negritud*, which occurs on many different levels. The creative process involves in most cases a breaking away from standard societal values, finding oneself in the African heritage, followed by a subsequent return to the mainstream, but on one's own terms.

Themes and Concepts

In addition to the basic themes prevalent in Afro-Hispanic literature, a number of key concepts underly this artistic output. As outlined by Richard Jackson and Martha Cobb, they are confrontation, dualism, identity, and liberation. Cobb defines these concepts in the following manner:

1) confrontation—with an alien and hostile society;
2) dualism—or a sense of division between one's own concept of self in conflict with the definitions imposed by the dominant culture;
3) identity—a search that embraces the who am I? of the present situation while at the same time it probes both African origins and historic bases in the Americas; and
4) liberation—political and psychical, which has been the predominating quest of black people since their historic confrontation with the West. [12]

Although this particular study by Cobb is designed for the Caribbean and the United States, the basic tendencies outlined are also applicable to the South American continent. Ethnicity, identity, self-affirmation in an internally colonized situation, and the myth of Africa are vital issues. This particular thematic approach represents, in the words of Richard Jackson, an attempt "to apply a critical framework to Afro-Hispanic literature built in part on the thematic model of the basic tenets of French *Négritude* and in part on the more recently defined literary characteristics of the black aesthetic, the cultural arm of Black Nationalism in the United States." [13] In a word, the definitions and concepts that I have discussed all lead in this direction.

In spite of the national cultural differences among black people in South America, there is at least one common denominator that most of their ancestors shared: the experience of slavery and the negative stigma attached to this institution. In an effort to find positive images and symbols in the colonial period, most writers examine the African connection—not in the sense of a physical retreat to Africa or things African but rather as a quest for a format upon which to construct a mythic world.

Myth, in this sense, represents a symbolic projection of a people's collective values and aspirations. Africa, and its meaning for New World black writers, has been the topic of discussion for Edward Kamau Brathwaite, who offers the following enlightened comments concerning the literary tradition in the Caribbean and, by analogy, throughout the Americas:

> There are four kinds of written African literature in the Caribbean; the first is *rhetorical*. The writer uses Africa as mask, signal, or *nomen*. He doesn't know very much about Africa necessarily, although he reflects a deep desire to make connections. But, he is only saying the word "Africa" or invoking a dream of the Congo, Senegal, Niger, the Zulu, Nile, or Zambesi. He is not necessarily celebrating or activating the African presence. There are also elements of this romantic rhetoric within the other three categories. The second is what I call *the literature of African survival*, a literature which deals quite consciously with African survivals in Caribbean society, but without necessarily making any attempt to interpret or reconnect them with the great tradition of Africa. Third,

there is what I call *the literature of African expression,* which has its root in the folk, and which attempts to adapt or transform folk material into literary experiment. Finally, there is *the literature of reconnection,* written by Caribbean (and New World) writers who have lived in Africa and are attempting to relate that experience to the New World, or who are consciously reaching out to rebridge the gap with the spiritual heartland.[14]

Most of the literature written by South American authors falls within the categories of rhetorical and African survival due to the separation in time and space from Africa. However, their preoccupation is important because it represents the recognition of an important element of their cultural heritage. The writers often use the African *nomen* to create a nostalgic, paradisiacal image that stands in ironic juxtaposition to the adverse social circumstances with which generations of blacks have had to contend in the Americas.

Related to Africa is the concept of time, linear and mythic. In a recent critical evaluation of time in both a traditional agrarian culture (Africa-mythic) and a highly industrialized culture (United States-linear) and time's relationship to the fiction of Africa, the Caribbean, and the United States, Bonnie J. Barthold arrives at some temporal parameters that are applicable to this study: "Thus the movement [Richard] Wright describes implies a movement from an emphasis on synchrony, from what other writers have termed 'mythic' or 'cyclic' time, toward diachrony, toward a preference for history in which time is seen as linear sequence."[15] Consequently, Barthold views the passage of time in three phases: cyclic time—myth; the interval of passage; and linear time—history.[16] These categories are evident in the majority of poets treated in this discussion. Specifically, mythic time for them is related to the African context, the place of origin culturally and literarily; the interval of passage represents both the transition from an African to a Hispanic identity as well as a search for literary roots; finally, linear time represents full participation in their national cultures as well as entrance into the literary mainstream.

The trajectory of most Afro-Hispanic writers begins with a work probing their origins and identity and moves progressively toward the Western literary tradition. Therefore, most of their first works were written during a personal interval of passage, which culturally assesses both synchronic and diachronic time with emphasis upon the former. Ironically, blacks are viewed as being in a temporal state of flux in regard to the past and the future. According to Barthold, they are "cut off and dispossessed from both the mythic cycle of Africa and the linear flow of Western time."[17] The sense of temporal estrangement expressed by this group of black writers from South America is compounded by the fact that their African heritage is constantly denied in the push for national homogeneity and miscegenation. When blackness at both the social and linguistic levels of signified and signifier becomes synonymous with negativity, a tremendous amount of pressure to conform is exerted. Therefore, to progress from the now of an existing negative state to a better tomorrow represents a constant artistic and human goal. This can be achieved, in most cases, only with a backward glance at the mythic past, a search for authenticity in the present, and a reaffirmation of self-worth for the future struggle.

The Writers

This study is an examination of selected volumes of poetry by nine major writers of African descent in South America: Virginia Brindis de Salas (Uruguay), *Pregón de Marimorena* (*The Call of Mary Morena*, 1946); Pilar Barrios (Uruguay), *Piel negra* (*Black Skin*, 1947); Nicomedes Santa Cruz (Peru), *Décimas* (*Décimas*, 1960) and *Cumanana* (*Cumanana*, 1964); Nelson Estupiñán Bass (Ecuador), *Canto negro por la luz* (*Black Song for Light*, 1954); Adalberto Ortiz (Ecuador), *Tierra, son y tambor* (*Earth, Rhythm and Drum*, 1945) and *Fórmulas* (*Formulas*, 1973); Antonio Preciado (Ecuador), *Jolgorio* (*Merriment*, 1961); and Jorge Artel (Colombia), *Tambores en la noche* (*Drums in the Night*, 1940) and *Antología Poética* (*Poetry Anthology*, 1979); Hugo Salazar Valdés (Colombia), *Carbones en el Alba* (*Coals at Dawn*, 1954) and *Rostro iluminado del Chocó* (*Illuminated Face of the Chocó*, 1980); and Juan Zapata Olivella, *Panacea: Poesía liberada* (*Panacea: Liberated Poetry*, 1976). These volumes embrace a span of forty years and most of the continent.

Although my main concern is the ethnic poetry of these writers, I do discuss poems on other themes in the volumes: the writers consider themselves poets, first and foremost, not polemicists. My study is based upon the hypothesis that in spite of temporal and spatial distances between writers there is continuity in the black poetic experience throughout South America, thematically, structurally, and ideologically. My discussion of each author, consequently, is preceded by an examination of the society of which he or she forms a part. I will concentrate upon the most significant volumes by each poet.

My approach to the writers consists of a culturalist evaluation of their poetry. Basic concerns to which this study addresses itself are *negritud*, the myth of Africa, miscegenation, ethnicity and identity, black culture, and the relationships between the black writers and their respective societies. Because of the nature of the materials studied, my critical method is eclectic, employing a combination of formalist, sociological, historical, dialectical, archetypal, and mythic criticism. The works are criticized both as poetry and as interpretations of reality. On the one hand, I arrive at a better understanding of the level of black consciousness in Spanish America. On the other, I examine some of the similarities and differences—technically, thematically, and conceptually—between black writers who are separated in time and space.

Therefore, my approach to these writers is in line with the theory of "common sense" criticism articulated by Catherine Belsey. "Common sense," she writes, "assumes that valuable literary texts, those which are in a special way worth reading, tell truths—about the period which produced them, about the world in general or about human nature—and that in doing so they express the particular perceptions, the individual insights, of their author."[18] These attitudes are certainly applicable to Afro-Hispanic poets from South America. Granted, a literary work is an autonomous structure or production. However, when viewed within its cultural context, outside of its formal, internal coherence, most literature achieves social significance. That is why the majority of the poetry of this particular group of Afro-Hispanic writers has to be analyzed as creative activity that interprets a concrete reality. Consequently, Brindis de Salas, Barrios, Santa Cruz, Ortiz, Estupiñán Bass, Preciado, Artel, Salazar Valdés, and Zapata Olivella, for the most part, poeticize from the perspective of expressive realism,[19] reflecting their perceptions of their individual cultures—each of which is represented in a separate chapter that traces the evolution of the contemporary black poetic tradition in that particular region.

This project also takes into account both development and stagnation in each writer's poetic trajectory and relates it to overall trends in Afro-Hispanic poetry. Primary emphasis is on the period from 1940 to 1980. Chapter 1 is an analysis of the poetry of Virginia Brindis de Salas and Pilar Barrios. Their works are examined within the context of the movement for Afro-Uruguayan identity that surfaced during the early decades of this century. Chapter 2 evaluates the poetry of Nicomedes Santa Cruz both within the popular Peruvian tradition and as it relates to international black awareness movements. Chapter 3 criticizes the poetry of two of the best-known Afro-Ecuadorian novelists, Adalberto Ortiz and Nelson Estupiñán Bass, as well as that of Antonio Preciado. Their works are discussed within the cultural traditions of Esmeraldas, one of Ecuador's chief ports. Chapter 4 treats Colombian writers Jorge Artel, Hugo Salazar Valdés, and Juan Zapata Olivella, three authors who approach the black experience from different perspectives but nevertheless offer equally valid interpretations. My conclusions assess the current status of Afro-Hispanic poets in South America.

1

Our Race:
Modern Afro-Uruguayan Poetry

The Social Context

The exact number of blacks in Uruguay today is not known. The most recent estimate is that there are sixty thousand in a nation of 2.8 million, less than 2 percent of the population.[1] From before the founding of the Republic of Uruguay in 1830, blacks have been consistently instrumental in the formation and the development of the nation. This was especially true in the wars for independence from Brazil beginning in 1825, when two slaves, Dionisio Oribe and Joaquín Artigas, were among the original thirty-three patriots who proclaimed liberty or death. Nevertheless, since the abolition of slavery in 1853, Afro-Uruguayans have remained second-class citizens. Although discrimination based upon color ceased to exist officially, blacks have found themselves economically impotent and excluded from the mainstream of Uruguayan life. Just as most blacks do throughout the Americas, Uruguayans find that the stigma attached to slavery is still a heavy burden to bear.

Over the years, the Afro-Uruguayan has been the target of some scholarly activity by renowned social scientists. Among works that treat the contemporary scene are *El negro en el uruguayo: Pasado y presente (The Black in Uruguay: Past and Present*, 1965) by Ildefonso Pereda Valdés; *Los afro-uruguayos (The Afro-Uruguayans*, 1967) by Carlos M. Rama; and both *El negro uruguayo: hasta la abolición (The Uruguayan Black: Until Abolition*, 1965) and *Estudios afros: Brasil-Paraguay-Uruguay-Ecuador (Afro Studies: Brazil-Paraguay-Uruguay-Ecuador*, 1971) by Paulo de Carvalho-Neto. All are solid studies that take into account the Afro-Uruguayans' historical trajectory as well as their presence in contemporary society. The two works by Carvalho-Neto are particularly interesting because *The Uruguayan Black* is a collection of the best cultural and historical articles available and *Afro Studies* includes the most complete annotated bibliography on Afro-Uruguayans. The studies by Pereda Valdés and Rama present a more recent assessment of the present situation of black Uruguayans. After commenting on their situation throughout the centuries, Rama devotes several pages to racism and discrimination, observing rather casually, "In recent years there have been isolated cases in professions such as teaching; or in the admission to public establishments that must be studied systematically. But the prejudice against Blacks as it is carried out in the Uruguayan social historic development is being replaced by the prejudice of classes, or functions on different levels that even shows its [prejudice's] modernity."[2] This argument is familiar, but it must be reiterated that in the Uruguayan context class prejudices are based upon color. Nevertheless, according to Rama, more tolerance of blacks and less color prejudice and tension has led to a reduction of the group classified as *negro* and has sped up miscegenation. Rama's noncommital attitude is maintained in his discussion of twentieth-century black intellectual and political movements that sought to foster equality, justice, and progress.

Rama speaks as if the achievements of black intellectuals were just the efforts of a few uppity ones instead of a concerted effort by the majority to have some say in their destiny. The activities of these black scholars, which Rama did not bother to investigate, have been studied recently by Rout, Jackson, Pereda Valdés, and others. Rama, then, views discrimination and racism against blacks as part of the normal Uruguayan social process. He seems to be saying that there is no need for alarm since soon there will be no blacks with whom to contend.

A realistic view of the situation of Afro-Uruguayans is presented by Pereda Valdés who makes the following assertion: "The standard of living of the colored man in Montevideo is poor, as can be appreciated by the menial functions that he carries out in society: doormen, soldiers, laborers, newspaper vendors."[3] Pereda Valdés uses recent statistical information to support his arguments surrounding the miserable black economic situation that is inseparable from their social level. His conclusion is that perhaps blacks are worse off now than they were during the epoch in which they were so valuable fighting in wars and protecting the national interest. Even normal, public service jobs are denied to blacks. The most important conclusion at which Pereda Valdés arrives after studying numerous case histories is one that has somehow escaped many Uruguayan social scientists:

> We believe that racial discrimination and prejudice very deeply imbedded in our society, with deeper roots than that which is supposed, is a barrier that thwarts the black people of Uruguay in their integral development. In Uruguay pertaining to the Black, Jim Crow is applied, not withstanding the guarantees of laws and the constitution, seeming to say to the Black we are equal but separate.[4]

Pereda Valdés does not hesitate to denounce racism and its impact in Uruguay. Also, his positive discussion of the black intellectual provides the basis for similar assessments by Richard Jackson and Leslie B. Rout in their discussions of periodical, artistic, and cultural activities. The reasons for our having such a small amount of published cultural materials by Afro-Uruguayans, according to Pereda Valdés, are that "the black writers in Uruguay do not have the possibility of finding editors for their books, they have not won prizes in literary contests even as a stimulus and they have not found the support they need from the State."[5] Therefore, it has to be considered a minor miracle that writers such as Virginia Brindis de Salas and Pilar Barrios were able to publish and distribute their works widely given the adverse social conditions they had to confront.

One of the most insightful assessments of the black situation in Uruguay is the series of interviews conducted by Alicia Behrens in 1956. In two articles, "What is the Situation of Blacks in Uruguay?" and "Racial Discrimination in Uruguay," she recorded interviews with blacks and influential employers and religious people in an effort to grasp the causes of Uruguayan racism and discrimination. One of her black informants was Ignacio Suárez Peña of the Centro Uruguay, a scholar and longtime observer of the social situation. After speaking of discrimination in stores, hotels, movies, casinos, and public transportation, he remarks:

> You will understand that being this way, that having many people who reject our company, it is almost impossible to find jobs where we have direct contact with the public, unless they are subordinate positions, like doorman, dishwasher or cook. In the stores no owner would dare hire a black salesman. You won't even find black waiters in the sweet shops or restaurants. As I say, discrimination exists and it is natural that it is this way. As for segregation, it is impossible to prove it, but they can always tell us we are not qualified to occupy high level jobs, or that the position has already been filled.[6]

Behrens documents these allegations of discrimination in her follow-up conversations with individuals in positions of power and influence. To what, then, can Uruguayan blacks aspire when they find decent jobs and the professions closed to them? Not very much. According to Behrens, "Whites can carry out any type of job, while Blacks only for being Black, without any examination, without considering their aptitude, no."[7] A great deal of this discrimination is supposedly based upon class; compound it with racism, and the future of Afro-Uruguayans does not appear very encouraging.

In an effort to counteract some of the oppression inherent in twentieth-century Uruguayan society, blacks banded together to form their own political, social, and literary organizations. In 1937 the Partido Autóctono Negro (Indigenous Black party) was founded with the idea of improving participation in the local political process. However, due to a lack of support by blacks, the party suffered a disastrous defeat in 1938. In 1944 it disbanded. A related social body was the Asociación Cultural y Social Uruguaya (Uruguayan Cultural and Social Association), organized in 1941, which provided an outlet for interaction among blacks until the 1960s.

In any serious discussion of Afro-Uruguayan literature and culture, the impact of a significant group of newspapers and periodicals has to be taken into consideration. It was in these cultural outlets that many aspiring writers, including Barrios and Brindis de Salas, published their first works. The publications include *La Conservación (Conservation)*, 4 August 1872–24 November 1872; *El Eco del Porvenir (Echo of the Future)*, 25 August 1901–15 October 1901; *La Propaganda (Propaganda)*, 3 September 1893–3 February 1895, 15 October 1903–15 January 1904, and 10 May 1911–12 April 1912; *La Verdad (Truth)*, 15 September 1911–31 July 1914; *Nuestra Raza (Our Race)*, 10 March 1917–31 December 1917 in San Carlos and 25 August 1933–September 1948 in Montevideo; *La Vanguardia (Vanguard)*, 15 January 1928–30 January

1928; *Rumbos (Directions)*, 25 August 1938–August 1945 in Rocha and August 1948–September 1950 in Montevideo; *Revista Uruguay (Uruguay Magazine)*, February 1945–October 1948; and *Revista Bahía Hulan Jack (Bahía Hulan Jack Magazine)*, May 1958 to the present.[8]

Throughout the decades, these publications have shared the common concern of improving the conditions of black people in Uruguay. Each contained social, literary, and historical information with the stated intent of making the black masses aware of their situation and role in a changing society. Toward that end the efforts of most of Uruguay's black intellectuals were directed. Blacks were constantly exhorted to participate as responsible citizens and to be cognizant of the culture of which they formed a part. As indicated in the length of existence of the periodicals, most fought a losing economic battle of survival, although the impact of each one was significant. *Our Race, Directions,* and *Uruguay Magazine* were the most successful. *Bahía Hulan Jack Magazine,* the latecomer, appears to have suffered always from a lack of direction in its attempt to champion national and international black causes, but it is still being published.

In addition to Pilar Barrios and Virginia Brindis de Salas, the most widely acclaimed Afro-Uruguayan writers, many others published their works in black-sponsored journals from 1872 to 1948. Included among them are Juan Julio Arrascaeta, Carlos Cardozo Ferreira, and Julio Guadalupe—poets contemporary to Brindis de Salas and Barrios. These lesser-known artists address issues of concern to most Uruguayans of African descent. Thematically, they assess black culture, the myth of Africa, their confrontation with Uruguayan society, the art and function of poetry, and other preoccupations. Arrascaeta, Ferreira, and Guadalupe are not currently publishing. The height of their activity came during the 1930s and the 1940s.

Julio Guadalupe was affiliated with *Directions* and published five poems in it between 1939 and 1942: "La madre negra" ("The Black Mother"), "Mi canto" ("My Song"), "Reflexión" ("Reflection"), "Adelaida" ("Adelaida"), and "Plenitud" ("Abundance"). Carlos Cardozo Ferreira's poetic output, what has come down to us, consists of six poems published in *Our Race* between 1936 and 1942: "Negro en la noche" ("Black in the Night"), "Negrita vive llorando" ("Black Girl You Live Crying"), "Hermano negro" ("Black Brother"), "Brindo" ("Toast"), "Invitación a negrita" ("Invitation to a Black Girl"), and "La chispa en el bosque" ("The Spark in the Forest"). Eight of Juan Julio Arrascaeta's poems were published in the *Uruguay Magazine* between 1946 and 1948: "El negro oriental" ("The Uruguayan Black"), "Tamborilero" ("Drummer"), "Ríe, ríe, moreno" ("Laugh, Laugh, Black Man"), "La muñeca" ("The Doll"), "La negrita" ("Black Girl"), "El gramillero" ("Gramillero"), "La comparsa" ("Rhythm"), and "Cuando ella recita" ("When She Recites"). As the majority of these titles indicates, their authors were operating within a framework of black cultural awareness. The number of poems actually published by these writers in no way accounts for their total production. As Pereda Valdés points out, black writers in Uruguay have neither found publishers for their books nor received prizes or support from the state. In a recent letter, Alberto Britos informed me that Arrascaeta is still writing.[9]

Our Race, Directions, and *Uruguay Magazine* took the initiative in providing a forum for literary expression and proved to be the impetus behind the drive for maintenance of cultural and ethnic awareness during the first several decades of this century. Out of this period of cultural fermentation emerged two black poets who were able to have their works published independently of the journal, Virginia Brindis de Salas and Pilar Barrios. Brindis de Salas is the author of *Pregón de Marimorena (The Call of Mary Morena,* 1946) and *Cien cárceles de amor (One Hundred Love Ballads,* 1949). Barrios, who was the editor of *Our Race* and a cofounder and supporter of the Indigenous Black party, has published three volumes of poetry: *Piel negra (Black Skin,* 1947); *Mis cantos (My Songs,* 1949); and *Campo afuera (The Outdoors,* 1959). The works of both poets have been reprinted since their original dates of publication. Unfortunately, not much is known about the current status of the works; references to Brindis de Salas and Barrios are not included in any studies of Uruguayan literature that I have seen by Uruguayans past or present. I will discuss the most significant volume of each writer: *The Call of Mary Morena* by Brindis de Salas and *Black Skin* by Barrios.

Virginia Brindis de Salas: The Call of Mary Morena

Virginia Brindis de Salas is the first black woman writer in South America to have two volumes of her poetry published and distributed widely. Like many other Afro-Hispanic writers, Brindis de Salas expresses concern for the black experience. Her interest is manifested thematically in an examination of the African origins of Uruguayan and Latin American culture, in questions surrounding ethnicity and identity, and in self-affirmation, as well as in other social topics common to black writers in the Americas. *The Call of Mary Morena* and *One Hundred Love Ballads* interpret the Afro-Uruguayan experience from slavery to the present day. Not all of her poems are concerned with personal ethnic situations, however, since her selections vary to embrace themes common to human existence.

The Call of Mary Morena, literally meaning *Brown Mary,* consists of four sections, "Ballads," "Calls," "Tangos," and "Songs," all of which contain compositions in free verse and suggest song and dance associated with the popular tradition. In the first part of this book, the poems vary thematically from love in "Madrigal" to a call for continental unity in "A la ribera americana" ("To the American Shore"). In between, Brindis de Salas comments upon artistic unity, "La hora de la tierra en que tú duermes" ("The Hour on Earth that You Sleep"); daily sustenance, "El pan legendario" ("Legendary Bread"); children and their social perceptions, "Prez para los niños sin canto" ("Prayer for Children without a Song"); nature, "El Cerro" ("The Hill"); war, "Sombras" ("Shadows"); and the black experience,

"Semblanza" ("Portrait"), "Es verdad, sí señor" ("It's True, Yes Sir"), and "Cristo Negro" ("Black Christ"). An analysis of several selections reflecting the thematic tendencies in this first section will suffice to demonstrate its poetic variety.

"Madrigal" is a brief but intense poem of desire:

> Tú miras mi carne morena
> con ojos que son dos ascuas;
> quisiera ser una fuente
> donde escancies sed de ansias.
>
> Quiero quemar la sangre
> de mis venas en el trópico
> de tu frenesí trashumante.
>
> (You look at my brown flesh
> With eyes that are two coals;
> I would love to be a fountain,
> Where you quench your anxious thirst.
>
> I desire to burn the blood
> Of my veins in the tropic
> Of your consuming frenzy.)[10]

From an internal, personal perspective, Brindis de Salas established a positive image of the black woman as desirable and sensual rather than as a mere rhythmic sex object, as presented by many *negrista* poets. Images of heat and passion underscore the sexual connotation here as she expresses the desire to be a repository for all of his frustrations. Apparently there is both physical and emotional distance between the poetic "you" and "I" since the relationship appears yet to be at the desire stage. The kinetic imagery is charged with longing—"coals," "burn," "tropic," "frenzy"—and if the poet has her way, there will be fulfillment. Metaphorically, the total essence of her being, flesh and blood, will serve as a reservoir, "fountain," from which the substance for a total physical and sentimental union can be drawn.

"To the American Shore" is a plea for continental unity among diverse ethnic groups. Midway through the work she states:

> Vamos por la ribera
> de esta América indígena y mulata
> en pos de la vereda
> que todo lo malo mata.
>
> El pecho fuerte y los brazos siempre abiertos;
> macho y hembra;
> multitud, barcos y puertos;
> y una bandera
> de un solo color
> hinchada al viento.
>
> (Let's go along the shore
> Of this indigenous and mulatta America

In pursuit of the direction
That all evil kills.

Firm chested and arms always open
Man and woman;
Multitude, ships and ports
And a flag
Of one color
Blowing in the wind.)

From Brindis de Salas's perspective, America should become a multiethnic community built on love and brotherhood. America should call upon her indigenous and mixed heritages to stress the positive in human beings. All components should work toward that end. She offers herself as an instrument of sacrifice to achieve harmony.

Hijos del suelo americano
blancos y negros hermanados;
tomad mi cuerpo,
gustad el sabor de mi carne morena;
quebrad el espasmo de la gruta del miedo
que a vuestra carne encierra!

(Children of America's soil
Blacks and Whites joined;
take my body,
enjoy the flavor of my brown flesh
break the spasm of the cave of fear
that surrounds your being!)

Through a combined effort involving all sexes and all ethnic groups, America can fulfill its potential as two continents of progress with emphasis upon human dignity and respect.

Another concern of Brindis de Salas's is war and its aftermath. "Shadows" is dedicated to the sailors of the Soviet Union, the United States, China, and Free France who have been victims of war:

Rostros sin una mueca
con manchas escarlatas
van y vienen en la noche
más densa del siglo veinte.

Labios sin una queja
en alas de blanda muerte;
bólidos surcando el cielo
zahiriendo al "Padre Eterno."

Cuerpos convulsos, magros;
bocas sin un sonido,
ojos que miran siempre
hacia la noche aguda.

(Faces without a grimace
with scarlet stains

go and come in the darkest
night of the twentieth century.

Lips without a complaint
on wings of soft death;
fireballs plowing the sky
provoking the Eternal Father.

Convulsive bodies, thin
mouths without a sound,
eyes that stare forever
toward the deep night.)

Anaphora with the negative sign "without" effectively accentuates this adverse picture of human destruction. All of the action in the first three stanzas takes place in the dreamlike, surreal ambiance of night. The most vital of human organs are disjointed as viewed in the "Faces without a grimace," "Lips without a complaint," and the "mouths without a sound." The arms of war—"fireballs"—are what determine human destiny. Morally, these acts are affronts to the worldly and divine orders. The surreal description concentrates upon individual parts of the body, separated as if in a giant puzzle. Aspects of normal daily life have long ceased to exist for the combatants. Finally, the poet injects herself into the scene while attesting to the fact that the victims were, indeed, Everyman. In negatively relating humans and nature in the stanzas that follow, pessimism reigns:

El mar al piélago arrastra
sus pobres humanidades;
y en la tierra socavada
de a centenares se pudren.

Cuando veas una sombra
en mitad de tu camino
y te hable, no te asustes
que no es fantasma, es un hombre.

(The sea to the high sea drags
its poor humans;
and in the caved earth
many hundreds rot.

When you see a shadow
in the middle of your path
and it speaks to you, don't be frightened
it is not a ghost, it is a man.)

Images of death persist because nature is involved in an adverse way as the sea destroys and the land consumes. At the end of "Shadows," the line between life and death is blurred completely as ghosts and men become inseparable. Through a combination of realistic and surrealistic imagery, Brindis de Salas achieves a stunning denunciation of war, presenting it as a destructive force whose impact is not limited to those directly involved.

Of the poems devoted to the black experience in the "Ballads" section,

"It's True, Yes Sir" denounces the social structure and attempts to link poetic and rhythmic traditions among blacks in Spain, the Caribbean, and Uruguay. "Black Christ" religiously advocates an eye for an eye, surmising that

> Sangre y llaga mucho enseñan
> Mejor amo es la Justicia
> que las lágrimas del valle del esclavo venerable.

> (Blood and wound teach a lot
> Justice is a better owner
> than the tears of the valley of the venerable slave.)

"Prayer for Children without a Song" criticizes poverty among black children in a slum area and "Portrait" describes a black woman.

"Prayer for Children without a Song" is an emotional poem in which the writer observes from a distance the children's activities. Spiritually, however, she is very near. The black children are joined by white children from the neighborhood and they sing together. But this does not improve the plight of the blacks because,

> En este patio inmundo
> todo destartalado
> no hay hamacas, ni muñecos . . .

> Si en sus cuartuchos viejos
> escasea el pan seco!

> (In this filthy yard
> poorly furnished
> there are neither hammocks nor dolls . . .

> Even in their dirty old rooms
> dry bread is scarce!)

What bothers the poet even more than the miserable physical conditions, which she portrays through negation, is the lack of love and affection for the children. The absence triggers a final outburst of sympathy on her part:

> Quiero la cabecita
> besar el niño negro
> y darle así mi tierno
> calor. Que circule su sangre
> en este amargo invierno.

> (I wish to kiss
> the head of the black child
> and give him that way my tender
> warmth. Let his blood flow
> in this bitter winter.)

Poverty and urban decay take a tremendous toll upon disadvantaged children. Within these depressing surroundings, physical and spiritual growth is stunted. The children's physical situation is reflected in the sense of frustration and humility apparent in the poet's perception of their circumstances. The miserable exterior surroundings mirror her own interior sentiments, thereby creating a metaphorical environment bent upon demonstrating the relationship between the real and poetic worlds.

"Portrait" presents several dimensions of a black woman:

¿De dónde provienes tú
pasionable y exaltada?

Tu sangre vio los ardores
de la Nigeria expectante.

Combada
y de ébano arrogante
el mapa de tu mirada.
Tus axilas aromadas
vegetación de la seiba.
Paso de culebra
tus caderas,
muchacha negra.

(Where are you from
excitable and hot-headed one?

Your blood saw the excitement
of expectant Nigeria

Bent
and of arrogant ebony
the map of your stare.
Your fragrant armpits
leaf of the seiba.
Movement of a snake
your hips,
black girl.)

In a positive sense, the black woman is presented as full of life, aware of her past, attractive, and possessing the proverbial rhythm as well as the desirable anatomical structure. The description ranges from the emotional—"excitable and hot-headed"—to the physical—"Movement of a snake / your hips / black girl"—in an effort to present a total picture in this "portrait." In this poem, just as with "Madrigal," Brindis de Salas succeeds in presenting a positive image of the black female. Also of significance is that in "Portrait" she mentions Africa for the first time as an important cultural source. Since ballads are narrative poems characterized by simple words and short stanzas, usually intended for popular consumption, the first section of *The Call of Mary Morena* reflects these tendencies in poems written for the masses.

The "call," by which street vendors announce their products, is defined by Nestor Ortiz Oderigo not as being "work songs as somebody erroneously classified them . . . with slight variations calls pass from one generation to another. Their poetry collects the most picturesque terms of colloquial speech."[11] After pointing out the differences between calls and work songs, Ortiz Oderigo examines the popular basis of this type of oral folkloric expression. Historically a large number of the street vendors have been blacks, and they were primarily responsible for the development of this art form in Uruguay. Calls represent cultural continuity among the people who are often classified as marginal and who do not participate fully in the official culture of the country but who are still legitimate sources of popular expression.

All three calls contained in this volume are concerned with various aspects of the daily experience of Mary Morena, a street vendor, for whom the poet feels a great deal of compassion, a sentiment that is prevalent throughout her poetry. The poet is so moved by the street scene that she feels it is her responsibility to soften the impact of the pain evident in the first call:

> Quiero tu angustia,
> quiero tu pena,
> toda tu pena
> y el tajo de tu boca
> cuando ríes
> como una loca
> Marimorena,
> toda ebria
> más que de vino
> de miseria.
>
> (I desire your anguish,
> I desire your pain,
> all of your pain
> and the shape of your mouth
> when you smile
> like a crazy woman
> Mary Morena,
> totally drunk
> more than from wine
> from misery.)

The poet is seeking a catharsis with Mary Morena in which the agony will be symbolically transferred to herself. "Anguish," "pain," "misery" have engulfed Mary Morena, who seems totally overwhelmed by her lowly social status. "Crazy" and "drunk" are images symptomatic of a social situation out of control, and in fact they exemplify the situation of this woman. The call that is most encompassing in this volume, "Número dos" ("Number Two"), is an indication of the dynamics of this type of artistic creation and its social function; it captures several moments in the daily life of Mary Morena as she peddles her wares from sunup to sundown. She covers all areas of the city from downtown to the popular barrios on the fringes. The pay is meager, the hours long, but nevertheless the spirit and voice are strong. After setting the street scene in a picturesque manner, the poet shifts her focus to the personal situation of the vendor:

Tú, negra, analfabeta,
Marimorena
día a día, jeta a jeta,
las calles llenas
con pregones sandungueros:
en la mañana primero
y por la tarde despúes
durante los treinta días
o treinta y uno del mes.

(You, black, illiterate
Mary Morena
day to day, face to face
the streets filled
with witty calls
in the morning first
and in the afternoon later
during thirty days
or thirty one of the month.)

Although she is identified as a crier of hope, the fact that she is black and illiterate has placed Mary Morena in a position of ceaseless toil from dawn until dusk, twelve months a year. The poem ends on a critical note as the following rhetorical questions are raised:

¿Qué harían tantos obreros
si su labor no vendieras?
¿Qué harían con el tiraje
sin tu pregón solidario?
Administradores y empleados
y otros cómodos sentados?

(What would so many workers do
if their labor did not sell?
What would they do with the press run
without your involved call?
Administrators and employees
and others comfortably seated?)

In spite of her seemingly unimportant status, Mary Morena is essential in the chain of supply and demand. No doubt employees from the highest to the lowest echelon all profit from her labors. She is being exploited by the social and economic systems, but her own interest in survival has prevented her from thinking in these terms. This critical interpretation of her situation is explicit in the last stanzas of the poem, in which black existence becomes analogous to service and sacrifice to the nation. The poet then is critical of a system that serves to exploit cheap black labor through illiteracy and economic dependency. Such is the case not just with the street vendors but also with many of the workers described by Ignacio Suárez Peña in his conversation with Alicia Behrens cited at the beginning of this chapter. For Brindis de Salas, the call becomes a popular instrument for critically depicting the plight of Afro-Uruguayans.

There are three tangos in this volume. The word *tango,* according to
Nestor Ortiz Oderigo, is a genuine Africanism that is "a corruption of the
name Shangó, god of thunder and of storms in the mythology of black
Yorubas from Nigeria in West Africa."[12] Ortiz Oderigo traces the African
etymology of *tango* as well as its transformations from a liturgical to a profane
dance through syncretism. In the New World, the combination of religious
myth and rhythm has been made into an expressive art form, which is
referred to in "Tango número dos" ("Tango Number Two") as a

> Danza
> que bailaron los esclavos
> parche y ritmo
> en su elemental rueda de gallo.

> (Dance
> that the slaves danced
> drum and rhythm
> in their rudimentary chicken ring.)

The specific drum mentioned in this poem, the *piano* (tenor), is also of
Afro-Uruguayan origin according to Ortiz Oderigo. Acoustically, the
sounds of "Tango Number Two" are *jitanjáforas,* an onomatopoetic mixture
of supposedly African sounding words, chants, and drumbeats. The night is
personified, has "hips of the tango" ("caderas del tango"), and in the last
stanza night has taken on the characteristics of other celebrants:

> ¡Qué ojeras
> tiene la noche
> que se va descaderando
> con un tango dormilón!

> (What eye rings
> has the night
> that goes shaking its hips
> with a sleepy headed tango!)

The tango, as Brindis de Salas views it, has evolved from the oppressive
conditions of slavery to become an important aspect of culture in the Río de
la Plata region. In related fashion, the first and third tangos both emphasize
the elements of sound and rhythm that are involved in this particular dance.

The ancestral drum, a sustaining cultural force, is of utmost importance in
"Tango número uno" ("Tango Number One"), providing a sense of history
and community. The social situation is described as that of a "tribe in
ostracism" ("tribu en el ostracismo"). A vital question is directed to Don
Rafael Sobremonte (a slave owner?):

> ¿quién los junta?
> ¿quién junta
> quién vio a tantos negros juntos
> alrededor de un tambor?

(Who unites them?
who unites
who saw so many blacks together
around a drum?)

Here the drum is a unifying factor among oppressed people and a positive symbol of *negritud*. Emphasis is placed upon "unites" and its variations because of the cohesive impact of the scene. Anaphora with "who" reinforces the attitude of mystery surrounding the dilemma of origins and identity for blacks. The scene has undoubtedly been re-acted many times in the quest for freedom and justice throughout the Americas.

"Songs," the final division of *The Call of Mary Morena*, consists of four poems: "Canto para un muchacho negro americano del sur" ("Song for a Black American Boy from the South"); "Unguet" ("Unguet"); "La conga" ("The Conga"); and "Aleluya" ("Hallelujah"). The first two selections are concerned with the black experience from Africa to adolescence in the New World. The latter two embrace rhythm and solidarity.

"Song for a Black American Boy from the South" interprets critically the slavery era, its impact upon black culture, and the subsequent search for an Afro-Uruguayan identity:

En los galeones negreros
vino
engrillado en sus sentinas
sin un adiós a la tribu
ni a la manigua.

(In the slaver galleons
you came
shackled in its bilge
without a goodbye to the tribe
or to the jungle.)

Of symbolic significance is use of the word *galleon* to identify the Spanish multidecked vessel of the sixteenth and seventeenth centuries. It becomes a negative signifier of degradation. The heartless process of uprooting and transporting slaves from Africa is dramatized here and strongly emphasized through alliteration in the original Spanish. Images of the arduous middle passage, "shackled in its bilge," for example, are used as points of reference during the years of bondage and afterwards, so that the young man is not allowed to suppress his Bantu heritage. Afro-Uruguayan popular culture and the family unit serve to maintain the link between past and present:

Abuelito
gramillero
díselo, díselo tú
a este muchacho americano
cómo era el bantú.

(Grandpa
gramillero

tell it to him
to this American boy
how the Bantu were.)

Throughout the arduous centuries, the grandpa (*gramillero*) has assumed the responsibility of keeping alive the collective memory of the past. The figure of the *gramillero* is important because he is a central actor in the Candombe, a symbolic Afro-Uruguayan dance. The ritual is described by Paulo de Carvalho-Neto as "a dramatic dance with well-defined characters, inherited by social transmission, across generations and generations of Negroes, and which manifests itself especially during the carnival."[13] Carvalho-Neto cites evidence linking the Candombe with the Congo or Congada, an Afro-Brazilian dance, as well as with other New World forms of African origin.

The *gramillero*, who is at the same time comic and serious in his actions, represents the king figure from the African past. Carvalho-Neto stresses this point when he raises the question, "Would we not have here an unconscious psychological displacement of all of them, which came to consider him, because he is 'old' as a substitute of the king who vanished from the masquerade?"[14] Rubén Carámbula expresses the opposite opinion concerning the *gramillero*, stating, "In his snakelike rhythms and savage reminiscences the *gramillero* is the symbolism of the witch of the African tribe in the River Plate."[15]

Carámbula tends to stress the exotic while Carvalho-Neto views the *gramillero* as a positive cultural force. In either case, the *gramillero* should be seen as a repository of Afro-Uruguayan folklore and culture, and as Brindis de Salas emphasizes in "Song for a Black American Boy from the South," he has the capacity to reconstruct the racial memory of Afro-Uruguayans. In this poem, the grandpa-*gramillero* achieves cultural continuity with Africa by stressing Bantu heritage and relating it to survival in Uruguay.

Much of the same imagery surrounding the African past is evident in "Unguet," an ode to a young woman. The poem begins with allusions to her jungle background and geographical origin. In subsequent stanzas, Unguet's portrayal goes far beyond the physical to assess her total composition as a human being.

Y que tú puedas decir
Benguela o Mozambique
sin tener que maldecir
el barco que se va a pique.

Unguet,
hija sureña
en el invierno
frío
en el verano
estío.

La vena tropical
de bisabuelo
seca y ancestral
Este es tu suelo.

(And that you can say
Benguela or Mozambique
without having to curse
the ship that is going to flounder.

Unguet
southern daughter
in the winter
cold
in the summer
hot.

The tropical vein of great grandfather
dry and ancestral
This is your land.)

In the Uruguayan context, Unguet is closely allied with the sea, the wind, and other elements of nature. She is a

recental de viejos seres
nacidos en la manigua,

(descendant of old beings,
born in the jungle,)

but in the present situation Unguet is reminded that "this is your land." The Afro-Uruguayan, according to Brindis de Salas, must never forget her origin but should use past experience as an impetus for present and future progress.

In her interpretation of the myth of Africa, Brindis de Salas's poetry is rhetorical as defined by Brathwaite because her direct experience with African culture is minimal due to time, distance, and cultural assimilation in the Americas. On the other hand, cultural maroonage is definitely an underlying concept in *The Call of Mary Morena*. This is apparent in a positive self-concept for blacks, folklore, music, dance, and other forms of cultural continuity.

Of the two remaining poems, "The Conga" is concerned with rhythm and the festive environment surrounding this dance. "Hallelujah!" the last selection, is a plea for ethnic solidarity:

Yo negra
tú blanca, mujder americana:
la misma sopa
habremos de comer
durante días y semanas;
lo mismo tú mujer
de Europa,
has de comer igual que yo
la misma sopa,
y tendrás la misma fe
y la misma ropa
y has de beber tu vino
en igual copa.
        ¡Aleluya!

> (I am black
> you are white, American woman:
> the same soup
> we must eat
> during days and weeks;
> the same you woman
> from Europe
> have to eat the same as I
> the same soup
> and you will have the same faith
> and the same clothes
> and you will have to drink your wine
> in the same cup.
>   Hallelujah!)

Sameness and equality are the human issues that have preoccupied blacks since their arrival in the Americas. Brindis de Salas's message is that black and white destinies are inextricably bound together in Uruguay and throughout the New World by social, religious, and economic realities. "Hallelujah" echoes sentiments expressed in "To the American Shore," which opens this volume. Thus the cycle is complete. Brindis de Salas recognizes that the destiny of Afro-Uruguayans is analogous to that of other ethnic groups in the country, but blacks must be able to confront their society with a strong, positive sense of self.

The Call of Mary Morena is significant for a number of reasons. Of prime importance, it is the first major publication by an Afro-Uruguayan writer. Second, Brindis de Salas is able to articulate a number of thematic concerns expressed by her countrymen, who include Carlos Cardozo Ferreira, Juan Julio Arrascaeta, Julio Guadalupe, Pilar Barrios, and others. Furthermore, certain experiential images that unify the black literary experience without regard for temporal or spatial limitations are evident in Brindis de Salas. These include, but are not limited to, mythic-paradisiacal Africa, the black woman as life-giver and sustainer, the constant struggle for liberation, and the strong desire to give positive values to blackness—all literary components of negritud.

In The Call of Mary Morena, Virginia Brindis de Salas emerges as a literary preserver of Afro-Uruguayan culture. She constantly affirms within a majority culture that seeks to negate. As a result, her cry is, above all, for respect and dignity—a call that began with one of the first published Afro-Uruguayan poems, "To Men of Color" by Timoteo Olivera. This poem, published in Conservation: Organ of the Society of Color on 22 September 1872, initiated a long process of literary consciousness raising and cultural awareness among the Afro-Uruguayan population. The Call of Mary Morena is an eloquent response to this challenge.

Pilar Barrios: Black Skin

It is virtually impossible to discuss the literary trajectory of Pilar Barrios apart from Our Race, the journal founded in 1917 by his brother Ventura and his sister María Esperanza in San Carlos. Pilar Barrios became an official editor with the seventh issue in May 1917 and served in some capacity until its demise in 1948. Some of Barrios's earliest poems, dedicated to love, nature, poetry, and patriotism, were published in this periodical during 1917. Several of these selections are contained in *Piel Negra: Poesías (Black Skin: Poetry) 1917–1947*—published through the efforts of friends of Barrios who were associated with *Our Race*—and they demonstrate how his poetic maturation is inseparable from his social and political growth. During the second epoch of *Our Race*, beginning in 1933, Barrios's poetic themes remained socially noncommital in the journal that was his principal artistic outlet. But as he became more involved in the worldwide struggle against racism, war, and fascism, the tone of Barrios's poems changed noticeably.

Undoubtedly the instrument most responsible for this modification of perspectives was the Indigenous Black party, which was affiliated with *Our Race:* Barrios was secretary of this organization. The party was created in June 1936, given official recognition on 5 January 1937, organized on 9 January 1937, and disbanded in July 1944. In spite of its pledge to represent black interests, however, the Indigenous Black party received minimal support. The platform was not radical by any means, although it did call for social equality, justice, and economic progress, principles set forth in "Why the Indigenous Black Party Was Founded," a document published in *Our Race:*

> We shall fight tirelessly and intervene inexorably in all social problems, our action being determined in favor of the underprivileged against the wealthy, in favor of the winning of a true social justice, which humanity is still, unfortunately, far from achieving.[16]

The party took great pains to demonstrate that its principal goals were inseparable from those of all Uruguayan blacks. In clarifying the party's position, the executive committee pointed out, "No foreign dogma or ideology inspires our calm and patriotic civic action but rather we aspire to congregate beneath the folds of this flag of order, peace and work."[17] Therefore, the push for a slate of candidates, headed by Mario Méndez, to participate in the national parliament was done within the established rules with the idea of gaining more concessions for blacks.

That economics was one of the overriding factors contributing to the discontent of black intellectuals is evident in the first part of an essay by Ildefonso Pereda Valdés, a nonblack, entitled "The Economic Situation of the Black Race in Uruguay." This essay appeared in *Our Race* on 27 March 1938, one day before the elections, with the obvious intention of stimulating Afro-Uruguayan thinking about the adverse social and economic situations. The ploy did not work, as revealed in the editorial assessing the outcome of the voting: "In Montevideo alone, there are approximately five thousand persons of color capable of voting. The final result of the election produced *Eighty Four* votes for the Indigenous Black Party."[18] The Indigenous Black party, in reality, never recovered from this humiliating rejection by Afro-

Uruguayans. Nevertheless, it remained active but without much impact until disbanding in 1944. The party appears to have had minimal impact upon blacks in terms of consciousness raising and integrating them into the national political process.

Pilar Barrios—as poet, the editor of *Our Race*, and an intellectual committed to the progress of Afro-Uruguayans—expressed his sentiments concerning their problems on many occasions. Vis-à-vis the elections of 1938, it is significant that his poem "Remedos" ("Imitation") was published in *Our Race* on 25 March 1938; it was only Barrios's second poem with social or political overtones to be published. The first, "Frente a la hora que pasa" ("Facing the Hour that Passes"), appeared during the furor of activity generated by the Committee of the Black Race against War and Fascism and the Indigenous Black party. The former group was founded in January 1936, and the organizational meeting of the Indigenous Black party was announced in December 1936 by the secretaries, suggesting a tremendous amount of organizational activity throughout the year and resulting in the decision by this group of black intellectuals to fight injustices wherever they might occur. Toward this end, Barrios published "Facing the Hour that Passes" on 25 September 1936.

This poem is an insightful look at the human condition in general, ethnicity, and the black experience. "Facing the Hour that Passes" consists of sixteen sestets, each of which begins with reference to biblical genocide, inequality, the basis of discrimination, and the humiliation and racism associated with blackness. Barrios's plea is for unity among black Uruguayans in the face of events transpiring in Europe and Africa. He goes one step further midway through the poem and appeals for armed resistance to the oppressive situation experienced by his people who have little hope of changing the social structure. But the poet recognizes that uncoordinated acts of armed resistance are futile and that because blacks are in the minority they will be decimated. The simile "as blades of grass before a brisk wind" ("como hierba ante un vendaval") is certainly appropriate in this instance. The solution, Barrios tells us, is in political sophistication that entails a reversal of the age-old pattern in which blacks have been used to fight other peoples' battles instead of bettering their own lot.

Justice, not hate, is his professed goal. Individual heroes will not suffice. Only when people worldwide give blacks the respect they deserve will Uruguayans profit. Barrios's attitude vacillates between militancy and mediation, a posture that prevails throughout his protest poetry. In "Facing the Hour that Passes" he implores whites to aid in eradicating stereotypes and misdeeds directed toward blacks in Uruguay. The poem is an important transitional piece for Barrios; it was the first published poetic presentation of his negative social and political perceptions.

Published in *Our Race* three days before the ill-fated election of 28 March 1938, "Imitation" demonstrates the growing social and political awareness of Barrios as well as his perceptions of the relationships between art and life.

A statement about art and its function, the poem serves as Barrios's announcement of his heritage and poetic trajectory, an indication of what to anticipate from Barrios as a poet. It defines his personal origins as well as how he views his literary production. His lyre, Barrios warns us, is different because of its rebellious, unsociable tendencies that will seem strange to unaccustomed ears. This has to do with the poet's background. Although he is from the countryside (Garzón, Department of Rocha), there still remain strains of the African past, which are conjured up in images of the jungle, wild beasts, and savage songs. The Uruguayan rural ambience and the African connection will provide physical and psychological inspiration for Barrios. He states in the third stanza,

> Mi lira es rebelde y está saturada
> con todo el bullicio que vierte el follaje,
> por eso es que a veces se exalta vibrante
> y pone al desnudo su arista salvaje.[19]

> (My lyre is rebellious and is saturated
> with all the excitement that empties the foliage,
> for that reason at times it exalts itself vibrantly
> and exposes its savage edge.)

Cloaked in rural, agrarian imagery is the implied threat of exposing the other side of his poetic persona. Barrios's poetry is at once rebellious, as he reiterates in the fourth stanza, and an imitation of the chirps of birds and of all things pleasant in the pastoral environment. "Imitation" is a statement to the effect that this combination of harsh and gentle poetry, which on the one hand is critical while soothing on the other, will be typical of Barrios's production.

Immediately following the disastrous elections of 1938, the poem "Esclavitud" ("Slavery") appeared in *Our Race*. Written in sestets, it reflects Barrios's interpretation of the unrest and anxiety of modern times. The tendency toward barbarism and hypocrisy evident in the first stanza is indicative of the moral disintegration of the human fiber. Human rights are constantly violated in an era of inhumanity and retrogression from the basic principles of dignity. Through a juxtapositioning of opposites in the second stanza (greed versus liberty and justice), this negative crescendo continues. Anaphora with "how much" ("cuánto") at the beginning of stanza three and the ensuing reiteration of the world's ills with the powerful descriptives "insidious, impostures, and vilification" ("insidioso, imposturas, vilificación") lead to the conclusion that Good has been usurped by Evil.

Not once in "Slavery" does Barrios mention Uruguay specifically. His country, however, is not exempt from the world's evils: it too participates in the human community. Therefore, the negative conditions outlined in the three preliminary stanzas are symptomatic of people everywhere. In the final stanza, Barrios focuses on slavery, which becomes a metaphor for physical and spiritual oppression:

Esclavitud del hombre en su afán de dominio,
desencadenamiento de odio y de exterminio
Como una ráfaga trágica van de uno a otro confín,
Esclavitud del vicio, vergonzante y sin nombre,
esclavitud oprobiosa del hombre sobre el hombre
mientras que Abel sucumbe a manos de Caín.[20]

(Slavery of man in his zeal of mastery,
an unleashing of hate and extermination
like a tragic burst they go from one extreme to the other,
Slavery of vice, shamefaced and nameless,
opprobrious slavery of man over man
while Abel succumbs at the hands of Cain.)

Slavery as defined and delineated throughout this poem, and especially in these last verses, is not just in keeping with the concept of physical bondage of an individual. It also embraces humans' innate negative qualities, which date to the origins of the race. Writing under adverse conditions in 1938, Barrios chose to universalize a concept that was playing such an important role in Uruguay, thereby lending more credibility to his art as criticism. "Slavery" is indeed a pessimistic poem, and Barrios's sentiments appear to be at low ebb. After this brief letdown, however, he resumed his normal publishing routine of dedicating poems to the most trivial as well as to the most important human concerns.

The three-year period 1936–1938 was crucial in the formation of Barrios as a poet, because there one can see his development from a writer with predominantly Spanish Golden Age literary tendencies to a bard capable of grappling with problems inherent within the Uruguayan context. Over the next decade, Barrios published less than a dozen poems in *Our Race, Directions,* and *Uruguay Magazine.* However, these early poems provided the lyrical basis for Barrios's publishing career and material for *Black Skin,* his most important work.

Black Skin (1947), representing thirty years of poetic activity, is a collection of forty-one poems on the following major topics: the art and function of poetry; ethnicity and the black experience; the rural ambience; black literary figures and heroes; death; love; and worldly concerns including poverty, war, and humanity in general. Given the title, one would expect the plight of Afro-Uruguayans to play a major thematic role, and it does. But Barrios is concerned first of all with being a poet, a position that he firmly establishes in this volume.

The first poem in this book, "Imitation," is an indication of what to anticipate from Barrios as a poet. His attitudes of artistic ambivalence are extended to a similar poem, "Mis versos" ("My Verses"), which also deals with poetic creation:

Mis versos son eso
nada más que un esfuerzo,

un montón de sonidos violentos
de la lira que vibra en mi pecho.

Pobre lira de rasgos humildes
saturada de aromas silvestres
que se exalta al impulso impetuoso
de un espíritu ardiente y vibrante.

(My verses are that
no more than an effort,
a mountain of violent sounds
from the lyre that vibrates in my chest.

Poor lyre of humble traits
saturated with rustic aromas
that is excited at the impetuous impulse
of a fiery and vibrant spirit.)

The image projected is one of a spontaneous, intense poet, bursting with creative energy. Verbs and adjectives—"vibrates," "impetuous," "fiery," "vibrant," "excited"—underscore the intense emotional level. Anger is very much in evidence as the poet reiterates:

Mis versos trasuntan
los distintos estados de mi alma,
y traducen en rudo lenguaje
el intenso dolor de una raza
que ha sufrido el mayor vilipendio
que nunca se viera.
Y que aún hoy, a través de los tiempos
perdura su influencia!

(My verses sum up
the different states of my soul
and translate in rude language
the intense pain of a race
that has suffered the greatest vilification
that has ever been seen.
And even today, through time
survives its influence!)

Barrios sees it as his duty to address the injustices perpetrated against Uruguayan blacks over the centuries. In no uncertain terms he reaffirms his position that the pain and suffering associated with slavery cannot be erased when these experiences are essential in tempering today's perceptions of blacks. His poetry, then—by admission in "My Verses"—are attempts to "tear away the stigma that weighs upon the race" ("arancar el estigma que pesa sobre ella"), which will be achieved through his "virile shout" ("grito viril") and "rude language," in other words, his committed poetic discourse. Barrios directly criticizes the institution of slavery and the people whose activities are responsible for the present adverse situation of Afro-Uruguayans. His aim is to give dignity to a people who have been suffering:

Desde el día que la mano del blanco
innoble e infame,
despiadada y grotesca,
para hacerla vivir el escarnio
más vil y humillante,
la arrancó de sus vírgenes tierras.

(Since the day that the hand of the white man
ignoble and infamous
ruthless and grotesque
to make it live the derision
most vile and humiliating
tore it away from its virgin lands.)

In poeticizing the social function of his verses, Barrios dwells on the institution of slavery and its negative impact on the present-day situation in
Uruguay. His dissatisfaction is vigorously expressed, in this instance,
through adjectival accumulation and his conviction that the poet is responsible to his people. The stigma sttached to slavery, in Barrios's estimation, is
responsible in part for the adverse conditions of Afro-Uruguayans in the
twentieth century.

Nevertheless, the conception of poetry as an art that expresses beauty as
well as criticism of social injustices permeates the verses of Pilar Barrios. He
is classic in the sense of his treatment of age-old poetic themes and modern
in his social preoccupations. The former interest is demonstrated in "La
idea" ("The Idea"), described as a

Vuelo del espíritu
expresión del estado del alma,
la idea no tiene
nacionalidades,
ni es privilegio
de climas, ni razas,
condición, ni clases.

(Flight of the spirit
expression of the state of the soul
the idea does not have
nationalities
neither is it the privilege
of climates, nor races
condition, nor classes.)

In this description of the ineffable nature of the thought process, Barrios
painstakingly points out that the ability of independent thought is granted
to all humans, without regard for historical or social circumstances. "Flight
of the Spirit" metaphorically supports the poetic assumption that the idea
represents one of the few free entities in a world of restrictions.

In short, it is possible to conclude that Pilar Barrios is a multifaceted poet
and not just a writer who pens black verse. Throughout his books, however,

the obvious problem of whether to subvert his work with social concerns or to practice art for art's sake is an issue. Near the end of *Black Skin*, Barrios seems to have arrived at a conclusion when he remarks in "¡Yo tengo una lira!" ("I Have a Lyre!"),

> Hay instantes que son un arrullo
> un sutil susurrar sus acordes,
> dijérase que son como ecos
> de aunados y dulces rumores.
> Pero en otros momentos sus cuerdas
> cobran el sonoro chocar del acero
> y sus sones se trocan entonces
> en vibrantes y recios acentos.

> (There are moments that are a lullaby
> a subtle whispering its chords
> one would say they are like echoes
> of mixed and sweet murmurs.
> But at other moments its strings
> acquire the melodic clash of steel
> and its sounds then change
> to vibrant and harsh accents.)

Alliteration with *s* in the first stanza is effective in demonstrating, from the poet's point of view, that he is capable of achieving the harmony between form and content necessary for good poetry. The negative contrast between "mixed and sweet murmurs" and "vibrant and harsh accents" underscores the basic preoccupations of any poet who is socially committed and concerned with his craft. In *Black Skin*, Barrios struggles to reconcile art, social reality, and the Afro-Uruguayan experience, but he arrives at the conclusion that poetry certainly has a critical social function that does not remove it from the realm of artistic creation. This principle is put into practice throughout *Black Skin*.

The poor, the hopeless, and the downtrodden are the protagonists of "Hay que ir allí" ("One Must Go There"), "Pueblo" ("People"), and "Voces sin eco" ("Voices without Echo"). This last poem is employed to interpret the situation of people without hope:

> Son voces sin eco
> las de los humildes
> y menesterosos,
> que pueblan la tierra
> gritando su angustia
> su dolor y su hambre.

> Voces sin aliento
> son todas aquellas
> que no hallan apoyo;
> pues son, se dijera,
> como gotas de agua
> que volatiza
> y evapora el aire.

(They are voices without echo
those of the humble
and needy
that populate the earth
shouting their anguish
their pain and their hunger.

Voices without breath
are all of those
that do not find support;
well they are, it is said,
like drops of water
that fade away
and evaporate in the air.)

Anaphora ("voices") serves to underscore the plight of the dispossessed worldwide, although the Uruguayans' context is the point of departure, where a tremendous process of depersonalization and dehumanization is taking place due to the impact of poverty upon people of the lower social classes. Whites, Indians, blacks, and orientals all share the debilitating effects of an unequal distribution of goods and services. What compounds this material problem, from Barrio's perspective is the

la vorágine
de la indiferencia,
y la egolatría
de los poderosos
de toda la tierra

(vortex of indifference
and the self-worship
of the powerful
of all the earth.)

The poor and the needy who cry out in their "anguish," "pain," and "hunger" populate an insensitive world that is not concerned with social equality, human dignity, or justice. In a powerful surrealistic image, the anonymous cries are presented as if they did not exist: "like drops of water," they "fade away / and evaporate in the air." Harsh imagery is used throughout "Voices without Echo" to dramatize the plight of the dispossessed. Negativism, "without," is constant in the descriptions because the protagonists are literally broken and their cries are in vain. But from Barrios's perspective, their situation is not limited to one ethnic group; it is shared by the poor in general. Until the disproportion in the distribution of wealth that inevitably leads to a structured society of class and privilege is solved, there will be misery and suffering.

In the transition from general to specific, the outcry is more strident in "One Must Go There," which concentrates upon a segment of the poor who live in a *tugurio*, or slum. Anaphora with "one must go" stresses the urgency to bring these conditions to public notice. It seems as if the people have been forsaken by both earthly and heavenly forces:

Hay que ir a esos lugares insalubres,
donde faltan calorías, sol y aire
y la desnutrición y desnudez del niño
son la obsesión constante de las madres.

(One must go to those unhealthy places,
where there is a lack of calories, sun and air
and malnutrition and nakedness of children
are the constant obsession of mothers.)

Not only is the economic situation deplorable because of a lack of food and clothing for the young, but Nature also seems to have turned its back on them because of an absence of sun and clean air. Of greater significance, the children described are disease ravished, which will retard and destroy future generations. "One Must Go There" is a powerful denunciation of a social system that demonstrates a lack of sensitivity to poverty by the people responsible for its presence.

The poet totally identifies with the situation of misery in "People," but the people's spirit seems to have been crushed:

cuyo nivel de dignidad rebaja
la condición misérrima en que vive.

([the] level of dignity lowers
the miserable condition in which they live.)

In "People," a poem replete with images of suffering and misery reflecting a sense of estrangement from society, the poet maintains his posture as a spokesman for the causes of human dignity and economic equity for all. "Voices without Echo," "One Must Go There," and "People" all demonstrate Barrios's strong identification with the masses, the dispossessed, sentiments that have prevailed from his early political involvement in 1936 to 1945 when the last of these selections was written.

The image of world destruction is as disquieting for Barrios as the specter of poverty, and several of the poems in *Black Skin* are dedicated to war and its aftermath. The most blatant antibellicose criticism is apparent in "Sombras inquietantes" ("Disturbing Shadows") and "Condenación" ("Condemnation"), the latter fervently attacking the problem:

¡Guerra! gritó con bronca voz el déspota.
¡Guerra! corearon mil blasfemos labios
Con expresión satánica y siniestra
en injurioso agravio.

A esa voz prepotente, yo respondo
Y le digo a mi vez, ¡Guerra a la guerra!
Con voz que arranco desde lo más hondo
que el corazón y el sentimiento encierra.

(War! shouted with gruff voice the despot
War! chorused a thousand blasphemous lips

With a satanic and sinister expression
in abusive wrong.

To that haughty voice, I reply,
and say it is my way, Wage war on war!
With a voice that I tear from the deepest
that the heart and feeling embraces.)

War, for Barrios, is a crime against all of humanity, a game of madmen and
despots who are described in the most negative jargon. The satanic, evil
expression of the first stanza is contrasted directly with the heartfelt sentiments of the second. The poet wishes to declare not just a moratorium but
war on the war machine itself. His strident cry for sanity, he hopes, will be
joined by other concerned individuals. This poem, written in 1946, presents
the poet as a witness to World War II and reflects both Barrios's antiwar
posture and his horror with human destruction and violence.

The adverse views of war are consistent with the ones expressed by
Barrios in 1934 in "Disturbing Shadows," which also raises questions concerning the existential anguish of modern man:

¿Quién podrá decirnos hacia dónde vamos?
¿Dónde llegaremos? ¿Dónde despertamos?
¿Quién le pondrá freno a tanta ambición?
¿Y la grave crisis que trastorna al orbe,
preocupación máximá que todo lo absorbe
quién vendrá a ponerle feliz solución?

(Who can tell us where we're going?
Where we will arrive? Where we will awaken?
Who will put a stop to so much ambition?
And the serious crisis that upsets the world,
maximum preoccupation that absorbs it all
who will impose a happy solution?)

The future of humanity is at stake because the world has the historical
precedent, the negative ambition, and the instruments of war to inflict
incalculable damage. In the first stanza above, "who" and "where" underscore the lack of direction in human destiny while questioning the motivational factors behind bellicose activities. From an existentialist perspective,
"Condemnation" and "Disturbing Shadows" stand as the overt testimony
of a man who has witnessed two world wars. For Barrios, some historical
events assume as much importance as his own ethnic situation, which
informs nearly a third of the poems in Black Skin, as they assess the ethnic
situation and the black experience in Uruguay.

"La leyenda maldita" ("The Damned Legend") is Barrios's central poetic
interpretation of the Afro-Uruguayan experience. It consists of fourteen
chants describing blacks' history in that country and shared black experiences throughout the diaspora. The first stanza sets the tone in recounting
the legacy of trials and tribulations as well as emphasizing the strengths of
black people:

Raza negra, noble raza;
raza humilde, sana y fuerte,
generosa y abnegada,
hecha a todos los rigores.
Como sientes inquietudes,
sabes también de dolores
del pasado y del presente.

(Black race, noble race;
humble race, healthy and strong,
generous and unselfish,
made from all the hardships.
As you feel uneasiness
you also know of pains
of the past and present.)

Since much of black history emphasizes the lack of real progress in human terms, the present mirrors the past without much hope for the future. Although a legacy of suffering and sacrifice is integral to the experiences of Afro-Uruguayans, there is always the drive to overcome and the spirit of resistance, a force

que nos habla y nos separa
de aquel ciclo ignominioso
de martirio y de penuria,
de vergüenza y de vejámenes
que llenó la vida esclava
desde los días remotos
que el prejuicio cruel e infame
y ambición de una raza,
con violencia te arrancara
de ese suelo codiciado
amplio, fértil y ardoroso
que es el Africa.

(that speaks to us and separates us
from the ignominious cycle
of martyrdom and of penury
of shame and of vexation
that filled the slave life
from the remote days
that cruel and infamous prejudice
and ambition of a race
with violence tore you away
from that coveted soil
ample, fertile and fiery
that is Africa.)

The black ethnic group is a complicated entity of human beings who have experienced their share of adversity. Nevertheless they forge ahead though always haunted by the specter of slavery, a system based upon racism and dishonor that violently uprooted millions of people. In this stanza, Barrios mentions Africa for the first time in *Black Skin* and reiterates an image that will become a central metaphor in his ethnic poetry. The idea of tearing away or obtaining through force or vehemence persists throughout most of his pieces that deal with blacks and their uprooting from Africa. Symbolically, they are orphaned from the archetypal center and condemned to wander in the Americas.

In stanzas two and three, Barrios turns his attention to historical lies surrounding black inferiority that persist despite scientific efforts proving that superior races do not exist. In stanza four, through his use of the rhetorical question, the poet emphasizes positive accomplishments of blacks in the arts, sciences, peace, and war. Stanza five presents the black as a morally superior being

> que contrasta
> con el bárbaro y grotesco
> de los amos.

> (who contrasts
> with the barbarity and grotesqueness
> of the owners.)

Nevertheless, one hundred years has not been enough time to erase the discrimination that Barrios vehemently opposes in stanza six. His call is for harmony and solidarity. Humans should be perceived as

> no núcleos aislados,
> sino hombre y mujeres de todo el universo,
> sin ver fronteras ideológicas, ni razas,
> se sienten hermanados.

> (not isolated nuclei
> but men and women of all the universe
> without seeing either ideological frontiers, or races
> they feel united.)

People should be striving for the highest possible ideals instead of wallowing in Hitlerism and other forms of degeneracy.

In this poem, Barrios poses the question, Do black Uruguayans have a future if they must plead for dignity rather than demand it? The idea of science being used to verify black inequality crops up repeatedly throughout "The Damned Legend," and as the title implies, eliminating the stigma is virtually impossible. Respect and dignity are hard to come by, but Barrios persists in his push for universal brotherhood in which all humans will participate in the world community. He believes that people are capable of transcending their socially ingrained views of inequality and discrimination. In his search for dignity and justice, Barrios manages to go beyond the Uruguayan situation to link the black experience to world decadence. His view of the global situation remains pessimistic—the world is totally consumed by the holocaust of war in the last stanza of "The Damned Legend." For Barrios, notwithstanding the individual capacity for transcendence, there is something evil innate in human beings. The same kind of perverseness that enslaves people is also responsible for the destructiveness of war. Both work to our disadvantage.

In the area of ethnic relations, Barrios constantly expresses a desire for harmony while taking a firm stand against discrimination and historical oppression. In "La lección del abuelo" ("The Grandfather's Lesson"), for example, a black grandfather calls upon his white grandson to recognize that they are all part of the same ethnic amalgam. This sensitive yet ironic poem seeks to teach a lesson not only to children but to all Uruguayans. "Hermano blanco" ("White Brother") is an open appeal to whites to understand that the poor are not necessarily a threat to them. Instead of repressing the disadvantaged, the majority culture should call upon its Christian heritage to aid the "redemption of the oppressed" ("redención del oprimido"). Barrios believes that affluent whites do have the capacity to become more sensitive to the less fortunate, and because they are in fact operating from a position of advantage, they should take the initiative in promoting harmony.

"Passing," a radical solution to discrimination, is the theme of "Cartas que recibimos" ("Letters We Receive"). Apparently a friend has advised the poet to bleach his face so that it would be "white and pretty" ("blanca y hermosa"), but the central question with which he retorts is

> al cambiar el color de mi epidermis
> se transforma también mi pensamiento?
>
> (on changing the color of my skin
> is my thought also transformed?)

A change of skin color does not necessarily alter the thought process, nor does it assure one of happiness. "Letters We Receive" rejects outright the idea of passing and strongly affirms the acceptance of one's ethnic identity. This poem's significance lies in its positive treatment of a sensitive issue confronting a hostile society.

The question of defending ethnic heritage is debated in "¡Negra!" ("Black Woman!")—a poem scrutinizing the intellectual basis of racism. Early on, there is an ironic manipulation of the verb "to know" in delineating the problem:

> que no saben, que no saben
> pero que creen saber.
>
> (but they do not know, that they don't know
> but they think they know.)

Through alliteration, by affirming and denying knowledge, the poet stresses that ignorance forms the basis of racism, because color does not denote the true essence of a human being. Biological functions among ethnic groups are identical; the difference is in societal hypocrisy. Interestingly enough, Barrios presents this problematic poem of identity from the point of view of a woman, stressing that sexism and racism are learned behavior and are not innate individual attitudes.

One of the most profound of Barrios's sonnets treating the question of ethnicity is appropriately titled "Raza negra" ("Black Race"). The poem encourages blacks to look forward to their destiny because it will be difficult to discover encouraging models in the past. "Black Race" is a positive poem, one that views blacks as historical martyrs but with the energy necessary to win future social battles.

> Por el martirologio que viviste,
> por toda la ignominia que sufriste
> en el dolor de tus antepasados.
>
> Yo te exhorto a luchar constantemente
> llevando hacia el futuro, del presente,
> todos los adelantos alcanzados.
>
> (For the martyrdom that you lived
> for all the ignominy that you suffered
> on the pain of your forefathers.
>
> I exhort you to fight constantly
> carrying toward the future,
> from the present all the advances reached.)

Barrios sees struggle as the route for Afro-Uruguayans to follow since it has been such an integral part of their experience. Martyrdom, suffering, and pain are realities of the past. Idealistically, the future does offer hope if it is built upon both past and present accomplishments. Unfortunately, Uruguay does not offer many positive models.

In spite of his obvious disenchantment and pessimism, Barrios is a poet of hope. A great deal of his positivism is revealed in "Tema racial" ("Racial Theme"), in which he encourages youth to seek the greater values embodied in spirit and mind. "Study, struggle, continue ahead" ("Estudia, lucha, sigue adelante") is the prevailing motif as blacks are encouraged to break down the so-called mental handicaps and stereotypes and to take advantage of natural gifts of intelligence. Brain power has no color. In exhorting the young, the poet points to successful people of the black diaspora worldwide to give his audience, in effect, an excellent cultural history lesson. "Racial Theme" stresses intellectual seriousness. Education and a positive self-image are among the poet's first priorities.

In his ethnic poems, Pilar Barrios interprets the black experience in Uruguay from slavery and martyrdom to the quest for respect and dignity. His attitude, however, remains ambivalent. In "Martirologio" ("Martyrdom"), for instance, the poet describes victimized blacks who

> vivió y sufrió con estoicismo heroico
> sin que haya paragón, la raza negra.

> (lived and suffered with heroic stoicism
> without there being a comparison.)

One disturbing aspect of this poem is that there is no apparent resistance to oppression. Survival, both spiritual and physical, is the key issue because blacks are a

> Raza que demostró ser adaptable
> a las evoluciones del progreso.

> (race that proved to be adaptable
> to the evolutions of progress.)

Progress is essential and there is no time for self-pity: but progress according to whose terms?

Through literary *negritud*, Pilar Barrios places positive emphasis upon the African heritage, although it might be from a rhetorical perspective. Barrios identified himself as an Afro-Uruguayan. Therefore, not only is the view of mythic homeland important but the pressures involved in being of African origin surface within the Uruguayan context. Thus, temporally, the interval of passage as delineated by Barthold is a difficult transition for Barrios as a poet; full participation in Uruguayan culture and entrance into the literary mainstream are denied to him. His poetic reaction is alienation, societal confrontation, an identity crisis, but most important, dualism—the dichotomy between self-concept and definitions imposed by the majority culture. Most of the poems in *Black Skin* interpret these issues as integral to the psychological composition of Afro-Uruguayans.

Barrios also reserves space in *Black Skin* for concerns such as love, memory, the passage of time, and the human condition. "Mi eterna tristeza" ("My Eternal Sadness") and "Sombras en la luz" ("Shadows in the Light") are memories of his mother and the past. "Triste impresión" ("Sad Impression") is about time, memory, and love. "Espejismo y fantasías" ("Mirages and Fantasies") is an exaltation of nature and an attempt to escape from wordly existence. "Mi oración" ("My Prayer") and "Betervide" ("Betervide") are elegies to Dr. Salvador Betervide, a spokesman for black progress and founder of *Vanguard* in 1928. "Opacidad" ("Sadness") and "Tedio" ("Tedium") describe weather and the seasons. Finally, there are two poems that probe the all-important question of the destiny of humankind, "Hombre" ("Man") and, for analysis here, "¿Qué somos?" ("What Are We?").

> Cruzamos el camino de la vida
> a través de la selva perfumada
> y al término final de la jornada
> llegamos con el alma dolorida.

> Porque si hay en la breve recorrida
> flores bellas, lozanas y divinas
> van más tarde trocándose en espinas
> que abren en nuestro ser sangriente herida;

y cuando al final de la jornada
muerto el placer que acariciamos tanto,
perdida la esperanza, muerto el brío.

¿Qué somos en la vida?—Somos nada,
somos miseria, sufrimiento, y llanto.
Despojos sólo, de un sepulcro frío.

(We cross the road of life
through the perfumed jungle
and at the final boundary of the journey
we arrive with the grieving soul.

Because if there is in the brief trip
beautiful flowers, haughty and divine
later they will change to thorns
that open in our being a bloody wound;

And when at the end of the journey
dead the pleasure we embraced so much
the hope lost, dead the vigor.

What are we in life?—We are nothing
we are misery, suffering, and weeping
mortal remains only, for a cold grave.)

This sonnet is dated 1919 and reflects the influence, perhaps, of baroque Spanish Golden Age poetry in the use of the flower as a metaphor for human existence. The last tercet brings to mind similar analogies in Sor Juana, Góngora, and Quevedo. In the first stanza, life's trajectory is contrasted between the affirmative "road of life" and the negative "final boundary of the journey." Paradoxically, the flower, which inevitably turns to thorns after briefly enjoying beauty and youth, exemplifies this journey. Thus the motif of carpe diem is suggested in the second stanza; life is to be enjoyed to its fullest. The first tercet emphasizes forcefully the negative with words such as "final," "death," and "lost." Life is essentially a path toward death, then, an ignoble death in fact. After all of life's pleasures and disappointments, a grave awaits us.

In direct contrast to this bleak picture of existence is the warm, sensitive "Sad Impression":

Las violetas aquellas que el domingo
recibiera de ti,
en un búcaro azul, frescas, lozanas,
hoy al pasar las vi.

Me intrigó la frescura que tenían
y entonces me acerqué
y entre mis manos trémulas, nerviosas,
una de ellas tomé.

(The violets those that on Sunday
I was to receive from you,

in a blue vase, fresh, haughty,
today on passing I saw them too.

The freshness they had intrigued me
and then I approached
and between my hands trembling, nervous,
one of them I took.)

In this nostalgic poem, two quartets with alternating eleven- and seven-syllable lines, a variation of the Spanish *lira,* the poet reflects upon a touching love scene. The action is all imaginary in that the scene painted is an assessment of the past. The preterite verbs of the first three stanzas reinforce the attitude of finality. The protagonist's mental hope and longing are stressed in the verbs "seemed," "had," and "offered," all imperfects suggesting indefiniteness. His basic preoccupation is love—and the memory of a past love affair that is triggered by the image of violets in the present. The fleeting nature of love and existence is symbolized by the fragile violet itself.

Yet the power of love is strong, and Barrios reserves a special place in his poetry for the black mother, especially his own, with "Poema de la madre" ("Mother's Poem") and "Shadows in the Light" being representative selections. The former poem was inspired by a question concerning the "false concept" ("falso concepto"), the

> absurda creencia
> de sangres y de razas superiores
> prejuicio vil, trágico y violento.
>
> (absurd belief
> about blood and superior races
> vile prejudice, tragic and violent.)

The poet commences a diatribe against inequality and concentrates upon the common experiences of motherhood and the double discrimination experienced by black women, who fit the archetypal image of Mother Earth:

> la madre es un cristal que el dolor quiebra
> cuya amplitud no tiene paralelo,
> la madre es, la realidad más pura
> ¡no excluye esa virtud a la madre negra!
>
> (the mother is a crystal that pain shatters
> whose amplitude has no parallel,
> the mother is, the most pure reality
> don't deny this virtue to the black mother!)

Motherhood is an experience shared by women across cultures, and its positive features should not be limited because of ethnic factors. The love, loyalty, and tenderness inherent in a mother's relationships with others transcend boundaries of class and culture. More importantly, the mother is the key figure in perpetuating the human race.

The theme of the mother is carried from the general to the specific in

"Shadows in the Light," in which Barrios commemorates his dead mother's birthday. The scene set in the first four sestets is that of a *locus amoenus*, a pleasant place whose natural environment is in perfect harmony. The only element not in tune with the situation is the poet, who is suffering from "a sadness that has no end" ("una tristeza que no tiene fin"). But his own sentiments are not allowed to disturb nature until the final contrast is made:

> hoy que la luz llena el campo y el río
> solamente hay sombras en el pecho mío,
> tan solo hay angustias en mi corazón!!

> (today when light fills the field and river
> there are only shadows in my chest,
> as there is only anguish in my heart!)

The entire poem places emphasis upon light until the realization comes that the poet is ironically juxtaposing life, "light," and death, represented by "shadows," "anguish," and the "sadness" mentioned in the first stanza. His emotions of sadness and sorrow stand in stark contrast to the harmony and the relative indifference of nature.

Other important sources of inspiration for Barrios are Afro-Uruguayans and their counterparts throughout the Americas and the Hispanic world. He dedicates poems to Langston Hughes in "Voces" ("Voices"); to the black Uruguayan painter Ramón Pereyra in "Carta abierta" ("Open Letter"); to "Nicolás Guillén"; to Federico García Lorca in "Duelo de las liras" ("Duel of the Lyres"); and to the most famous Afro-Uruguayan, Ansina, the constant companion of José Artigas, Uruguay's national hero, in "Mi ofrenda" ("My Offering") and "Ansina." The man is a symbol of fidelity and endurance:

> Ni los dolores, ni desengaños,
> esa gran brecha que abren los años
> ora en lo físico y en lo moral,
> sintió más íntimo ni más profundo
> que al expresarse: "Hasta el fin del mundo
> yo lo acompaño, mi General."

> (Neither the pains, nor disappointments,
> that great breach that the years open
> now in the physical and in the moral,
> he felt more intimate neither more profound
> than upon expressing himself: "To the end of the world
> I will accompany you, my General.")

In this poem of homage, Barrios extols Ansina's loyalty to Artigas, his attempts to present a positive impression of a group of people maligned since biblical times, and his subsequent historical lionization. Throughout the Uruguayan struggle for independence and nationhood, blacks were always on the front line, willing to sacrifice themselves for the good of the nation. Their patriotic attitudes of self-sacrifice are paradoxical indeed when contrasted to the social situation experienced by their descendants. In mute testimony to the years of black patriotism, struggle, sacrifice, and discrimination is the bronze statue by Belloni dedicated to Ansina, which bears the inscription: "I will accompany you my general, even if it is to the end of the world!" Uruguayans have a very short memory, it seems, in terms of their indebtedness to black warriors.

"Voices" acknowledges Langston Hughes's unending fight for black dignity throughout the world. Perhaps Barrios was inspired by some of his more militant writings, those from a Marxist perspective that concerned social class and economics and appeared in *New Masses* and *The Negro Worker* in the 1930s. The Hughes portrait is one of energy, awareness:

> Id, luchador incansable,
> generoso trotamundos
> de la tierra
> y de los mares,
> sobre tu potro rebelde
> desgranando tus cantares.
> Que tu voz ardiente y férrea
> demarcadora de rumbos,
> sepa que en estos lugares
> y en este rincón de América
> que baña el Río de la Plata,
> hay conscientes multitudes
> y voces que se levantan,
> y anhelos, ansias e inquietudes
> y conciencia proletaria.
>
> (Go, tireless fighter,
> generous world traveler
> of the earth
> and of the seas
> on your rebel horse
> shelling out your songs
> that your fiery and steely voice
> demarcator of directions
> know that in those places
> and in this corner of America
> that bathes the River Plate,
> there are conscientious multitudes
> and voices that raise,
> and longings, anxieties and worry
> and proletarian consciousness.)

The phrases "tireless fighter" and "world traveler" aptly describe Hughes, who fought for respect and human rights in both the New and Old worlds. Although he did not travel to Uruguay, that did not prohibit his being a model writer for Barrios and for those who wished to stimulate the masses, which calls into question the assumption that there was no communication between black writers of North and South America. Barrios wants to make it clear that in spite of physical distance, Hughes's sentiments are echoed among people in the most remote corners of the Americas. Barrios, for example, is motivated by the same unrest about which Hughes sings, as is clearly demonstrated in Barrios's poems to the disadvantaged and on the Afro-Uruguayan experience.

In an interview in 1948 between Pilar Barrios and Ceferino Nieres (Repórter), the following exchange took place concerning Barrios's commitment to the betterment of the Afro-Uruguayan's plight:

R.—In the struggle for our problems do you believe one can arrive at something?

B.—Always there is the possibility of arriving when one departs, my friend, even when mistaken paths are taken. What is not possible is to carry out a journey without first understanding it . . . I am optimistic in spite of disagreements and prevailing pessimism.[21]

In an oblique manner in this rare interview, Barrios expresses his eternal optimism concerning the future of Afro-Uruguayans. From the publication of his first poems in *Our Race* to the appearance of *Black Skin* and beyond, Pilar Barrios formed an essential part of that long struggle for Afro-Uruguayan cultural affirmation. The publication of *Black Skin* was, judging from advance publicity in *Our Race* and *Uruguay Magazine*, the single greatest achievement of the *Our Race* group of intellectuals. Its positive impact upon the black community throughout Uruguay and Argentina is documented in the many critical responses afforded the book, an important example of Afro-Uruguayan solidarity.

As a writer undergoing his personal interval of passage, Pilar Barrios's attention to black causes is understandable, since Afro-Uruguayans have not been fully integrated into the national culture. Barrios recognized early on that positive values must first be found in blackness before the transition could be made to being just another Uruguayan. *Our Race,* the Indigenous Black party, and *Black Skin* were all steps in that direction.

*   *   *

In sum, Virginia Brindis de Salas and Pilar Barrios are but two of a number of Afro-Uruguayan writers who flourished during several decades of this century, elevating blackness to a literary plane heretofore unachieved in Uruguay. Metaphorically, *The Call of Mary Morena* and *Black Skin* represent both an assertion of identity and a call for harmony, two crucial issues that remain socially unfulfilled, a fact that is more a testimony to the nature of Uruguayan society than to the aspirations of individual poets.

2

From Cañete to Tombuctú: The Peruvian Poetry of Nicomedes Santa Cruz

The Social Context

The only recent general historical treatment of contemporary Afro-Peruvians in Peru is found in *The African Experience in Spanish America: 1502 to the Present Day* (1976) by Leslie B. Rout, Jr. After a discussion of the presence of blacks and their role during the colonial period, Rout concentrates upon emancipation, the Afro-Peruvian since emancipation, the Afro-Peruvian in the national culture, and the future of the Afro-Peruvian. These subjects are covered in ten pages. However, this attention represents a step forward, since Peruvian historians tend to ignore blacks completely.

In his study, Rout offers positive comments about only two twentieth-century Afro-Peruvians who have had an impact upon Peruvian society, Agustín Vallejos, a labor leader, and Nicomedes Santa Cruz, an artist. Rout's conclusions are not optimistic:

> Unfortunately, the literary and cultural effects of Santa Cruz, Gamarra and a few others do not seem to have had much influence upon the mass of Afro-Peruvians. In this regard, the observation of George Schuyler, an Afro-American newspaperman, would still seem to be essentially valid. Writing in 1948, Schuyler concluded that Peruvians of negroid ancestry were about where the free Negroes were in our northern states in 1776, and as a group they are not going forward.[1]

Because of a lack of numbers, common goals, and racism, black Peruvians are being pushed further into obscurity by the ethnic forces at work within the country. Blacks represent approximately 1 percent of the population, or eighty thousand persons, and are decreasing proportionately because of miscegenation and the indigenous migration to Lima. The tragic dimension of this situation is the possibility that blacks will become extinct without their history ever being written.

A brief survey of widely circulated histories will substantiate the view that Peruvian historians have not seen fit to comment upon the role of blacks in the nation's evolution. J. M. Valega in his *Historia general de los peruanos (General History of Peruvians)* is unique in that the book contains a picture of and a poem by Nicomedes Santa Cruz.[2] Perhaps the reason for the omission of references to blacks is found in Jorge Basadre's *Historia de la república del Perú: 1822–1933 (History of the Peruvian Republic)*. Basadre offers the following assessment of "Las Razas" (The Races) after contrasting the Peruvian brand of racism with that of the United States and South Africa:

> The freeing of slaves in Peru was a relatively easy event. All that does not mean that there does not exist prejudice against Indians, Mixed, and Blacks. But those prejudices are not sanctioned by laws, and more than a deep racial sense they have an economic, social and cultural character. Color does not prohibit an aborigine, a half breed, or a blackish person from occupying high positions if he manages to accumulate a fortune or conquers political success.[3]

Basadre also comments upon the social distance between ethnic groups that is historical instead of racial. The economic difficulties as well as the political maneuvering surrounding manumission in Peru have been well documented by Rout and other enlightened historians.[4] In spite of the official version of ethnic relations in Peru offered by Basadre, it is obvious that historical determinism is an important factor. Discriminatory laws are not necessary to impede the progress of blacks if they are systematically denied access to fortune and political success. This is and has been the situation in Peru, where covert and overt discrimination reign.

Sociological studies of the first half of this century, by Felipe Boisset and José Carlos Mariátegui, for example, have not been favorable to Peruvian blacks. However, three later evaluations do give a more complete and balanced view of this population: *Negros en el Perú (Blacks in Peru,* 1947) by Roberto Mac-Lean y Estenós; *Poder blanco y resistencia negra en el Perú (White Power and Black Resistance in Peru,* 1975) by Denys Cuché; and *Tugurio: La cultura de los marginados (Slum: The Culture of the Marginal,* 1978) by Luis Millones.

Negros en el Perú is an assessment of Peruvian blacks during the sixteenth, seventeenth, and eighteenth centuries. Its primary concerns are with slavery, acculturation, attempts to emphasize positive aspects of culture, emergence of the mulatto class, and the subsequent "disappearance" of blacks from the Peruvian social fabric. This is the best sociological study, with a historical bent, of blacks during the early decades of their Peruvian experience. The documentation of early reactions by blacks to the Peruvian environment is the most valuable aspect of *Blacks in Peru.* No attention is given to modern-day Afro-Peruvians except for the 1940 census information.

Mac-Lean meticulously documents atrocities committed against the bondsmen and their reactions to harsh treatment in the form of creative expression through song, dance, and religion. He is at a loss, though, to explain the decline in the black populations in the first several decades of the twentieth century. The difficulty with determining the present number of blacks in Peru is directly related to internal migration patterns. The periods immediately preceding and following World War II saw the greatest influx of rural dwellers to the cities where most blacks lived. This migration of indigenous peoples in search of a better life further diluted the declining numbers of Afro-Peruvians, through intermarriage, and greatly accentuated the problem of being a recognizable ethnic entity. Combined with the absence of black immigration and low birth rates, migration and miscegenation helped to speed up the decline in the Afro-Peruvian population. One of the major problems facing Peruvian blacks is how to adjust to the bleaching process that is taking place.

White Power and Black Resistance in Peru by Denys Cuché is the best sociocultural study of Afro-Peruvians available. Cuché's original intention was to conduct "an anthropological interpretation of historical events" ("una interpretación antropológica de los hechos históricos").[5] In the process, Cuché examines the black presence in Peru from the Spanish conquest to the twentieth century, and unlike most scholars who have treated the topic, he does not devote most of his attention to slavery. That the author is French allows him to approach the material objectively and to arrive at conclusions that Peruvian scholars have been either unable or unwilling to set forth in terms of the positive dimensions of Afro-Peruvian culture. Cuché's study firmly verifies the process of cultural maroonage as the foundation of the contemporary Afro-Peruvian experience. The book is divided into fourteen chapters, treating topics such as slavery, economics, occupations, racism, miscegenation, sexuality, revolts, politics, and social organization.

The last two chapters, "Religious Deportment of Blacks" and "Folklore and Cultural Resistance of Blacks," examine vital aspects of the black experience with the intent of demonstrating how black Peruvians react posititively to combat cultural genocide. In discussing "black resistance and religious syncretism" in the first of these chapters, Cuché shows how blacks were able to combine Christian teachings with their own African religions to develop a system of worship that would benefit their spiritual needs. Imposed religion did not fill this void. Cuché concludes that blacks did not accept Christianity as it was taught; instead, they used Catholicism to express their own religiosity.[6] What blacks did succeed in achieving, through their religious syncretism, brotherhoods, and other religious outlets, was the development of religious symbols that sustained them through difficult times and some of which have survived to the present day. In the last chapter, Cuché contrasts imposed artificial folklore to spontaneous and authentic folklore. Dances, such as those celebrating the victories of Christians over Moors, and bullfights and cockfights served to demonstrate white superiority over black and to sublimate the desire for violence or resistance to the system of slavery. On the positive side, dances, the oral tradition, music, food, and language were cultural factors that aided Afro-Peruvians in being themselves. Cuché assesses the overall impact of acculturation, maintaining that black acculturation in the the nineteenth century was more material than formal. As a reaction to imposed folklore, blacks merely selected what was of significance to them. Today, remnants of black culture are in a state of siege because of the nationalistic tendency to view everything as Peruvian and because of the prevailing hostile attitude toward most black societal contributions regardless of their nature.

In sum, *White Power and Black Resistance in Peru* is a lucid analysis of the development and status of one of the major Peruvian ethnic groups. Cuché has begun a modern discussion of a problematic element at work within the Peruvian ethos. His study clarifies many uncertainties concerning blacks in Peru but leaves unanswered many questions concerning the dynamics of ethnicity and social class.

Slum: The Culture of the Marginal by Luis Millones delves into the sensitive area of interethnic relations in Huerta Perdida, a *barriada* (enclave) of Lima. In 1971, Millones and his colleagues surveyed 341 families, and their results are disturbing in terms of both the present status of blacks and the manner in which they are perceived by people who share similar socioeconomic conditions.

Racism is still alive and well but in the most unexpected quarters. The attitude toward blacks maintained by other marginal people seems to be the old attitude that we are poor also but our lighter color makes us superior. The attitudes expressed by Peruvian social historians of the early twentieth century are still echoed by the common people. Millones finds even deeper implications that paradigmatic activities associated with slavery such as laziness, cowardliness, agility, and physical strength are still applied to blacks.[7] Afro-Peruvians continue to bear the burden of slavery because in the minds of others they do not possess the positive qualities necessary to improve their social status. The slavery model remains implanted upon the mentality of the majority culture, thereby prejudicing that culture's perception of the Negro. Since the mixed and indigenous peoples are themselves receiving pressures from those who consider themselves whites, the blacks by default become the objects of their scorn.

Millones's premise is supported in subsequent observations by the people themselves, who appear to be aware of and very opinionated concerning the ethnic question. The author maintains, "The majority of our interviewees classified themselves as 'creole' or 'mixed' and demonstrated superiority toward the 'highlander' [Indians] and contempt toward those with bad hair [blacks]"; the majority sees itself as being "A good race, hard working, noble and healthy; creoles descendants of Spaniards, neither Indian nor Black; Peruvian race, of the Peruvians of long ago, of all of us, a legitimate race, a mixture of races."[8] For this particular group of people the "drop of Spanish blood" allows them to assume an attitude of superiority.

The hierarchal social structure becomes more obvious as the other two major ethnic groups, Indians and blacks, define their social roles. The Indians are "provincials . . . born in the highlands, descendants of the Incas, legitimate nationals, with indian blood, of the Peruvian, a pure race, the race of Peru"; the blacks or coloreds define themselves this way "because [their] parents were colored, black, nappy hair, without mixture, a strong race, a peaceful and quite race, native and frank."[9] The mixed and the Indian call upon what they believe to be glorious aspects of their past, Spanish and

Inca, respectively, to justify their superiority in relationship to the black who does not have an American past. It is precisely this lack of a documented historical past in Peru that denies the Afro-Peruvian a future.

This brief survey of historical and sociological interpretations of Afro-Peruvians is useful in that it provides an indication of how they have been perceived throughout the centuries. Moreover, these opinions call to question prevailing attitudes concerning existence of Peruvians of African descent, that there is no problem. As with most descendants of slaves throughout the Americas, black Peruvians find themselves still combating the stigmas attached to experiences acted out years ago. Needless to say, prevailing social attitudes are also manifested in the literary arena where, historically, very few Afro-Peruvian writers have published. Nicomedes Santa Cruz is an exception, but his trajectory has been far from ideal.

Décimas

In Peru, Nicomedes Santa Cruz suffers from a lack of critical exposure. This is not due entirely to the age-old distinction between popular and erudite poets. Rather, the issue is more fundamental, relating to politics and discrimination. For example, in his *Introducción crítica a la literatura peruana* (*Critical Introduction to Peruvian Literature*, 1974), Luis Alberto Sánchez discusses such mundane interests as women and poets of the people. The former discussion centers on women writers of the nineteenth and twentieth centuries. The poets of the people are classified as "young people charged with extinguishing social injustice with their verses, they ended up giving life to a poem-discourse, eloquent, declamatory, from whose influence few were saved."[10] Sánchez discusses poets of the last several decades, reserving his greatest praise for Javier Heraud, the poet-guerrilla, who was killed in 1963 while exercising the latter profession. Ironically, Heraud only became worthy of such positive critical acclaim after his death, when he was no longer a threat to the Peruvian power structure.

Yet none of the popular poets discussed is of the caliber of Nicomedes Santa Cruz—who is not even mentioned by Sánchez or any other Peruvian literary critic in a major publication. This is rare for a person who is widely read and recited throughout Peru and abroad and who has been the most popular poet of the people. How are we to explain this lack of critical attention? Santa Cruz is aware of the problem and in a response to my inquiries informed me that he does not belong to the literary elite in Peru.[11] Also, any black man who is capable of independent thought, especially from a leftist point of view, should be avoided whenever possible. The popularity that Santa Cruz enjoyed as a private performer at upper-class social occasions during the late 1950s and early 1960s waned as the rich began to listen to his messages. The dearth of serious critical attention to his work is apparently no surprise to Santa Cruz since years ago his father was denied a literary prize solely on the basis of color. Peruvian literary critics seem to be imitating their historian counterparts in not documenting positive contributions of Afro-Peruvians. Abroad, Santa Cruz has been the object of scholarly discussion in the form of numerous articles and a doctoral dissertation by Otis Handy, who places Santa Cruz's work within the *décima* tradition of Spanish America.

Nicomedes Santa Cruz has published three major volumes of poetry: *Décimas (Décimas,* 1960); *Cumanana (Cumanana,* 1964); and *Canto a mi Peru (Song to My Peru,* 1966). Most of the selections from these books form the core of two anthologies, *Ritmos negros de Perú (Black Rhythms of Peru,* 1971) and *Décimas y poemas: Antología (Décimas and Poems: Anthology,* 1971). Santa Cruz's publications have enjoyed outstanding success both at home and abroad, and he currently resides in Spain. There are three separate books of *Décimas.* A promotional edition containing eight poems appeared in 1959.[12] *Décimas* (1960) is the poet's first major publication and consists of sixty-nine poems. A revised and corrected edition of *Décimas* was published in 1969 with a prologue by Ciro Alegría. It contains the same poems as the earlier editions, along with a glossary and explanatory notes, as well as a thematic grouping of the material. Many of Nicomedes Santa Cruz's poems are repeated in several of his works. Therefore, for the sake of clarity and continuity, I will outline some of the basic themes encountered in *Décimas* and elaborate upon them in the same poems when they are present in other works. The 1960 edition of *Décimas* is my focal point. It is convenient to approach this work thematically, dividing it into five sections: the *décima* tradition; the black experience; religion; sports; and diverse topics.

It is interesting, first of all, to examine how the poet views the poetic process in general and the *décima* tradition in particular. There are two versions of the poem "Al compás del socabón" ("To the Beat of Guitar Melody"), both of which seek to define the *décima*. Conceptually related is "A todo canto de monte" ("To All Mountain Songs"), which attempts to justify the presence of this art form and to explain the techniques involved. The *décima* is generally characterized by ten-line stanzas of eight syllables, rhyming *a b b a a c c d d c* in consonance. The *décima* treats topics of a religious *(a lo divino)* and of a secular nature *(a lo humano).* The second version of "To the Beat of the Guitar Melody" links the Peruvian *décima* tradition with popular poetry worldwide:

> Van trazando mi camino
> nuestras criollas estampas
> Como le inspiran sus pampas
> al payador argentino
> Como cantara el beduíno
> a su famoso laúd
> Como coplero andaluz
> o trovador italiano
> Yo canto como peruano
> con décimas del Perú.[13]

(They go tracing my path
our creole sketches
As he inspired his pampas
the Argentine gaucho singer
As the Bedouin would sing
to his famous lute
as an Andalusian rhymer
or an Italian trovador
I sing as a Peruvian
with décimas from Peru.)

Most civilizations have spawned a tradition of popular poetry, and Peru is no exception. Not only is Santa Cruz following the steps of his Peruvian predecessors in terms of heritage, but he is also finding inspiration in daily activities just as the Argentine *payadores,* or gaucho poets, did. The relationship between the gaucho poet and the *décima* singer is a close one; both belong to a tradition that emphasizes spontaneous verbal competition. In this regard, Nestor Ortiz Oderigo relates Afro-American popular poets in the Río de la Plata region to the *trovadores* of the Middle Ages, the *minnesinger, the African jilli keas,* and the Afro–North American *minstrels.*[14] Moreover, adds Ortiz Oderigo, "The Black reigned absolutely in this verbal art. And not only in our country. He also did it under different skies of the New World in which the African element exercised some social or esthetic force."[15] Popular poetry has been accepted throughout the ages as creative art. As Ortiz Oderigo points out, the black has always been prevalent in such spontaneous poetic activity. This is certainly true for the *décima* tradition in Peru, where Nicomedes Santa Cruz represents the current state of a long and dynamic process concerned with viewing Afro-Peruvian culture in a positive light.

The question of *negritud* in the poetry of Nicomedes Santa Cruz has been treated in an article by Teresa C. Salas and Henry J. Richard.[16] *Negritud* is out of necessity modified to conform with cultural and national contexts.[17] Due to the complexities of cultures and peoples in Latin America, a single concept of *negritud* is not applicable indiscriminantly. There are, however, certain common denominators shared by black peoples separated in time and space.

In his penetrating article "Saludo y despedida a la negritud" ("Hello and Goodbye to *Negritud*"), René Depestre questions and reaffirms some of the basic premises of *negritud* while advancing his ideas, from a Marxist perspective, concerning progress toward Americanism.[18] The study is worthy of discussion here because Depestre and Santa Cruz share some fundamental ideas concerning the black experience. The present-day search by Afro–Latin Americans for identity and positive cultural values is rooted in the adverse impact of the colonial experience. According to Depestre, "The colonial system wishes to make of Africans and their descendants Anglo Saxon and Latin byproducts from Europe in the Americas. Not only would the slave lose his liberty but also collective memory and the facility to transmit cultural continuity."[19] This process is what Depestre terms *zombification*, the psychological as well as the physical destruction of blacks in the name of the capitalist system. The intent was to create a subhuman by robbing from blacks their past, their history, their self-confidence, their legends, their family, their beliefs, and their art, as well as concepts of beauty associated with blackness. Slavery and the dehumanizing process that it perpetuated served to strip the victim of many positive cultural traits. As a defense mechanism, slaves resorted to cultural maroonage. Despite the negativism associated with slavery, some positive cultural values managed to persist despite the odds. But, as Depestre points out, cultural maroonage could not save the African languages or the African judicial, political, and economic systems because of total immersion in the socioeconomic realities of America. Nevertheless, positive cultural attitudes "saved from zombification all that could be saved in religion, magic, plastic arts, dance, music, and, of course, the capacity for resistance to oppression."[20]

Cultural maroonage is vital in that it halted the process of complete dehumanization and total loss of ethnic identity. More importantly, it established the basic frame of reference for *negritud* from which many Afro–Latin American writers, especially Santa Cruz, operate today. Their works continually extol positive virtues and remnants of African culture associated with religion, magic, plastic arts, dance, music, oral literature, and other aspects of popular culture.

In this article, Depestre does not deny that *negritud* is and has been vital, but he sees it as an intermediate step toward Americanism. For him, Nicolás Guillén is the exemplary model in the Spanish-speaking world, because "racial sentiment comes integrated by Guillén to Cubanity—to the historical essence of the country—, it has not been a literary mode, but a mode of being Cuban, Antillean, American."[21] Guillén and Cuba, however, represent a type of cultural and historical synthesis that is not prevalent throughout Latin America. No doubt many blacks would like to be integrated totally into their national societies as the situation is alleged to be in Cuba, but, unfortunately, they are not and there is no indication they every will be.

Nicomedes Santa Cruz's treatment of the black experience is parallel to some of the concepts outlined by Depestre. He writes of the colonial experience, cultural maroonage, *negritud*, Americanism, and Pan-Africanism, and he has demonstrated his concern from his earliest poems—"Ritmos negros del Perú" ("Black Rhythms of Peru," 1956), for example—to his most recent—including "Madre Angola" ("Mother Angola," 1976). In *Décimas* alone, there are fifteen poems devoted to the Afro-Peruvian experience. Collectively, they interpret the black experience from slavery to the present, concentrating upon culture, color, and language.

The question of whether an Afro-Peruvian creole language developed among the slaves has received the attention of several scholars, with the consensus being that the language mixture of Spanish and African did not pass the pidgin stages. However, a number of words of the *replana* (slang) remain. These words and their meanings are the topic of the *décima* "En la era colonial" ("In the Colonial Era").

> Mezcla de hispano caló
> con dialectos africanos,
> jerga de negros peruanos
> Fue la que antaño se habló:
> "Misioma" remplazó al ¡Yo!
> del pronombre personal,
> y hablando de igual a igual
> "susioma" fue justed! o ¡tú!
> para el negro del Perú
> en la era colonial.

> (A mixture of Hispanic slang
> with African dialects
> popular speech of black Peruvians
> Was what was spoken long ago:
> "Misioma" replaced the "I"
> of the personal pronoun,
> and speaking among equals
> "Susioma" was "You"
> for the Peruvian Black
> in the Colonial era.)

In *El lenguaje peruano (Peruvian Language)*, Pedro M. Benvenutto Murrieta, who reflects the typical Peruvian attitude, is reluctant to admit that any words in Peruvian Spanish are of African origin. Benvenutto gives a list of eight words of which he is sure and another dozen or so with possible African roots. Oddly enough, none of the words pointed out by him appears in the poem by Nicomedes Santa Cruz. The important question posed by Benvenutto is whether the *replana* was "the exclusive language of Blacks or the argot of the Peruvian underground?"[22] Denys Cuché is of the same opinion as Nicomedes Santa Cruz: "The *replana* had syncretic forms but it had been created by the Blacks."[23] It has been well documented in many countries that during slavery blacks created their own forms of secret verbal communication because of the oppressive system. Are we to believe that in Peru it was any different?

Of the thirty-one words of African origin present in the poem "In the Colonial Era," the majority have passed on to slang usage and can be found in the book *Argot limeño o jerga criolla del Perú (Limeñan Argot or Creole Slang of Peru*, 1977) by Guillermo E. Bendezu Neyra, a publication considered to be the most authoritative treatment of Peruvian popular language. Other words not included in this publication but present in the poem by Santa Cruz are *tecla* (elderly lady), *ganchurime* (with close friends), *remia* (move up), *tomba* (stomach cavity), *ánima gurfia* (crow), *jamar* (to eat), *me aparro* (I approach), and *palisio* (guitar). Although it may seem as if a list of words from the past is insignificant, one needs only to think of the one phrase from *Roots* that was of such great impact culturally for the Haley clan.

In the first section of *Décimas*, many of the poems are concerned with the African connection: "Mi dios, mi Zanahary" ("My god, My Zanahary!") and "Ritmos de la esclavitud" ("Rhythms of Slavery") are the most indicative of this tendency. The former poem discusses the impact of slavery upon the systems of worship and the beliefs of the slaves. Baptism of the individual and prohibition of former religious practices did not change the African mindset, at least not during the first several generations. There was a constant conflict between new and old ways of relating to the cosmos. Therefore, the practice of religious syncretism evolved, since the slaves wished to maintain some of their own religious practices while assimilating new cultural values.

> Amuleto de la muerte
> era el grigrí de los bantos
> y Zanahary en sus cantos
> el dios bueno, justo, y fuerte.
> En esta tierra de muerte
> poco sirvió aquella fe.
> Una cadena en el pie
> y empezó a perder su influjo
> el más importante brujo:
> poderoso Karambé.

> (Charm of death
> was the *grigrí* of the Bantus
> and Zanahary in his songs
> the good, just, and strong god.
> In this land of death
> For little served that faith.
> A chain on the foot
> and he began to lose his influence
> the most important sorcerer
> powerful Karambé.)

The image of death predominates in this stanza, not just physical death but the passing of religious tradition. The ensuing conflict of physical and spiritual realities accentuates the degree of pain and suffering inherent in the colonial experience. Resistance to the religious norms of the majority culture was punished institutionally.

> Con la Inquisición se pierde
> hasta el último hechicero,
> lo juzgan por embustero,
> lo azotan y el polvo muerde.

> (With the Inquisition was lost
> even the last sorcerer,
> they judged him a deceiver,
> they beat him and he bit the dust.)

African rites proved not to be strong enough to cope with the dehumanizing practices of slavery and the Inquisition, institutions whose major objective was to change people into things devoid of cultural or religious concerns (zombification). The slave's major preoccupation was survival. Coupled with religious persecution and torture by organized religion, Zanahary, Karambé, and the *hechicero* (sorcerer) were systematically eliminated. Along with these myths and symbols, many rites and practices associated with Africa disappeared.

From Santa Cruz's point of view, understanding the experiences of slavery and the history of blacks to the present is essential if one is to perceive anything positive in their contribution to Peruvian culture. Therefore, he constantly evokes the African past in an attempt to place the black experience in its proper perspective. "Black Rhythms of Peru" is his best-known attempt toward this end. It is a poetic introduction to the trauma of being a slave, from the brutal uprooting in Africa to the new home on the plantation:

> De Africa llegó mi abuela
> vestida con caracoles,
> la trajeron lo' españoles
> en un barco carabela.
> La marcaron con candela,
> la carimba fue su cruz.
> Y en América del Sur
> al golpe de sus dolores
> dieron los negros tambores
> ritmos de la esclavitud.

> (From Africa my grandmother arrived
> dressed in sea shells
> the Spaniards brought her
> in a caravel ship.
> They marked her with fire
> the brand was her cross.
> And in South America
> to the beat of her sorrows
> the black drums gave out
> rhythms of slavery.)

Images of humiliation and degradation abound in the poem. The initial symbol of depersonalization, systematic branding, a common practice, reveals the inhumanity involved in the flesh traffic as human beings were converted into property.

"Black Rhythms of Peru" continues to relate the experiences of Afro-Peruvians during slavery, explaining that oppression led to creative expression in the form of song, dance, and other elements of folklore. The first two strophes deal with the inhumanity of the flesh traffic, while the third and fourth enumerate modes of expression. The sad *socabón* is a guitar melody that accompanies the singing of traditional *décimas* along the Peruvian coast. The *Zaña* is an orgiastic dance and song routine originally performed by slaves from the Zaña area in Chiclayo.

Unfortunately all of these song and dance routines were performed to the rhythm of chains. Above the sounds of the *zamacueca*, a song and dance representative of miscegenation, and the *festejo*, an Afro-Peruvian coastal dance, one heard echoes of the *panalivio*, a song-lament. Throughout the experience of slavery there were moments of joy and celebration, but these were overshadowed by the realities of being a slave. Geographical polarities are established between which Santa Cruz's ethnic poetry will gravitate, "From Cañete to Tombuctú / From Chancay to Mozambique." Cañete is a southern coastal town with a sizable black population, while Chancay's black element has been assimilated. Santa Cruz juxtaposes them to the African *nomen* (Tombuctú, Mozambique) to demonstrate his constant backward glance for answers during his search for meaning in the Peruvian ethos.

In "Black Rhythms of Peru," Nicomedes Santa Cruz shows how the system of bondage, in a negative sense, gave rise to cultural and folkloric values still prevalent today, a process that is indeed reflective of cultural maroonage. Similar sentiments are expressed in "Del ritmo negroide añejo" ("Of the Old Blackish Rhythm"), in which the only outlet for sad experiences is song and dance.

Three of the poems in this section of *Décimas* are dedicated to the black woman: "Que mi sangre se sancoche" ("Let My Blood Boil") and two poems treating the popular Pelona, a woman who has forgotten her humble beginnings. The best known of these latter poems is a plea for reason on the part of a disillusioned man. It begins,

> Cobo has cambiado; pelona,
> cisco de carbonería,
> Te has vuelto una negra mona
> con tanta huachafería.

> (How you have changed, Pelona,
> coal dust from the coal yard,
> You have become a cute black woman
> with so much uppishness.)

As far as the man is concerned, the woman is living above her social status, and he is envious of her new attitudes and habits. The word *pelona* is derogatory; it also refers to her short nappy hair, described as "head of a witch" ("Cabeza de bruja"). Wearing heels, smoking, and dieting are habits that the man fails to comprehend. A long list of other "vices" are enumerated as she must not forget that she is coal black, which for him demands another set of values. This poem points out a crucial social dilemma. For the woman, it is possible for her to improve her social status, often temporarily, by enhancing her appearance and mingling with people of other ethnic or social groups. For the man, even this possible exploitation of physical features is often denied.

In "How You Have Changed, Pelona," the attitude is ambivalent and apologetic; after much ridicule the posture is one of mockery:

> Perdona que te critique
> y si me río perdona.

Antes eras tan pintona
con tu traje de percala
y hoy, por dártela de mala
te has vuelto una negra mona.

(Pardon if I criticize you
and if I laugh pardon.
Before you were so desirable
with your suit of percale
And today, in a change for the worse
you have become a cute black woman.)

The woman has apparently outgrown her socioeconomic situation, and the man does not approve of the idea that he will be left behind. Change appears to be in store for him also, since he will either have to accept her leaving or improve his own social status. "Now I Don't Love You, Pelona" is on the same theme of rejection, but now the Pelona has been cast aside by someone of a higher social standing. The man's negative perceptions concerning upward mobility have apparently been justified.

"Let My Blood Boil" stresses the tantalizing effects of a woman upon her companion in both the physical and the spiritual dimensions:

¡Negra . . . ! ¡Grupa de repisa!
¡Cinturita de cuchara!
En la noche de tu cara
hay media luna de risa . . . !
Esta noche tienes prisa
por provocar algún boche:
Me miras como en reproche,
con todo el cuerpo me miras,
y deseas—cuando giras—
que mi sangre se sancoche.

(Black woman! Wide rump!
Waist of a spoon!
In the night of your face
there is a half moon of laughter . . . !
This night you are in a hurry
to start some kind of uproar:
you look at me as a reproach,
with all of your body you look at me,
and you wish—when you gyrate—
that my blood boil.)

The woman, with all of her positive attributes, is an intoxicating presence, provoking with her entire body. Her blackness is amplified by the many images of night projected throughout the poem. Highly expressive poetic language is weaved masterfully throughout. The evocation of time is indicative where there is a personification of the lamp—"licked" ("lamió"), "lips" ("labios")—which is achieved through imagery related to human tiredness—"shut up" ("calló"), "yawning" ("bostezando"). Also, alliteration with the liquid *l* gives the impression of a long, drawn out process. This image of time signals the transition from one locale to another by the speaker who begs, "let them serve me more night" ("que me sirvan más noche").

The protagonist is determined to return after he is beaten and to achieve his goal—even if this persistence costs him his money and his life. The obsession with possessing this woman has taken him beyond the realm of reason. Conceited and unobtainable as she might be, still she represents the maximum challenge:

> y me matan o te bebo
> en mi copa de mañana.

> (and they will kill me or I will drink you
> in my morning cup!)

His physical condition is not clear at the end of the poem; there is an ambiguous red buttonhole in his shirt. Either he has been physically harmed or his emotional wound is profound.

In the two Pelona poems and "Let My Blood Boil," the black woman is presented as an elusive but highly desirable figure for the black man. This attitude calls for a measure of ambivalence in her characterization because there is unreciprocated desire that inevitably leads to resentment in "How You Have Changed, Pelona" and to self-destruction by the male in the latter.

Miscegenation is the theme of both "Hay negra y negra retinta" ("There is a Black Woman and a Jet Black Woman") and "Desde la negra retinta" ("From the Jet Black Woman"). Each poem is an ironic interpretation of the biological consequence of interethnic union. The latter poem begins with an allusion to Ricardo Palma and represents a summary of the phenomenon of miscegenation:

> Al que de inga no le toque
> le tocará de mandinga,
> todo es la misma jeringa
> con diferente bitoque.
> Algún fulano que enfoque
> su genealogía extinta
> de ascendencia cuarta o quinta
> por ramajes paralelos
> hallará entre sus abuelos
> desde la negra retinta.

> (He who is not touched by the Inca
> will be touched by the Mandinga
> it's all the same garbage
> with a different guise.
> Some so-and-so who traces
> his extinct genealogy
> from fourth or fifth generation
> through parallel branches
> will find his grandparents
> from the jet black woman.)

The Peruvian process of miscegenation is a complex one, and any claims to pure blood are questionable due to the biological exchanges that have taken place over the centuries. "Garbage" and "guise" suggest how ridiculous the situation is.

The mulatto quadroon presents a problem; he has a choice as to his ethnic identity and consequently makes the more beneficial one:

> pero niega el mestizaje
> de abuelos color carbón.
> Busca al tío chapetón
> y al negro le hace una finta.

> (he denies the mixture
> of black grandparents
> He searches for the Spanish uncle
> and fakes out the Black)

Miscegenation in Peru has been a bleaching process whose purpose is to negate blackness. The ironic dilemma faced by Afro-Peruvians is whether to deny one's color, a form of ethnocide, for the sake of greater material access. The issue remains unresolved. In a society in which the lighter one's skin is, the more privileges one is afforded, where possible the mulatto will suppress the African part of his heritage in favor of the European. The poet is not alarmed by this fact, but he takes pride in his blackness and comes out vehemently against racism.

Within Santa Cruz's poetry, Afro-Peruvian folklore encompasses mainly music, poetry, dance, and religion. In an article published in 1957, entitled "Black Folklore of Peru," César A. Angeles Caballero outlined the following folkloric categories: oral literature; dances and musical instruments; beliefs and superstitions; and celebrations and traditional ceremonies.[24] In an interview with me, Nicomedes Santa Cruz maintained that "black folklore" does not exist but that "Peruvian folklore with black aspects" does, since Peruvian culture is made up of many components.[25] Nevertheless, elements of categories two (music, rhythm) and four (ceremonies, celebrations) play an important thematic role in Santa Cruz's poetry as it interprets the black experience in Peru. Indeed, there is an attempt on the poet's part to educate the public about black contributions to Peruvian culture. "Dios perdone a mis abuelos" ("God Pardon My Grandparents") is illustrative and deals with the Zaña. This song and dance, it appears, had an irreverent beginning, growing out of slavery, a situation that the priest attempted to soothe with religion. A black who was not attuned to the religious mores dubbed the Catholic Mass "patraña," a hoax, and paid with his life.

The teaching "Before God, we are equals" is a joke for the slaves because they know what the real situation is. Consequently,

> . . . De este modo tan austero
> nació en Zaña aquel cantar,
> satírico protestar
> de la liturgia y el clero.

(. . . from this very harsh mode
was born in Zaña that song
a satirical protestation
of the liturgy and the clergy.)

Like so many other protest songs and dances among blacks, the Zaña, a type
of blues, was born out of a situation of exploitation and degradation, of toil
and misery that typified several centuries of early Afro-Peruvian life.

"Cantando acuricanduca" ("Singing Softly") relates one of the most
popular Afro-Peruvian dances, the zapateo—a version of the tap dance—to
the folkloric tradition:

Desde su cuna a la tumba
zapateó el negro africano . . .

(From his cradle to his grave,
tap danced the black African . . .)

The zapateo, which is viewed as another form of the African majumba,
remains an essential element in the Peruvian coastal tradition by being
passed on from father to son. This same concern for cultural transmission is
expressed in "Apuesta hasta mi pellejo," "Voy a cantar un palmero," and
"Por ser la primera voz" ("I Bet Even My Skin," "I'm Going to Sing a Palm
Song," and "Being the First Time").

Both "Soy un negro sobrasón" ("I Am a Fiery Black") and "De ser como
soy me alegro" ("Being As I Am Pleases Me") are personal poems that reflect
upon attitudes surrounding being black in Peru. The latter poem is an appeal
for human dignity and a request to go beyond color and surface impression
to look at the real person since

Ni el color ni la estatura
determinan el sentir.

(neither color nor size
determines feeling.)

In poems dealing with questions of ethnicity and identity, Nicomedes
Santa Cruz expresses his concern for the preservation of Afro-Peruvian
culture. Out of necessity his poems are elegiac because he is in the ironic
position of witnessing the loss of what he is trying so desperately to affirm.
In these poems from Décimas, Santa Cruz has been assessing the Afro-
Peruvian experience historically, grappling with the problems of self-
definition, finally arriving at an acceptance of his own Afro-Peruvian
identity.

Religious themes also play a part in Décimas. "Todo lo que se asegura"
("All That Is Assured") is an ironic view of how religion is perceived by
people who have divergent attitudes concerning the creation of humankind.
The poet is critical of the intellectual person who lacks faith and who tries to
disprove the biblical version of the Creation. Nevertheless, ironically, this
person will pray for salvation when death approaches. In his religious
fervor, the poet calls for more faith and fewer theories. Throughout his

poetry, Santa Cruz reveals strong religious sentiment along traditional Roman Catholic lines. "En la época primera" ("In the First Epoch"), for example, is concerned with God and his infinite powers.

Two religious symbols related to the Afro-Peruvian experience that are prevalent throughout Santa Cruz's poetry are San Martín de Porres and El Señor de los Milagros, both of whom evolved from slavery and have subsequently been transformed into Peruvian religious myths. The figures of San Martín de Porres and El Señor de los Milagros are of prime importance in the Afro-Peruvian's interpretation of religion throughout the centuries. They serve as images that grew out of slavery and remain vital, being used by many to relieve present-day burdens. Nicomedes Santa Cruz is calling upon a sense of tradition and profound spirituality when he treats the themes of San Martín de Porres and El Señor de los Milagros. He is, in essence, examining cultural and religious continuity that has provided strength for black Peruvians throughout the centuries. He hopes that these traditions will continue their positive functions as Afro-Peruvians continue to hang on to vestiges of their culture.

Martín de Porres, an Afro-Peruvian saint, is the subject of "Santo demi devoción" ("Saint of My Devotion"):

> ¿Milagros? El hizo tantos
> como peces tiene el mar,
> de empezarles a contar
> no acabarían mis cantos.
> Este Santo entre los Santos
> del Cielo recibío el don.
> A su canonización
> —que aguarda el mundo cristiano—
> sabré que en el Vaticano
> no hicieron segregación.
>
> (Miracles? He performed as many
> as the sea has fishes,
> to begin telling them
> my songs would never end.
> This Saint among Saints
> from Heaven received the talent.
> At his canonization
> —that the Christian world awaits—
> I will know that in the Vatican
> they didn't tolerate segregation.)

The poem is a call for more respect for San Martín de Porres who, according to the poet, is commonly referred to as Brother Martín (Fray Martín), Mulatto (Mulato), or Colored Man with the Broom (Moreno de la Escoba). Because of San Martín's love for humankind and attitudes toward ethnic harmony, he deserves the same respect and equality as other saints.

In the same vein, "Paso a Nuestro Amo y Señor" ("Passage to Our Lord and Savior") describes the annual anniversary parade on 21 October celebrating the contribution of a painting of Christ the Redeemer by a slave, El

Señor de los Milagros (Man of Miracles). The permanent presence and significance of this religious symbol forms an important part of contemporary Peruvian religious mythology. Raúl Banchero Castellano tells the history of this very important Peruvian religious figure in the following manner: "An inspired slave of Angolan origin driven by unpredictable and superior impulse painted on the wall of his brotherhood's socializing place the image of the Crucified Redeemer for patronage and guidance."[26] Painted with great difficulty over a wall that was not ideal by a slave who had no art training, the mural survived the devastating earthquakes of 13 November 1655, 17 June 1678, and 20 October 1687. Its durable quality in the face of adversity was considered miraculous. Sebastían de Antunano y Rivas initiated the first procession and religious ceremony with an image of El Señor de los Milagros in the neighborhood of Pachacamilla following the quake of 1687. His purpose was to provide an outlet for the faithful to worship.

This is precisely the religious thrust of "Passage to Our Lord and Savior." The poem begins with a description of the procession and terminates with an imploration for divine grace:

> Sobre el lienzo de Jesús
> la tarde pinta una sombra.
> Sobre las frentes se nombra
> señal de la Santa Cruz.
>
> . . . .
>
> a Ti, Señor, me consagro,
> y de tus perfiles magros
> venga a nos tu Redención
> que nunca negó perdón
> el Señor de los Milagros.
>
> (Upon the canvas of Jesus
> the evening paints a shadow
> Upon the foreheads is engraved
> the sign of the Holy Cross.
>
> . . . .
>
> To You, Father, I dedicate myself
> and from your lean profiles
> come to us your Redemption
> that never denied pardon
> the Man of Miracles.)

Appropriately shrouded in religious symbolism, "Passage to Our Lord and Savior" represents a traditional Catholic and Afro-Peruvian cultural synthesis; Savior and slave merge in the painting. The search for positive sustaining myths has led, not surprisingly, to religion, which blacks have always viewed as essential in the process of spiritual liberation. Appropriately, religious devotion is part of the process of validating Afro-Peruvian religious heroes to whom they could turn for relief from intolerable social conditions. This quest for heroes extends to the secular level as well.

Black athletes and their impact upon Peruvian culture are also of prime importance in the poetry of Nicomedes Santa Cruz. Soccer, volleyball, and boxing are sports that at one time or another have been dominated by blacks. Alianza Lima, a soccer club whose outstanding players are and have been blacks, receives a great deal of poetic attention. In the introduction to his study *Minorías étnicas en el Perú (Ethnic Minorities in Peru)*, Luis Millones relates an interesting anecdote concerning the manner in which Alianza Lima and its players are perceived by the general public. At the end of a soccer match between Alianza Lima and Sporting Cristal, a fan of Sporting Cristal expressed outrage at the players of Alianza Lima: "He called them 'black slaves' and attributed the defeat to the massive presence of them on the team." Milliones was dismayed by this attitude because both teams seemed to have the same number of black players. Upon inquiring further, he was told, "Those with Cristal are *zambos*, those with Alianza are all shining niggers."[27] The attitude revealed is no different from the universal racist one in which black athletes are acceptable as long as they are on our side and we are winning. Millones adds that the nonblack public blamed even the internal problems of Alianza Lima on the preponderance of blacks.

The poem "Valdivieso, Rostaing, Soria" by Santa Cruz is a tribute to the many great players of Alianza Lima:

> Ni en Chile, ni en Argentina,
> ni en Uruguay ni en Brasil
> ha salido un cuadro al field
> como el del "Alianza Lima" . . .
> Cuando alcanzaron la cima
> los Negros de La Victoria,
> formaban la marcatoria
> de la zona posterior
>
> . . . .
>
> Valdivieso, Rostaing, Soria.
>
> (Neither in Chile, nor in Argentina
> nor in Uruguay nor in Brazil
> has a team gone onto the field
> like that of Alianza Lima . . .
> When they reached the top
> the Blacks of La Victoria
> made up the scoring line
> of the rear zone
>
> . . . .
>
> Valdivieso, Rostaing, Soria.)

The poem captures the sense of competition in the game, extolling the virtuoso movements of "the Blacks of La Victoria," a reference to the players and their neighborhood. Names indicate that the time period is the 1940s, and Santa Cruz has recorded some of the greatest moments in their careers. Black athletes in Peru have had a long and disinguished history, especially in

Lima and Chincha from which most of them come. As has been the case worldwide, athletics have provided an escape from poverty and assured fame, fortune, and social mobility for many.

Chincha, located in the district of El Carmen, continues to be the Peruvian city that has the largest enclave of blacks outside of Lima. The El Carmen district (where El Carmen, a black settlement, is located) was created in 1916, and as far as population is concerned there are "10,121 inhabitants according to the census of 1972, for the most part of the black race."[28] A textbook description of Chincha by Jaime Marroquín says, "Chincha is synonymous with large estates, good wine and excellent cotton, urban progress, great athletes, championship race horses and invincible fighting cocks."[29] In a cultural survey of this region, Marroquín states that the majority of Chincha's great sports figures were affiliated with the Cilloniz Sports Club on the San José estate. Some of the athletes, from an impressive array of boxers and soccer players, were accorded national and international fame as they played important roles in the Peruvian sports structure. They included Bombón Corona, Mauro Mina, Victor Lobatón, Roberto and Felix Castillo, and Cornelio Heredia.

Most Afro-Peruvian athletes, however, pass into obscurity and poverty after playing for love of the game, glory, and patriotism rather than money, as dramatically illustrated by the case of Cornelio Heredia, "Chocolatín" ("Chocolate Man"), eleven times captain of the Peruvian national soccer team and upon whom hard times have fallen. In an interview with Hernán Velarde, Heredia maintains that he was a slave of Alianza Lima, his former team. After detailing the many broken promises and disillusions experienced during his playing career, Heredia sums up the attitude of the club owners toward him: "They have become my enemies. The other day I went to ask Mr. Souza Fereyra for a pass and he didn't give it to me. 'There is nothing for the enemies of Alianza,' he told me."[30] A sad commentary, indeed, upon the situation of one of the greatest soccer players ever to have lived. His usefulness gone, he has been cast aside like any other worn-out part.

Santa Cruz's other topics for *décimas* include war, death, the cities, Santa Cruz family history, the bullfight, basketball, faith, and music. Outstanding among the last three is "En su estilo jaranero" ("In Its Merry Style"), a discussion of the black influence upon Peruvian music and dance. The evolution of the waltz in Peru is symptomatic of what happened to most dances, and for that matter people, in a country of continuous cultural and biological exchange:

> El vals—oriundo de Viena—
> se hizo cholo en el Perú:
> la seda perdió el frufrú,
> cambió a percala morena,
> aroma de hierbabuena,
> cuartito sin claraboya . . .

Así el vals se desarrolla
entre humilde y pobre gente
y pese al precario ambiente
cada vals es una joya!

(The waltz—native of Vienna—
became mixed in Peru:
silk lost the exotic
changed to brown percale
the smell of mint
a little room without a skylight . . .
This way the waltz develops
among humble and poor people
and in spite of the precarious environment
each waltz is a jewel!)

In a world of constant human reciprocity, even the most elite manifestations of culture are not immune to outside influence and transformation. The process of cholofication (enculturation) is evident in the change from silk to percale and the development of the waltz among humble and poor people. This change in constituency has in no way detracted from the overall importance of the dance. Indeed, its cultural viability has been enhanced.

In the remaining poems, Peru—the country, its people, and its institutions—is the primary literary focus. A sense of Peruvianess permeates the poetry of Nicomedes Santa Cruz in these *décimas*. Santa Cruz's first major publication is important because it lays the thematic and ideological frameworks of his subsequent poetry, which also embraces all aspects of human concerns, from the most trivial to the most profound. Because Nicomedes Santa Cruz conceives of poetry as being of the people, his work understandably reflects their sentiments.

Décimas reflects a profound sense of *negritud*, as well as the poet's reaction to the problems inherent in being black in Peruvian society. The issues of identity, dualism, and the ultimate confrontation with a hostile society tender the tone of his poetry. In the effort to reconcile mythic time with his present historical situation, Santa Cruz seeks to expound upon positive manifestations of Afro-Peruvian folklore and traditions.

Cumanana

Cumanana, published in 1964, is Nicomedes Santa Cruz's second major collection of poetry. In addition to new materials, the book contains poems written in the poet's early formulative stages, some of which first appear in *Décimas*. *Cumanana* is divided into four sections: "Al compás del socabón" ("To the Beat of the Guitar Melody"); "Décimas de pie forzado" ("*Décimas* of Short Lines"); "Poemas" ("Poems"); and, again, "Poemas" ("Poems"). Thematic concerns range from the black Peruvian experience to the international ethnic situation, with ample time given to Peruvian and other human problems.

"To the Beat of the Guitar Melody" is devoted primarily to the black experience. Twelve poems compose this section, eight of which are included in *Décimas*. The four new compositions are "El café" ("Coffee"), "Oiga usted, señor dotor" ("Listen Here, Mr. Doctor"), "Velorio de un negro criollo" ("Wake of a Black Creole"), and "Meme neguito" ("Cradle Song"). These are some of the most frequently anthologized poems of Nicomedes Santa Cruz because of his tendency to stress the affirmative in the black Peruvian experience in the historical evolution from slavery to the present.

The Afro-Peruvian trajectory is symbolically treated in "Coffee," which compares the destinies of a man and coffee. This poem is written in the *décima* form as a dialogue:

> Tengo tu mismo color
> y tu misma procedencia,
> Somos aroma y esencia
> y amargo es nuestro sabor.
> Tú viajaste a Neva York
> con visa de Zimbambué.
> Yo mi trópico crucé
> de Abisinia a las Antillas.
> Soy como ustedes semillas.
> Soy un grano de café.

> (I have your same color
> and your same origin,
> we are aroma and essence
> and our taste is bitter.
> You traveled to New York
> with a visa from Zimbambué.
> I crossed my tropic
> from Abyssinia to the Antilles.
> I am seeds like you.
> I am a grain of coffee.)

The poet identifies totally with coffee, as origins and destinies are linked through colonial times to freedom. Coffee is not only the impetus for the armed struggle but provides inspiration for the poet as well. As the poem ends, destinies have run full circle:

> ¡Vamos, hermanos, valor
> El café nos pide fe;
> y Changó y Ochún y Agué
> Piden un grito que vibre
> por nuestra América libre,
> libre como su café!

> (Let's go brothers, courage
> The coffee asks us for faith;
> and Changó and Ochún and Agué
> demand a cry that vibrates
> throughout our free America,
> free as her coffee!)

Here, African deities are invoked in the struggle for liberty as Changó, Ochún, and Agué are spiritual bridges between the New and Old worlds. "Coffee" is a complex poem, elaborating an ironic contrast between the black man and coffee and their parallel destinies. But through personification, coffee becomes a metaphor for freedom cloaked within two images of blackness.

"Listen Here, Mr. Doctor," on the other hand, shows a black man determined to maintain dignity in his household before the anticipated arrival of a white man. The former is a chauffeur, and the latter, his boss, has been invited to a festive occasion. Certain words and jokes are taboo and even manners have to be altered:

> mande al diablo el tenedor
> y deje vacío el plato!
> Son buenos guisando gato
> los pobres de mi color

> (to the Devil with the fork
> and leave the plate empty!
> They are good at cooking cat
> the poor people of my color.)

This poem demonstrates some of the negative perceptions and stereotypes about blacks. The superiority-inferiority dichotomy is maintained throughout, here with an ironic twist. Afro-Peruvians, too, use utensils and are not in the habit of cooking cat. Social norms are to be respected in that the doctor's wife, not his girlfriend, is invited and the host's daughter is not fair game. The doctor hopes to spend a quiet evening with honorable people. Yet Santa Cruz is saying that pride, respect, and dignity are not limited to the upper class. Plain does not mean ignorant.

"Wake of a Black Creole" assesses the different attitudes prevalent during a wake. Anaphora with the descriptive "black" helps to underscore the presence of death. Both the joy and the sadness of the ritual are presented in the introduction. Inside, there is mourning, while on the outside, alcohol is being used to soothe the sorrow and to ward off the cold emanating from the corpse.

At the other end of life's spectrum is "Cradle Song," narrated from the point of view of the father. Through the use of *jitanjáforas* (meaningless, rhythmic alliteration), the poet captures, tenderly, a brief bedtime exchange between father and son. Emphasis is on the positive as the image of a jewel relates the child to all that is precious. The words are to serve as balm for the absence of a mother.

> se fue antianoche
> —dicen que subió en un coche . . . —
> ¡pero tiene que volvé!

> (she left night before last
> they say she got into a car . . . —
> but she has to return!)

Warmth, gentleness, and fatherly concern are the salient characteristics of "Cradle Song," traits made even more significant with the parents' traditional roles being reversed. As do the other poems in "To the Beat of the Guitar Melody," "Cradle Song" is a continuation of themes concerning the black experience, the cultural and historical dimensions, begun in *Décimas*.

National issues become the primary thematic focus in the subsequent part, "*Décimas* of Short Lines," which consists of twelve *décimas*. In these poems, emphasis is placed upon time, death, and Peru. As a theme, the latter is represented by "Talara" ("Talara"), which speaks out against foreign attempts to dominate the petroleum region. Related is "Tu voto" ("Your Vote"), which stresses the need for the Peruvian citizenry to participate in the electoral process. "El Porvenir" ("The Future") assesses the urban barrio experience and calls for solidarity among the antagonistic forces within the urban milieu, as well as for an end to the exploitation of human beings.

"Indio" ("Indian") and "Agro" ("Countryside"), two forceful poems, assess the indigenous situation, past and present, years filled with exploitation, degradation, and mistrust. In "Indian" the poet pleas for the opportunity to understand and to be understood:

Indio de la Cordillera
en tu desconfianza pienso
pero penetrar quisiera
a tu corazón inmenso.

(Indian of the mountain range
I think of your distrust
but I would like to penetrate
your immense heart.)

The legal and political processes have not alleviated the distrust of officialdom that has been prevalent since the conquest. The immense cultural gap results from the inability to incorporate the indigenous peoples into the nation as equals. After so many misdeeds against them, they continue to be ignored. In a call for solidarity and a recognition of their dignity as human beings, the poet exclaims:

¿Indio? No: ¡Inca! o 'Peruano!
Voy hacia tu muda queja,
acerca a mi voz tu oreja
que no hablaremos en vano:
Yo, tu hermano; tú, mi hermano,
frutos de un dolor intenso!

(Indian? No: Inca! or Peruvian!
I go toward your mute complaint,
My voice nears your ear
let us not speak in vain
I, your brother; you, my brother,
fruits of an intense pain!)

The title "Indian" is not appropriate since it is a name of disrespect; "Inca" or "Peruvian" would imply more dignity. The poet calls for brotherhood based on shared experiences. The "intense pain" is the process of forced labor and subjugation experienced by two ethnic groups, Indians and blacks, throughout Peruvian history. This crisis in confidence remains a problem in communication and understanding among blacks and Indians and accounts for some of the poetic tension expressed. A desire to hide the past, expounded in the last stanza, is not a realistic solution to the situation. Rather, the move should be toward positive action on the part of the indigenous, in harmony with other oppressed peoples.

"Countryside" confronts the problem in a more direct fashion:

Por todos los indigentes
que del nacer al morir
se han condenado a vivir
como esclavos y sirvientes,
a ustedes, terratenientes,
estas décimas dedico.

(For all the indigenous
who from birth to death
have been condemned to live
as slaves and servants
to you landowners,
these poems I dedicate.)

The agents of oppression, the landowners, come under direct attack as "Countryside" continues the arguments advanced in the previous poem. Exploitation, for the indigenous, is synonymous with life. The insensitivity involved in the system is beyond comprehension, but "Countryside" ends on a positive note: in the immediate future,

veremos al campesino
forjar su propio destino
con la razón en la mano:

(we shall see the *campesino*
forge his own destiny
with reason in his hand.)

Only through armed resistance will the indigenous people be able to take what is rightfully theirs. The yoke of oppression has to be removed forcefully, just as it was implanted against their will.

Throughout the poetry of Nicomedes Santa Cruz there is recognition of and strong identification with the plight of indigenous *campesinos* (country folks). His concern reached its maximum level of expression in "Campesino Songs," a compilation of poems on the indigenous question. From the poet's point of view, a complete change in the socioeconomic order is overdue. A number of these poems were written during years of turmoil when many indigenous communities attempted to recapture communal lands that had been taken over by owners of huge estates and by corporations such as

Gildemeister, Grace, and Cerro de Pasco. The process of consciousness raising, unionization, and strikes began in 1958 and reached its high point in 1962. Much of this activity was confined to the so-called "Mancha India" ("Indian stain"), the Departments of Ancash, Apurimac, Ayacucho, Cuzco, Huancavelica, and Puno, in which the majority of the indigenous population live. The issues were recognition of unions, higher wages, recovery of land, and an end to servitude. Numerous communities were adversely affected by official reaction and repression.

As a poet of the people, the responsibility of Nicomedes Santa Cruz is to give voice to those who have none. This exteriorization of indigenous sentiment is also evident in the first section of "Poems," four of which continue the realistic portrayal of the indigenous peoples' plight.

"Exodo" ("Exodus") is a commentary on the destinies of man and bird and one of Santa Cruz's strongest indictments of poverty:

> El hambre arrojó al indígena
> de los Andes.
> El hambre arrojó al pelicano
> de los mares.
>
> Se cruzaron en Lima
> siguiendo un rumbo opuesto:
>
> Sobre el Puente de Piedra
> el indígena pide una peseta
> y junto al agua prieta
> el pelicano busca una anchoveta.
>
> Después . . .
>
> Volando hacia la puna
> cayó el alcatraz
> y el hombre de las cumbres
> murió al pie del mar.
>
> (Hunger hurled the indigenous
> from the Andes.
> Hunger hurled the pelican
> from the seas.
>
> They crossed paths in Lima
> going in different directions:
>
> On the Stone Bridge
> the indigenous begs for a quarter
> and near the dark water
> the pelican searches for an anchovy.
>
> Afterwards . . .
>
> Flying toward the highlands
> the pelican dropped dead
> and the man from the mountains
> died at the seashore.)

The poem is structured on a series of incongruities, implicit affirmations, and negations in terms of expectations and realizations. Hunger on both land and sea dominates the first stanza, The verb "hurled" is one of expressive force capable of conveying the idea of uprooting, dislocation, and migration. At the foundation of this tragedy lie economics and racism, the failure of the indigenous peoples to be integrated into the social system. The creation of a class of people dependent upon handouts assures the permanence of the oligarchical system that forced the migration in the first place. The commonality of the villager's and pelican's experience is maintained throughout as Lima proves not to be the promised land. The effort to encounter a new mode of existence ends unsuccessfully as the bird dies en route to the sierra and the villager expires by the sea. "Exodus" is an ironic look at the destinies of both man and beast in a country where it is estimated that one-half of the population suffers from malnutrition and where the unemployment rate is extremely high. In this poem, the poet agonizes over the destiny of those who migrate to the city expecting betterment, only to meet the ultimate defeat, an everyday occurrence in Lima.

The continuing saga of the indigenous peoples in terms of their inability to find better living conditions is the subject of "Los comuneros" ("Sharecroppers"), in which the people of Uchumarca, Pacoyán, and Chinche, historical villages, in their search for dignity and property, are brutally repressed by the armed forces. "Palo" ("Stick") is related to "Sharecroppers" in that it is a plea on the poet's part for the troops to recognize that soldiers, too, are part of the people and should join the rebellion against the real oppressors. Once there is more identification with the masses on the part of people who have guns, the chances of violence are reduced. Since most of the troops come from the working classes, there is an ideological rather than a social gap. "Coca" portrays the coca leaf in its cultural function as social anesthesia that has sustained indigenous peoples through centuries of oppression.

The last segment of "Poems" represents another step forward in Nicomedes Santa Cruz's trajectory toward international *negritud*. As an exponent of black culture he has an immense burden to bear; he has taken it upon himself to vindicate the black Peruvian or to make known to the world positive aspects of this side of Peruvian reality. Not only is Santa Cruz writing in a vacuum, without the benefit of other similarly committed writers, but there has also been a lack of critical feedback in his own country surrounding his works. Nevertheless, Santa Cruz's views on the situation of black people worldwide have been consistent. The fourth section of *Cumanana*, also called "Poems," is a comparative assessment of black struggle in Africa and the New World.

"Muerte en el ring" ("Death in the Ring") concerns the exploitation of athletes and the death of Benny "Kid" Paret in particular. It is an emotion-packed chronicle that charts the progress of black boxers from discovery to ultimate defeat. The fighter is caught in an unending chain of exploitation:

My challenger
es negro, como yo.
Si pierde le espera lo mismo.

> (Aquí los únicos que nunca pierden
> son nuestros managers y el promotor.)

> (My challenger
> is Black, like me.
> If he loses the same thing awaits him.
> [Here the only ones who never lose
> are our managers and the promoter.])

The issues of physical talent versus marketing sophistication are ones that dominate certains sports. Many are willing to be exploited in the hope of achieving fame and fortune. This poem is critical of the gladiator mentality that often begins as hype but ends in tragedy. In combat, both participants are placed in the situation of having to win, but the eventual loser pays with his life. The use of parentheses in the poem adds to the dramatic impact. They function as asides and are employed three times; each time the reference is to a vital element of survival and serves to indict managers and promoters. The mixture of Spanish and English adds a realistic touch to the scenes since boxing is an international sport. Moreover, there is cohesiveness between form and content in the structure of the poem whose lines vary from one to twelve syllables, controlling the speed of the action and bringing into clearer focus some of the problems involved in athletics.

"La Noche" ("The Night") is a glorification of night, which for twelve hours supposedly makes all people the same color. It is a good thought, but the world does not function in this manner. The poem shows the insecure side of the poet regarding color, and it is also escapist in nature. Night will not eliminate racism, but enlightened mentalities will help toward that end.

"Juan Bemba" is in the form of a dialogue in which the protagonist responds to several questions concerning his existence. His situation is so pathetic that the earth laughs at him. Food, clothing, and the very garbage from which he makes a living have been denied to Juan Bemba.

"Ay mama" ("Oh Mama") and "Formigas pretas" ("Black Ants") reflect the impact of Brazil upon Nicomedes Santa Cruz. The former is an expression of sheer joy at physically being in the environment. Palm trees are related to "Mulatto palms" ("palmas mulatas"), which, in this case, are the women to whom the poet reacts in the following manner:

> Me muero al verlas venir,
> me mata verlas pasar.

> (I die watching them come
> it kills me to see them pass.)

The idea of being surrounded by so many black people is an unforgettable experience since he is not accustomed to a majority of this color. "Black Ants," on the other hand, deals with toil and suffering throughout the black experience. The blacks of Bahía in their daily activities bring to the poet's mind his own past sufferings as he contemplates the scenes of people working like ants. Toil and struggle, as the poet sees it, are facts of life characteristic of the black experience worldwide, in which all blacks bear the weight of being descendants of Cam, the biblical Ham. In these two poems there is solidarity and identity with black Brazilians as the poet is in the process of expanding his own ethnic horizons through personal experiences with other black people, which in turn inspires his creative activity.

It is in "Congo libre" ("Free Congo"), "Sudáfrica" ("South Africa"), and "Johanesburgo" ("Johannesburg") that Santa Cruz registers his strongest protest about injustices against blacks. "Free Congo" discusses the difficulties of being born black in a European colony. Throughout the poem, analogies are drawn between different types of people and their national situation, with color in many instances determining their social status. In a racist society, life's chances are far from being equal and the downtrodden always suffer. Only complete liberation will put an end to these inequities:

>Africa ha sido la madre
>que pariera en un camastro
>al niño Congo, sin padre,
>que no desea padrastro.

>(Africa has been the mother
>who gave birth in a large bed
>to the child Congo, without a father,
>who does not need a stepfather.)

Personification, in this instance, is a rhetorical device serving to humanize the process of liberation. Just as the child, Congo, is capable of managing on his own, so is the country, Congo, which does not need outside interference from a white stepfather. "South Africa," which treats the same themes evident in "Free Congo," manifests perpetual identification with the country's problems of colonialism and racism. The poet is committed to do battle with the last drop of black blood in his body.

"Johannesburg" is by far the most forceful poem of the three. It commences with

>Una voz ancestral
>un tambor africano
>y un verso elemental
>peruano

>(An ancestral voice
>an African drum
>and an elementary Peruvian verse.)

Initially, the poem recounts the black experience in Peru through slavery and the process of miscegenation, adding that since blacks are no longer slaves they are not suffering. This attitude is questionable, but the poet proceeds to describe the plight of blacks in Cuba, the Dominican Republic, Panama, Haiti, Brazil, the United States, and Africa. The problem implicit within the poem is that in a number of countries there is more overt racism compared with the covert sinister practices in Peru, where the aim is to eliminate Peruvian blacks in the name of miscegenation. For the poet, the symbol of this ethnic negativism is Johannesburg. He desires a concerted effort to change the situation:

>Cuando en Johanesburgo
>llegue el "Día de Sangre"
>debemos estar todos
>Hijos de negra madre!
>
>Con la voz ancestral
>El machete en la mano
>Y el verso elemental
>peruano.
>
>(When in Johannesburg
>arrives the "Day of Blood"
>we must all be there
>sons of a black mother!
>
>With the ancestral voice
>the machete in hand
>and an elementary Peruvian
>verse.)

Needless to say, it will take a collective effort to liberate South Africa. It is significant, in a rebellious sense, that the *tambor* (drum) at the beginning of the poem has been replaced by a machete. "Johannesburg," moreover, announces the return to Africa in a collective liberation effort, which will be the theme of Santa Cruz's most important poem of the 1970s.

In *Cumanana*, the poet turns next to the situation in the United States with poems dedicated to two opposite personalities, George Wallace and John Kennedy. "De igual a igual" ("From Equal to Equal") reflects the poet's desire to engage Wallace in combat, preferably after assuming a native African tribal posture. His only desire, as reflected at the beginning of each stanza, is to eliminate this vestige of racism in the United States. "Llanto negro" ("Black Cry"), written on the death of President Kennedy, is a tearful lament extended to blacks worldwide. Images of sorrow and suffering abound as blacks are implored to "cry," "moan," and "sob" ("Llorad," "Gemid," "Sollozad") in order to soothe the pain of such a great loss. Whereas Wallace is presented in totally negative light, Kennedy is given the opposite treatment. Emphasis is laid upon John F. Kennedy's force and positive efforts toward civil rights, black equality and dignity.

These international poems provide Santa Cruz with the opportunity to verbalize some of his frustrations concerning the black situation worldwide. Like the Afro-Uruguayan poets, Santa Cruz recognizes that there is commonality in the experience and that boundaries do not eliminate basic human problems.

Cumanana ends with the poem thought by many to be Nicomedes Santa Cruz's finest expression of Latin American brotherhood, "América Latina" ("Latin America"). The poem is a call for ethnic harmony and solidarity:

> He aquí mis vecinos
> He aquí mis hermanos.
>
> Las mismas caras latinoamericanas
> de cualquier punto de América Latina:
>
> Indoblanquinegros
> Blanquinegrindios
> y negrindoblancos
> Rubias bembonas
> Indios barbudos
> y negros lacios.
>
> (Over here are neighbors
> Over here are my brothers.
>
> The same Latin American faces
> from any point in Latin America:
>
> Indianwhites and blacks
> whites and blackindians
> and blackindianwhites
> thick-lipped blondes
> Bearded Indians
> and straight-haired Blacks)

This particular process of miscegenation of the three principal ethnic groups has created the Latin American, a type recognizable in all countries of the Western Hemisphere. Common ethnic identification and cultural synthesis are the key elements in hemispheric solidarity. For that reason, the poet is harmonious in response to questions concerning his origins:

> Nací cerca de Cuzco,
> admiro a Puebla,
> me inspira el ron de las Antillas,
> canto en voz argentina,
> creo en Santa Rosa de Lima
> y en los Orishas de Bahía.
>
> (I was born near Cuzco,
> I admire Puebla,
> Antillean rum inspires me.
> I sing in an Argentine voice,
> I believe in Santa Rosa of Lima
> and in the Orishas of Bahía.)

From this posture of solidarity, the poet envelopes the continent in a Latin American embrace. In "Latin America," Santa Cruz maintains that ethnic and cultural differences are minimized by the prevalence of so many shared experiences throughout Latin America.

Cumanana is Nicomedes Santa Cruz's second complete volume of poetry and his finest. In it, he establishes Latin America's ethnic identity and miscegenation as two of his prime concerns. Just as important are the themes of *negritud*, Pan-Africanism, and national problems, embracing primarily the indigenous peoples and agrarian reform. *Cumanana* continues the thematic trajectory and poetic evolution of Santa Cruz who, in subsequent publications, has refined and developed many themes more fully.

One of Nicomedes Santa Cruz's most recent poems was published in 1976, commemorating the successful Angolan struggle for independence. It is entitled "Madre Angola: El retorno" ("Mother Angola: The Return") and represents the product of a twenty-year poetic cycle for Santa Cruz, beginning in 1956 with the poem "Ritmos negros de Perú: La ida" ("Black Rhythms of Peru: The Departure"). The historical and ideological implications are clear. Angola needs all of her sons and daughters of the diaspora in order to wage a never-ending war against oppression:

> Retorna mi carabela,
> torna a su lugar de origen
> pues nuestra presencia exigen
> Cabinda, Luanda, Benguela.
> Proa Allá y a toda vela
> vuelvo en un nuevo velero
> que ni es barco ni es negrero
> ni tiene un tratante al mando
> ¡Mi retorno es navegando
> en comando guerrillero![31]

> (My caravel is returning,
> it returns to its place of origin
> it demands our presence
> Cabinda, Luanda, Benguela.
> Prow forward and full sail
> I return in a new boat
> which is neither ship nor slaver
> nor has a slaver in command
> My return is navigating
> as a guerrilla commando!)

The poetic "I" has undertaken a mission of self-fulfillment in order to repay an old debt, a task that was physically carried out by Cuban troops.[32] In contrast to the first trip to America as a slave, the return journey is a product of free will and self-determination. The mode of transportation is, significantly, a caravel instead of a slave ship. Thus the transformation is complete—from slave to guerrilla.

> Hemos forjado fusiles
> de nuestras rotas cadenas
> y es furia de nuestras venas
> la que escupen los misiles
> y aquí venimos por miles

en cada atlántica ola
a decirte Madre Angola,
República Popular.
que tus hijos de ultramar
no pueden dejarte sola.

(We have forged firearms
from our broken chains
and it is the fury of our veins
that spits out the missiles
and to here we came for miles
in each Atlantic wave
to tell you Mother Angola
Popular Republic,
that your children from across the sea
cannot leave you all alone.)[33]

That weapons have been forged from chains makes the fight that much more significant and symbolic. The imagery is harsh; the fury from within will be metamorphosed and spat out in the form of destructive forces. The journey is difficult, but the ideal is worth fighting for. The poet is not just concerned with the bellicose state in Angola as an instrument of liberation. Another goal is to recapture the lost center of his existence in an effort to overcome the sense of orphanhood that has been present since slavery. The struggle provides an opportunity for reintegration of the psyche and resolution of the identity problem:

Por la Victoria Final
han de confundirse aquí
Túpac Amaru y Martí,
el Che y Amílcar Cabral
y en esta lucha frontal
contra el vil imperialismo,
vive Angola el heroismo del
gran pueblo vietnamita,
dejando con sangre escrita
la verdad del Socialismo.

(For the Final Victory
they must come together here
Tupac Amaru and Martí
Che and Amílcar Cabral
and in this frontal assault
against vile imperialism
Angola lives the heroism of
the great Vietnamese people,
leaving written in blood
the truth of Socialism.)[34]

Third World revolutionary figures of the nineteenth and twentieth centuries are positive models in the all-out effort against "vile imperialism," with

"Socialism" as the ultimate goal. In many cases, success has been written dramatically in blood. If Vietnam was successful against overwhelming odds, why not Angola? Hence:

> Nuestra victoria es segura
> tan cierta como el manaña
> de esta Unidad Africana
> que es la esperanza futura.
> Larga etapa de amargura
> es la que ahora termina
> una gran Revolución
> que consolida esta unión
> que consolida esta unión
> afroamericalatina!
>
> (Our victory is assured
> as certain as the tomorrow
> of this African Unity
> which is future hope.
> A long stage of bitterness
> is what we now finish
> a great Revolution
> that consolidates this union
> Afrolatinamerican!)[35]

"Afrolatinamerican" is a concept that allows the poet, as a black man, to reaffirm his identity and his origin. All of this is done within a revolutionary context in an effort to overcome some of the negative implications of Afro-Peruvian existence. He has the will as well as the capacity to repay the country that engendered him. Victory in Angola symbolizes African unity, majority rule, and Afro–Latin American involvement in a struggle for liberation.

*   *   *

Africa and the international dimensions of the black experience appear to be two of the future directions for Nicomedes Santa Cruz. In the aforementioned interview with Roberto Remo, concerning whether he intends to abandon the theme of Peru, Santa Cruz responds:

> No. That's not it. It happens that being Black is, at times, admitting a type of diaspora, a universality of blackness. But at the same time you feel that this land where you were born is your homeland, that you did not come here by your own will, but that all the initial richness of this people was won with your sweat . . . for others. Well then, fighting for a national integration and fighting against those who do not want it forces me toward the reality of the universal Black, involving me with my brothers from Africa and the United States, but without losing sight of my reality of a Peruvian committed to the cause of his people.[36]

The twenty-year period that separates "The Departure" and "The Return" demonstrates the maturity of Santa Cruz in terms of his ideological acumen.

No longer is he merely lamenting the injustices and inhumanity of Peruvian slavery; he has elevated his awareness of the black experience to a revolutionary Third World level. Wisely, though, Peru remains his point of departure for participation in international black liberation.

3

From Esmeraldas to Eternity:
Afro-Ecuadorian Poetry

The Social Context

For the most part, Afro-Ecuadorians have not fared well when scrutinized by their countrymen, but some foreigners do recognize their contributions to the culture. In his assessment of Afro-Ecuadorians, the Ecuadorian social scientist Alfredo Espinosa Tamayo presents a turn-of-the-century perception of the black population, citing the bad influence of this element in the national mixture, especially their "mentally inferior qualities"; the Afro-Ecuadorian belongs to a "servile race created in slavery . . . the least capable of incorporating itself to civilization and tends to disappear easier than the aborigines, absorbed by the rest."[1] The racism of this passage is obvious and reflects the author's ignorance in matters of color. The idea of blacks being absorbed into the melting pot by "bleaching" is not new either. Since it is unlikely that blacks will totally disappear from Ecuadorian society, the question has to be dealt with in terms of degrees or shades of color. Nevertheless, Espinosa Tamayo expresses commonly held stereotypes regarding blacks, their motivation, mental capacity, and cultural impact in the Americas, as well as their adverse influence upon Ecuadorian regionalism.

The image that has been projected of Afro-Ecuadorians by nonblack Ecuadorians varies from the stereotype—childlike and playful—to the negative—retarded and mentally incompetent. Alfredo Fuentes Roldán summarizes both attitudes when he portrays the black as happy, fun loving, and oriented toward music and dance, but at the same time, he cites "apathy, indolence, retarded psychic reaction, vagrancy and a lack of interest" as essential components of his makeup.[2] While Fuentes Roldán recognizes some positive contributions by blacks in the fields of music and popular culture, his attitudes toward Afro-Ecuadorian participation in the national culture are compatible with those expressed by Espinosa Tamayo forty years earlier. Without belaboring the point, it is safe to say that blacks in Ecuador and in Peru have much in common, being perceived as ethnic obstacles. Fuentes Roldán does admit, however, that this segment of the population has not been given the opportunity to realize its potential.

As Leslie B. Rout, Jr., and others point out, the number of people in Ecuador of African descent is not known.[3] The census no longer classifies people according to ancestral line. If they do not exist officially, it is much easier to ignore their participation in Ecuadorian life; in other words, legislate them out of existence.

The editors of the *Area Handbook for Ecuador* attempt to shed some light upon the current numerical and socioeconomic status of the Afro-Ecuadorian population. They maintain, "Negroes and mulattos together probably number no more than 500,000. . . . Negroes hold a slightly higher social position than that of the indigenous population. Racial barriers do not prevent the Negro from engaging in other than agricultural activities, but socio-economic circumstances do keep him from doing so."[4] Most informed scholars are aware that there is a strong relationship between Ecuadorian socioeconomic circumstances and racism. Blacks in that country are victims of historical determinism, as they are throughout the Americas. Otherwise, how are we to explain that they are part of the lower social strata unless there is a correlation between these observations in the *Area Handbook* and those advanced by Fuentes Roldán and Espinosa Tamayo. These attitudes place the responsibility for the victim's plight squarely upon his own shoulders and absolve a hostile society of assuring equality for all of its citizens.

Because blackness bears a negative connotation in Ecuador, people are often hard pressed to find a way to combat existing attitudes. The route that has been followed for centuries is miscegenation, which often assures one of more social respect while maximizing cultural loss. Norman Whitten addresses the color dilemma and relates it to the economic status of Afro-Ecuadorians in one of the most comprehensive cultural studies of this group of people:

> In the position taken here it does not matter that some members of the black category will rise in status with or without the "lightening" genes; what matters is that the social category defined by a national cultural criterion of blackness is cognitively relegated to the bottom of the economic and social hierarchy. When racial features are associated with class and cultural category, then the viability of a particular Afro-Hispanic mode of cultural adaptation is blocked or limited by racist social constraints. That such a social constraint—whiteness is superior to blackness—is the very one invoked in the North American industrial-capitalist complex is equally relevant. It is this very North American complot that is now instrumental in developing nations such as Colombia and Ecuador, and extracting their resources such as timber and oil.[5]

What should also be pointed out here is that the "North American indus-trial-capitalist complex" is not totally responsible for racist attitudes prevalent in Spanish American society. Rather, the push for economic wealth and political power associated with capitalism has helped to bring dormant negative social attitudes into the open. These symptoms have rarely been pointed out because of the paucity of black people capable of articulating their frustrations via the print media and other outlets.

One of the few Afro-Ecuadorian scholars to tackle the problem of racism directly is Wistting Fierro Ruiz in *Los ecuatorianos despreciados y humillados (The Despised and Humiliated Ecuadorians)*. In scathing antiracist rhetoric, Fierro Ruiz maintains, "Here in our country the division of races and classes go together; the Black is segregated because of the race he represents and besides for being poor and ignorant. Racism in Ecuador takes a different form than known in the country of the Yankees; but in the end it is hidden and paternalistic racism in which violence is substituted for human exploitation."[6]

Black creative writers in Ecuador, though few in number, have also consistently attacked the racism and discrimination, based upon color, experienced by Afro-Ecuadorians. Pablo Adalberto Ortiz Quiñones, Nelson Estupiñán Bass, and Antonio Preciado Bedoya, novelists and poets from Esmeraldas—where most blacks in Ecuador live—are the most visible. They are, moreover, the most eloquent exponents of Afro-Ecuadorian literary expression to receive critical attention beyond their national borders and to raise critical literary issues.

Ortiz, Estupiñán Bass, Preciado: The Black Poets of Esmeraldas

In the introduction to *La lírica ecuatoriana actual* (*Present Ecuadorian Lyric Poetry*), Violeta Luna mentions Adalberto Ortiz, Nelson Estupiñán Bass, and Antonio Preciado not just in passing but as figures integral to the development of Ecuadorian literature over the past several decades.[7] Her remarks are directed toward the earlier socially oriented poetry of Ortiz and Estupiñán Bass, after which there has been an identifiable transition from their black poetry to less committed verse. Antonio Preciado is situated by Rodrigo Pesántez Rodas, another critic, within the Generation of the 1960s, along with Carlos Eduardo Jaramillo, Ana María Iza, Rubén Astudillo, Carlos Manuel Arizaga, and Fernando Cazón Vera, a cadre of social poets.[8] Regarding the social dimension of these younger poets, Luna maintains that the purpose of their poetry is to "unmask and satirize all that is false, ridiculous or unjust. The poet wishes to fight shoulder to shoulder with the common people using the word as an effective arm."[9] These introductory remarks by Luna have a strong Marxist bent, and many of her observations pertaining to the class structure in Ecuador are applicable to the early poetry of Ortiz, Estupiñán Bass, and Preciado. Because the education of the general public about blacks, past and present, has not been adequate, at one junction in their careers, each poet deemed it necessary to enlighten the uninformed majority of people.

The poetry of the three writers under consideration reveals a discernible movement from socially critical poetry to a concern for pure aesthetic creation. This is true in spite of the fact that the two older poets are *mulatos* and their younger compatriot, Preciado, is a *negro*. Perhaps due to the writers' changing socioeconomic status they view the world differently, or, as with many writers, they want to be considered as poets, period. Whatever the reasons, unlike the situation with black writers in Uruguay and Peru, these Afro-Ecuadorians have been incorporated into the national literary tradition; their works have been reviewed and are being published by establishment institutions, including the Casa de Cultura Ecuatoriana, which subsidizes and distributes at no charge numerous books.

This raises an important question: Should one subvert one's identity and not be vocal in matters of color and thereby appease the majority culture? The problem has been discussed by many critics, including Wilfred Cartey. Preceding his three-page discussion of Adalberto Ortiz in *Black Images*, Cartey makes some interesting, if not altogether true, assumptions concerning Afro-Hispanic poetry. Cartey has in mind poets who have been accepted by and feel themselves part of the establishment.

> In the poetry of South America and the Antilles, the inner quality of Negritude, the poet's involvement in being Negro, is less felt. The less forceful the seeking after acceptance and assimilation into society, the more the poet of black verse seems able to relate to the condition, to the native, and the less self-revelatory is his poetry, the less subjective. If the United States stands on one side of the balance, then Brazil stands on the other. There the poet of Negroid stock attempts to ignore his inner Negritude and to be primarily aware of being Brazilian. The Negro Brazilian poet, since he is thought of first as a poet and not first as a black man who is a poet, relates then to his racial identity. His work is thus in the mainstream of his country's literature, not, as in the United States, a separate, suspended body.[10]

These images of Brazil are erroneous, the ones projected by the uninformed, naive persons who are not aware of the country's social dynamics. Only recently have Brazilian blacks begun to assess their own situation and to express their profound displeasure with it. They do not fit the above description. Certainly the comments by Cartey cannot be applied to the situations of Afro-Uruguayans or to Afro-Peruvians, who obviously do not try to ignore their inner *negritud*. The dilemma faced by these writers is multidimensional. Not only are they faced with the possibility of not having a publisher, but often there is not even a sympathetic, educated audience in the country. They run the risk of being ostracized socially, economically, and politically if too much attention is devoted to matters of ethnicity.

Just because all of the displeasure is not documented does not mean that it is not there. Certainly in the cases of Uruguay and Peru, such work is not a part of the mainstream. The opposite is true in Ecuador and Colombia, where the Afro-Hispanic writer has been criticized and anthologized. However, in all of the writers studied here, there is a conflict between ethnic identity and national identity due to the cultural dimension of Spanish American societies. From the southern tip of South America to its northern boundaries, one element that Afro-Hispanic writers share, to varying degrees, is their sense of blackness, of which *negritud* is the central feature.

In his discussion of *negritud*, Ortiz places this concept squarely within the American context when he states, "*Negritud* for us Americans, cannot now be a 'return to Africa' nor an exaggerated apology of African culture, but rather a process of ethnic and cultural miscegenation in this continent, which can be appreciated now not only in the somatic manifestations of miscegenation but also in literature, popular music, and beliefs and superstitions."[11] Ortiz's attitude toward *negritud* is a practical one given the present status of blacks throughout the Americas and especially in Ecuador.

Africa will always be the mother country, but the realities of the national culture require a judicious combination of past and present in order to face the future successfully. Both ethnic and cultural amalgamation will continue the integration of blacks into the Ecuadorian ethos. Ortiz believes that he has achieved such a state of equilibrium in his poetry with the distinction between his earlier Afro-Ecuadorian works—*Juyungo (Juyungo, novel, 1942)* and *Tierra, son y tambor: Cantares negros y mulatos (Earth, Rhythm and Drum: Black and Mulatto Poems, 1945)*—and his other publications—*Camino y puerto de la angustia (Road and Port of Anguish, poems, 1945), El vigilante insepulto (The Unburied Watchman, 1954), El animal herido (The Wounded Animal, 1959), and Fórmulas (Formulas, 1973). Earth, Rhythm and Drum, Road and Port of Anguish,* and *The Unburied Watchman* contain original poems, while *The Wounded Animal* and *Formulas* are anthologies that contain old, revised, and new poems by Ortiz. There is a discernible trajectory in his poetry from the social, ethnic poetry of *Earth, Rhythm and Drum* to the more cerebral selections in *Formulas.* Ortiz maintains that his latter works "are better classifiable as manifestations of a literature we can call White and Western."[12] It is significant that Ortiz's poetic trajectory, from its published beginnings in 1945, begins to develop in both the African and the white Western traditions. While *Earth, Rhythm and Drum* is concerned with Afro-Ecuadorian culture, *Road and Port of Anguish* emphasizes the opposite pole of his poetry. On the one hand, then, Ortiz stresses ethnicity; on the other, he affirms his ability to participate in universal poetic movements. His poetry, as a result, is a search for identity, or at least for a set of norms that will allow him to feel at ease with all of his cultural complexities. Most of these same tendencies are perceptible in the literature of his Afro-Ecuadorian counterparts.

Adalberto Ortiz: Earth, Rhythm and Drum

In a comparative study of Nicolás Guillén, Luis Palés Matos, and Adalberto Ortiz entitled "Antecedents of Negritude in Spanish American Literature," G. R. Coulthard draws interesting thematic and stylistic parallels.[13] He goes on to cite specific poems of the three writers that are related in terms of theme, ambience, and technique. Coulthard concludes, not surprisingly, "Ortiz is closer to Guillén: he employs the same strong tone of protest with respect to the exploitation of the Black and racial prejudice. This trait is almost totally absent from the poetry of Palés Matos. On the other hand, he shares with the latter the vitalizing power of Afro-American primitivism in contrast with the debilitating intellectualization of bourgeois art."[14] These comments clearly demonstrate the basic differences between a poet of *negritud* such as Guillén and the *negrista* writings of Palés Matos. The former poet manages to combine, literally, a social protest against exploitation and prejudice with his "primitivism," while the latter remains on the surface, describing dances and rhythms, at the margin of black culture.

Coulthard's observations are directed more toward Ortiz's earlier works, specifically *Juyungo* and *Earth, Rhythm and Drum*, books that have as their primary concern black cultural identity and spiritual liberation. As far as Ortiz being more "Africanizing" than Guillén and Palés Matos, all three of them fall within the rhetorical category established by Brathwaite, with the former two demonstrating some African survival. Ortiz's criticism of Ecuadorian society is much more subdued than the attitudes projected by his counterparts in Uruguay and Peru. This is possibly due to the relative social positions of the writers, as well as to the fact that Ortiz comes from a province where blacks are in the majority, a rare situation in Spanish-speaking South America.

Earth, Rhythm and Drum is divided into two sections, "Cantares negros" ("Black Songs") and "Cantares mulatos" ("Mulatto Songs").[15] The first division consists of nineteen poems and the second of thirteen. It is a provocative book that thematically varies from the black experience to nature, love, and the physical surroundings of Esmeraldas. "Black Songs" can be thematically approached from the perspectives of the African connection, dance and rhythm, rituals and folklore, New World adaptation, and black-white relationships. Because the image of Africa dominates much of this volume, it is appropriate to begin with that theme.

"Breve historia nuestra" ("Our Brief History") criticizes the uprooting in Africa as well as the inhumanity of slavery in America. It is, in essence, a poem of survival:

> Eramos millares.
> Eramos millares,
> los que oíamos la CH de la chicharra
> en la yunga de Dios.
> Eramos millares
> los que leíamos en los ríos
> la J de los cocodrilos
> y escribíamos en los árboles
> la S de todas las serpientes.
> Cuando la cacería se cuajó en nuestras muñecas,
> rastreamos el paso de Colón
> y los blancos arroparon nuestro torso
> con un cuero de cebra,
> porque la pestilencia no hacía caso a las cadenas.
>
> (We were thousands
> We were thousands
> those who heard the C of the cicada
> in the jungle of God.
> We were thousands
> those who read in the rivers
> the J of the crocodiles
> and we wrote on the trees
> the S of all the serpents.
> When the hunting party manacled our wrists,
> we traced the step of Columbus
> and the whites tied our torso

with zebra skin
because the disease did not notice the chains.)

The first stanza concentrates, through alliteration and anaphora, upon the physical environment of Africa, including the fauna and flora. The scene is harmonious, with all of God's creatures coexisting. This is interrupted, however, by the advent of slavers and their dehumanizing practices, exemplified by cacophony with *c* in verses ten and eleven in Spanish. It is ironic that the slaves are following the "step of Columbus" who set out to broaden the world's horizons. The "zebra skin" is a permanent, symbolic identity stamp that the trials of slavery have ingrained into black people sharing this experience. The image is negative in the sense that it does not lighten the burden that they are condemned to bear. In "Our Brief History," Ortiz employs the rhetorical device of metonymy, a Jakobsonian "figure of equivalence" in his interpretation of the African presence. The animals and their physical environment become synonymous with a continent and a sad chapter in its history.

Images of imprisonment persist in the following stanza.

Nuestras manos engrilladas
henchidas de Dios,
se elevan a Dios,
claman a Dios.
Cuando la huella creció en la playa
nos subimos con los ojos a los árboles gigantes
para tragarnos el paisaje de América.

(Our shackled hands
filled with God
raised to God
cried out to God.
When the trail grew on the beach
we went up with our eyes on the giant trees
for the American countryside to swallow us.)

The "wrists" and the "chains" are now "shackled hands." A triad of emotionally charged verbs—"filled," "raised," "cried"—underscores the unsuccessful appeal to God for liberation. Confrontation with the new physical, spiritual, and cultural realities of America is the important priority:

La tierra nueva
no era de todos.
Perdidos en catacumbas metálicas
charlábamos con las congas nigérrimas
para saber que no se nos quita el cuero de cebra
ni en los cañaverales ni en los cauchales
ni en los algodonales.

Y nuestras manos encallecidas
dudaban de Dios.
Estrujaban a Dios.

(The new land
was not for everybody
lost in metallic catacombs
we talked with the dark drums
to find out that the zebra skin has not been removed
neither in the cane fields nor the rubber forests
nor the cotton fields.

And our callused hands
doubted God
Crushed God.)

There is a cultural dialectic involved in affirmation, with the drums as positive modes of communication, while negation surrounds the image of zebra skin that reinforces the stigma of slavery, a burden blacks cannot shed. Still, the back-breaking labor in the rubber, sugar, and cotton industries causes doubt concerning divine interest in the plight of blacks. They are pictured as lost souls without any hope for salvation except in the form of physical liberation by those same callused hands that crushed the white god. The only positive outlet is drumming, which represents authentic culture as opposed to the exotic zebra skins imposed upon them. Perseverance remains the principal issue:

Ya no somos millares,
somos millones.
Millones con una brocha y un machete,
que soñamos bajo todas las palmeras
que somos hombres,
hombres, sí, libres.

Eramos millares . . .
somos millones . . .

(Now we are not thousands,
we are millions.
Millions with a brush and a machete
who dream beneath all the palm trees
that we are men,
men, yes, free.

We were thousands . . .
we are millions . . .)

While the legacy of toil has not diminished, neither has the promise of manhood been fulfilled. The numerical increase from thousands to millions has been achieved through cultural adaptation and the black's capacity for survival. In the penultimate stanza, the dreams of manhood and freedom have not been totally realized. The contrast between a negative past and present potential suggests that "Our Brief History" is an ironic poetic voyage to nowhere. Until profound social changes are made, manhood and freedom will remain dreams.

The theme of Africa as the maternal source is extended to "Contribución"

("Contribution"), but in this poem it remains at the level of a paradisiacal state violated by European aggression. Since the poem is concerned with cultural reciprocity, much of Afro-Ecuadorian popular culture is presented as evolving from pain and suffering.

> Siempre han partido los látigos
> nuestra espalda de cascol
> y con nuestras manos ágiles
> tocamos guasá y bongó.

> (The whips have always parted
> our black back
> and with our agile hands
> we played *guasá* and *bongó*.)

Ortiz manages to find something positive even in the miserable conditions of slavery by concentrating upon positive cultural contributions of blacks in the forms of music, miscegenation, exoticism, and exuberance.

In terms of technique, "Contribution" consists of the successful implementation of consonance, free verse, anaphora, and alliteration. Final syllable *o* in the Spanish accentuates the onomatopoetic quality. In addition, ironic word play in the last several lines underscores the positive dimension of the black experience in Ecuador: "encadenada" ("chained") is converted into "canela" ("cinnamon") and "candela" ("fire"). Juxtaposed, however, is the negative image of whites

> invade la sangre cálida
> de la raza de color.

> (invading the hot blood
> of the colored race.)

Reaction to the New World is symbolically treated in "Son del trópico" ("Rhythm of the Tropics"), a poem of rhythmic polarities between up and down, woman and man, copper and steel. A scene of harmony and tranquility is set throughout the first three stanzas as humans, nonhumans, and nature are in tune. Abruptly, the problematic nature of existence is introduced in the fourth stanza:

> En el cauchal
> hay sangre de negro.
> En el platanal,
> mil balas de acero.

> (In the rubber forest
> there is the blood of Blacks.
> In the banana grove
> a thousand steel bullets.)

The implication here is that blacks have been exploited and killed through their labor in the rubber and banana industries. The ironic clash in the poem is between appearance and reality, which serves to underscore the violence

perpetrated against blacks. The river, symbolic of human existence, paradoxically demonstrates this fact:

> Por sobre el río
> las ondas giran.
> Bajo del río
> las piedras gritan.
>
> (On top of the river
> the waves churn.
> Beneath the river
> the stones shout.)

On the surface, life goes on in a normal fashion; underneath, however, there
are many historical grievances that need to be redressed, mainly the exploitation and oppression of blacks.

"Son del monte" ("Rhythm of the Forest") scrutinizes the impact of
black-white relations upon popular culture and miscegenation. The setting
is a forest, and many facets of ordinary life—such as plants, animals, songs,
and legends—are present. Parallelism exists between each of the eight
quintets, verse five in each stanza enumerating a practical element in life.
These elements are all components of the physical environment, the ecolo-
gy, and the social life of Esmeraldas. Overshadowing the external aspects of
existence are important biological factors of the milieu. The genetic consequences of blacks, whites, Indians, and their interrelations prevail:

> Mi dicen que tengo
> de negro mi canto,
> de blanco mi llanto.
> . . . .
>
> El negro y el zambo
> que talan la yunga,
> se van a la tumba.
>
> (They tell me that I have
> of the Black my song
> of the White my cry
> . . . .
>
> The Black and the *Zambo*
> who work the jungle
> go to the grave.)

"Rhythm of the Forest" is also a poem of survival and adaptability written in
the style of the *son*, a rhythmic poem with alternating assonance and consonance featuring onomatopoetic chants prevalent in each stanza. While this
son affirms the rhythmic dimensions of popular culture, it questions the
positive impact of interethnicity upon Afro-Ecuadorian culture.

The issue of ethnic relations is also treated in "Antojo" ("Whim"), "Lo
verán y lo veremos" ("You Will See It and We Will See It"), and "La
despedida" ("The Farewell"). "Whim" is a conversation between a black

mother and daughter concerning the latter's relationship with a white man. The daughter is worried about money and appearances as well as bettering her social status. Her mother is quick to bring the daughter into the real world, however, as she reminds her of the possibility of pregnancy and physical abuse, but more importantly,

> tu' sijo son casi negro,
> tu' sijo son casi blanco.
> Tu' sijo ya no son náa.
>
> (your children are almost Black
> your children are almost White
> your children are now nothing.)

The poem's title demonstrates that the deeper implications of the relationship have not been thought out by the daughter. After the novelty of the union wears off, the questions of respect and parenting will have to be faced. The consequences of having mulatto offspring in Ecuador are overstated, however, and the daughter's quick change in attitude to re-embrace blackness is forced.

"You Will See It and We Will See It" places the breach between black and white in a different context, with economics the point of contention. The Afro-Ecuadorian remains a source of cheap, unskilled labor exploited now by the *gringo*. The implications are that multinational corporations have elevated the national labor force to international participation. The dichotomy between physical and monetary power is contrasted in the first stanza. While the *negro* "cleans" ("limpia") and "plants" ("siembra"), the *gringo* can "buy" ("compra") at his own price, pointing up the basic difference between the powerful and the powerless. But the exploitation of blacks is built into the system:

> Que el pobre negro se endeuda
> para plantar guineales,
> que el gringo rechazará
> para aumentarles sus males . . .
> de cierto é
> verdadero é.
>
> (That the poor Black will get in debt
> for planting bananas
> which the *gringo* will reject
> to compound his evils . . .
> surely is
> truly is.)

Use of both "surely" and "truly" stresses the inevitable results of the present system of inequality. The picture, then, is that of a person who because of the economic structure is both in debt to and manipulated by the *gringo*. The poet foresees a change, though; sometime in the future justice will reign and blacks will be compensated for past atrocities. Verbs in the future tense accentuate this mandate, which will be carried out in plain view of all.

The negativism associated with the *gringo* reaches its high point in "The Farewell," in which emphasis is placed upon cultural loss. The poetic voice laments the falling of dances and musical instruments into obsolescence with the arrival of outsiders. The changes are most evident in the realm of popular culture. The people are dancing "mambos" and singing "boleros," and "there are black women who say 'well' " ("Hay negras que dicen well"). Intolerance to progress has caused the protagonist to seek shelter in a world more of his own rather than face the arduous process of adaptation to another dominant culture. This points to the fact that often material progress entails a loss of values.

Several of the poems in "Black Songs" deal with Afro-Ecuadorian folklore and rituals. Popular work songs are incorporated, such as in "Canción del pescador del río" ("Song of the River Fisherman") and "Faena y paisaje" ("Toil and Countryside") in which rhyme and rhythm function to capture the motion involved in the task. "Contra e' culebra" ("Against the Snake") is related in that it details a reaction to snakebite incurred in the work place.

The legend of La Tunda is the theme of two poems by Ortiz. According to Tomás García Pérez, the legend can be traced to the seventeenth-century battles between blacks and Indians for dominance in Esmeraldas. Apparently, the Devil himself intervened in the fighting:

> He appeared in the form of a black prince named Macumba, and with his bewitching arts helped the Blacks win the war. But the Devil, who was ready for war, destruction and death, is at last conquered by love; well a beautiful black princess changed him into a peaceful family man. This union of Devil and black woman produced in time many children, this way giving origin to the hellish beings that make up the black mythology of Esmeraldas, among which we find: "El Cuco," "El Duende," "El Ribiel," "La Gualgura," "El Bambero," "El Marinero," and "La Tunda."[16]

It is culturally significant that this legend, now a true Esmeraldas myth, arose out of the initial Afro-Ecuadorian confrontation with the hostile realities of America. Blacks have so few New World myths upon which to call in their attempts to make life more meaningful. García Pérez continues his description:

> "La Tunda" is a horrible, deformed black woman with an enormous mouth and a disfigured foot. Because of her hybrid character she cannot have children and this is the motive for which—in order to satisfy her maternal instinct—she steals strange little black children, especially cry babies and disobedients; she carries them to her lair of thorns and there, with her devilish magic and shrimplike tail, drives them mad, bewitches them.[17]

It is this last aspect of the legend that allows parents to use her practically: to instill fear, responsibility, and respect in the young.

Ortiz treats both the sensational side of La Tunda, in "La Tunda, tunda que en entunda" ("La Tunda, witch that bewitches"), and the practical application of the legend, in "La Tunda para el negrito" ("La Tunda for a Little Black Boy"):

Cuando llegués a sé hombre
vos tenes que trabajá.
Porque si viene la tunda,
la tunda te va a llevá.

No quiero que seas un bruto,
sino que sepás leé.
Que si te coge la tunda,
la tunda te va a comé.

(When you become a man
you will have to work
because if La Tunda comes
La Tunda will carry you away.

I don't want you to be ignorant
but that you learn how to read.
If La Tunda catches you
La Tunda is going to eat you.)

Here the concern is not for grotesque descriptions but rather for common sense in the maturation process. As with most of his conversational pieces among blacks, Ortiz manages to capture the language, tone, and emotions of a given situation. In this instance, the mother still maintains rhythm and melody while teaching an important lesson based upon a cultural symbol that has persisted throughout the centuries.

"Sábado y domingo" ("Saturday and Sunday"), "Jolgorio" ("Merriment"), "¿Qué tendrá la Soleda?" ("What's Wrong with Soledad?"), and "Sinfonía bárbara" ("Barbarous Symphony") are picturesque manifestations of culture through music, dance, and ritual. While the first three poems are concerned with merriment and its aftermath, "Barbarous Symphony" makes a connection between African and American cultures. "Merriment," on the other hand, fuses violence associated with work to that between man and woman, while reproducing the onomatopoetic sounds of musical instruments. "Saturday and Sunday" recaptures the hipswaying, inebriated environment of a weekend celebration. "Soledad" appears to be a disenchanted woman. Of these four poems, "Barbarous Symphony" clearly demonstrates the most depth in terms of culture and its relationships to rhythm:

Se escucha un retumbante trepidar
sobre el gran tambor del mundo:
¡Bómbom—Búmbum!
¡Bómbom—Búmbum!
¡Bómbom—Búmbum!
Trajeron los mandingas candombe y calabó,
rugieron los tantanes en tierras de Colón:
la conga, la bamba, la rumba, la bomba
y sus fuerzas telúricas en sombra.
Aé—airó,
aé—airó.

Ecos salvajes de africana tempestad.
Condensación de un gran espíritu bantú
Aé—ajujú,
aé—ajujú.
y el bombo, rebombo, retumba.
Engendros horrorosos de totem y tabú.
¡Oh dioses primitivos de madera y de marfil!
¡Máscaras de brujos de impulso vegetal
ofician los rituales con hálito viril
y hay lúbricas faenas la noche de San Juan!

(A resounding vibration is heard
upon the great drum of the world
Bómbom—Búmbum!
Bómbom—Búmbum!
Bómbom—Búmbum!
The Mandingas brought *candombe* and *calabó,*
The tom-toms roar in the lands of Columbus:
The Conga, the Bamba, the Rumba, the Bomba
and their telluric forces in darkness.
Aé—airó,
aé—airó.
Savage echoes of an African storm
Condensation of a great Bantu spirit.
Aé—a ju jú,
aé—a ju jú.
And the drum, rumbles, resounds,
Horrible offsprings of totem and taboo.
Oh primitive gods of wood and ivory!
Masks of sorcerers with vegetable impulse
Officiate the rituals with virile breath
and there are lewd activities the Night of San Juan!)

"Barbarous Symphony" thus pays dramatic tribute to the drum-and-mask culture that Ortiz considers an essential ingredient in *negritud*. These events on the Night of San Juan transpire in an environment of primitiveness occasioned by the nature of the activities themselves. This has to be viewed as a poem of African survival since the ritualistic elements reflect back on that continent. For instance, the Bomba, according to Benjamin Nuñez, is "An African drum which is given sexual attributes," but more significantly it is "a black dance held on Sundays at which the spectators formed the chorus for response singing. The music was supplied by two drums, maracas, and two sticks tapped on a bench. The rhythm was set, not by the drummers, but by the lead dancer. The form of the *bomba* was like many African dances in which the voices start out unaccompanied and then are joined by drums, which come in with dramatic effect."[18] There are evident echoes of this definition in "Barbarous Symphony" in the call-and-response relationship between human voices and musical instruments. Although the scene is intoxicated with rhythm, its images are also charged with meaning as the dancers seek to reaffirm cultural links. "Their telluric forces in darkness" and "Condensation of a great Bantu spirit" suggest negation that can only be affirmed through the "primitive gods of wood and ivory."

What is striking throughout the poem is the alliteration and onomatopoeia with *m, b, g, t,* and other consonants that capture the explosive impact and rumble of the ancestral drums. African culture is presented as being transplanted and imposed upon the "lands of Columbus." The "Savage echoes" represent an amalgamation of the Bantu spirit and the New World reality. In this phase of acculturation, however, there is still a clash between the new and the old ways of perceiving the universe. The "primitive gods" and the "masks of sorcerers" are very active on the Roman Catholic Night of San Juan, a fact that inevitably leads to religious syncretism.

In the first two stanzas of "Barbarous Symphony," there is the initial cultural confrontation that will eventually entail acceptance, rejection, or compromise of societal values. The poem continues with a different thrust.

> Macumba, macumbero, macumba.
> Macumba, macumbero, macumba.
> Por las copas rijosas de las palmas,
> bajo el polvo tranquilo de la estrella,
> se clara la liturgia de Oxalá,
> y el bombo, rebombo, retumba.
>
> Danza guerrera vino,
> danza guerrera va.
> Kombumá—candombe—kombumá.
> Kombumá—candombe—kombumá.
> Uá—uá.
> Danza guerrera llegó
> danza guerrera que fué,
> danza guerrera quedó.
> Y la lanza que se hunde
> y la rabia que se funde,
> en nosotros está,
> en nosotros irá.
> Y el bombo, rebombo, retumba.
>
> (Macumba, sorcerer, Macumba.
> Macumba, sorcerer, Macumba.
> Through the sensuous treetops of the palms,
> under the quiet dust of the star,
> the liturgy of Oxalá brightens,
> and the drum, rumbles, resounds.
>
> A warlike dance came.
> A warlike dance goes.
> Kombumá—candombe—kombumá
> Kombumá—candombe—kombumá
> Uá—uá.
> A warlike dance arrived
> a warlike dance left,
> a warlike dance stayed.
> And the lance that is buried

And the rage that is fused
in us it is,
in us it will go.
And the drum, rumbles, resounds.)[19]

The poem now switches from a Caribbean focus to Brazilian ceremonial practice. *Macumba,* according to Nuñez, is "a fetishistic ceremony in which the black congregation invokes the gods and the spirits of ancestors. It is accompanied by dances, songs, and prayers to the sound of the drum," and the *Macumbero,* a high priest and sorcerer, "often engages in the preparation of aphrodisiacs and in sexual incantations."[20] These definitions are in keeping with the structure and meaning of the poem because Oxalá is "an Afro-Brazilian bisexual deity symbolizing the reproductive energies of nature."[21] The ritualistic bellicose nature of the "Barbarous Symphony" is thus related to a sensual dimension of natural forces, as participants and environment are in harmony.

The *Macumba* ceremony is one form of spiritual liberation. By imploring gods such as Oxalá, the priest is seeking salvation from oppressive circumstances. Here the rite is not treated totally as some exotic ceremony but as a liturgy within a metaphorical setting. Yet the religious liturgy is only one phase of the rite; it is followed by a war dance designed to kill real and imaginary enemies. The expected result is physical liberation prompted by the lance and the rage that will transform the present deplorable situation ("in us it is") into future advances ("in us it will go"). Consequently, the poetic posture is

No amarrados como árboles,
sólo sueltos como pájaros.
En nuestras muñecas nunca más.
Antes que hierro,
primero muertos.
Canto guerrero que fué,
canto guerrero quedó,
Kombumá, candombe, Kombumá.
Uá—uá—uá.
Y el bombo, rebombo, retumba.

(Not bound as trees
but free as birds
On our wrists never again
Before steel,
death first.
A warrior song that was
a warrior song it remained,
Kombumá, candombe, Kombumá.
Uá—uá—uá.
And the drum, rumbles, resounds.)

The contrast between past ("bound") and present ("free") continues in a last call for liberation in spite of the odds. The final posture is a positive one, death before chains. All of these acts will be realized within an Afro–Latin American cultural context enhanced by ancestral rituals and religion.

That Ortiz is aware of and not satisfied with the adverse black situation in Ecuador is revealed in two other poems, "Yo no sé" ("I Don't Know") and "Romance de la llamada" ("Ballad of the Call"). They are opposites in that the first is of passive acceptance while the second deals with positive assertion. "I Don't Know" poses a significant question concerning black existence:

> ¿Po qué será,
> me pregunto yo,
> que casi todo lo negro
> tan pobre son
> como yo soy?
> Yo no lo sé.
> Ni yo ni Uté.

> (Why is it,
> I ask myself,
> that almost all Blacks
> so poor are
> like me?
> I don't know
> neither I nor you.)

Money, color, and class are the issues in this plain, direct poem, as an uneducated but sophisticated black contemplates his social circumstances. His perceptions are the same as society's in general, as he relates poverty to blackness and affluence to whiteness. And the narrator is astute enough to make the connection between social status and color, a situation that money cannot change in Ecuador. He realizes that the Afro-Ecuadorian is condemned to occupy a lowly social position, thereby revealing a sophistication well beyond the level of discourse employed.

"Ballad of the Call" views the black situation from the perspective of one who desires change:

> Quebranta ya tu silencio
> y en tu machete perdura.

> (Break now your silence
> and survive with your machete.)

This initial stanza asserts that clinging to the past in terms of tradition and culture is not productive, given the present-day situation; memories of suffering and toil are helpful only when they provide the impetus for progress. Afro-Ecuadorians must understand who they are and where they are going:

> Eres hombre y eres negro,
> mal descendiente de esclavos,
> esclavo para ser libre
> en el monte desolado.

Olvida más tu marimba
y arroja al suelo tu vaso,
cuelga también la guitarra
y empuña tu propia mano
Desde antes que el alba llegue
tu bandera está esperando.

(You are a man and you are Black,
evil descendant of slaves,
slave to be free
in the desolate mountains.
Forget now your marimba
and throw down your glass,
also hold your guitar
and tighten your own fist
Before the dawn arrives
your flag is awaiting.)

"Ballad of the Call" stresses black pride while seeking to motivate Afro-Ecuadorians to change the existing social and economic orders. First of all, acceptance of blackness and the responsibilities of manhood are in order. This will entail moderation in traditional festivities such as music and drinking, especially when they are for escapist purposes. Self-hate and in-group violence should be halted. The future, the symbolic flag, belongs to those who seize the advantage and profit from it. Force, symbolized by the machete, is a distinct possibility as the poet advises blacks to take matters into their own hands. Institutions have not aided Afro-Ecuadorians in the past. Couched within a militant frame is some sane advice for black people throughout the Americas, an attitude that is carried over into "Mulatto Songs."

The poems in this section are concerned primarily with ethnicity, miscegenation, love, poetry, death, and nationalism. As demonstrated in previous selections, miscegenation is one of the major thematic preoccupations for Adalberto Ortiz. In "Mulatto Songs," this tendency is exemplified in "Casi color" ("Almost Colored") and "Sobre tu encuentro" ("Upon Meeting You"). A poem of affirmation, "Almost Colored" has been anthologized and has received critical attention; it is a positive treatment of color and the values of Pan-Africanism:

Aun recuerdo su voz fraternal que me decía:
Que no quiero ser negro.
Que no quiero ser blanco.
Es mi grito silencioso:
Quiero ser más negro que blanco.

. . . .

He vivido en Congo
y he soñado en Harlem:
he amado en Caledonia
y he dormido en Chiclaya
y siempre un mapa de África

en todos los ojos enlutados,
en todos los ojos sin color.

(I still remember your fraternal voice which told me:
That I don't want to be Black
That I don't want to be White.
My silent shout is:
I want to be more Black than White.

. . . .

I have lived in the Congo
and I have dreamed in Harlem:
I have loved in Caledonia
and I have slept in Chiclaya
and always a map of Africa
in all the mourning eyes,
in all the eyes without color.)

The first stanza presents the basic conflict of a mulatto—whether to accept the white heritage over the black or vice versa. The problem is an internal one that results in placing more emphasis upon blackness. Stanza two is an enumeration of positive qualities associated with Afro-Ecuadorians. A great deal of stress is placed upon the relationship between humans and nature, albeit from a negative point of view at times. The stanza terminates with a dynamic simile that captures the black's universal association with joy.

As Nicomedes Santa Cruz will do twenty years later, Ortiz portrays the Afro-American experience as not being temporally bound in references to Africa and to North and South America. But a tricontinental picture of pain and suffering is written on the black countenance. As Everyman, the narrator has experiences that he has shared with blacks everywhere, but Africa is still the common ground in spite of present-day suffering.

The poem grows more intense as the poet describes the atrocities of slavery. He speaks of "infinite pain" ("dolor infinito") and the "caress of lynchings" ("caricia de los linchamientos"). But an aware black person must cast aside past cruelties. The poet escapes into his world of blackness in an effort to solve the dilemma of mixed ethnic heritage:

Para olvidarme de todo
quiero ser negro.

(To forget everything
I wish to be Black.)

"Black" is encased within a crescendo of anaphora and similes in the effort to emphasize color but, most of all, humanity—an idea implied in the last line, "Black with blood—blood" ("Negro con sangre—sangre"). Therefore, the poet will be able to experience blackness directly and not merely comment upon it from a distance. Miscegenation is an essential ingredient in the quest for identity, but in "Almost Colored," the conflict is presented from an internal perspective derived from a clearly defined historical focus.

"Upon Meeting You," on the other hand, is a poem of identity and love

that presents the question of miscegenation from a dual perspective. It
begins and ends on the same note:

> Negros y blancos vinieron hasta mí
> negros y blancos irán después de mí
> después de ti.

> (Blacks and Whites come toward me
> Blacks and Whites will go after me
> after you.)

In the background, the situation of being a mulatto threatens to interrupt the
speaker's relationship with a woman he totally adores.

Directly related to the poems on miscegenation are "Mosongo y la niña
blanca" ("Mosongo and the White Child"), "Mosongo y la niña negra"
("Mosongo and the Black Child"), and "Mosongo y la niña china" ("Mosongo and the Chinese Child"). Mosongo is the poetic alter ego that stresses the
positive qualities of each woman with the stated purpose of a physical
relationship. The poet is not so sure of himself in either case; as he addresses
them, he sees the necessity to apologize to each individually for being a
mulatto. This ambivalence about his heritage surfaces in many poems of
Adalberto Ortiz and demonstrates his inability to reconcile ethnic identity
with social reality, a dilemma experienced by many Afro-Ecuadorians.

Love is another of the themes that surface in "Mulatto Songs." It is a
theme expressed in several *romances* (ballads) and in "Monotonía de un
paisaje" ("Monotony of a Countryside"). The latter poem etches an amorous scene that is reinforced by the natural setting:

> Hasta el patio de tu casa
> llegan los vientos del Sur,
> y en la pared de mi estancia
> dibujo un amor en cruz.

> Cuando el crepúsculo muere
> se acaba el cuadrado azul:
> sólo queda una palmera
> mirando mi amor en cruz.

> En el patio de tu casa
> hay un cuadrado de luz,
> y en el fondo hay un lucero
> igual a mi amor en cruz.

> Tú, el lucero.
> Yo, la palmera.

> (Up to the patio of your house
> arrive the winds from the South
> and on the wall of my dwelling
> I draw a love-shaped cross.

> When the twilight dies
> the blue square is finished
> there only remains a palm tree
> looking at my love-shaped cross.

In the patio of your house
there is a square of light
and in the background there is a star
equal to my love-shaped cross.

You, the star.
I, the palm tree.)

In this lyrical, emotional poem, the poet emphasizes the ability of love to transcend temporal and spatial limitations. The cross, a universal symbol of love, is juxtaposed with light, the south wind, and palm tree, all positive images, throughout the poem. The change in scenery from "my dwelling" to "your house" occurs subtly and within the mental realm. Finally, the poem's allegorical overtones are revealed as "You" becomes the morning star, transcending the physical situation, and "I" is transformed into the palm tree. In this instance, the poet, through metaphor and metonymy, is projecting his sentiments upon the harmony, balance, and universal love of nature.

In the three *romances*, too, there is a close harmony between humans, nature, and sentiments. In "Romance vulgar" ("Popular Ballad"), the moon is a source of inspiration; in "Romance de luz marina" ("Ballad of Sea Light"), it is the sea; and in "Romance de lo irreparable" ("Ballad of the Irreversible"), memories of death and defeat are cloaked within imagery associated negatively with nature:

Y en el puente del dolor
se paró a ver la laguna
y una y una y otra vez
contemplaba las burbujas
del abuelo que murió
perdido en la selva oscura,
y monte adentro se fué
tratando de hacer fortuna.

(And on the scaffold of pain
he stopped to see the lake
and time and time again
contemplated the bubbles
of the grandfather who died
lost in the dark jungle,
and into the forest he went
trying to make a fortune.)

This poem is positive in that it stresses the tendency to continue forward in spite of tragedy, fear, and doubt. The "dark jungle" that killed the grandfather encourages a double reading because of the references to both death and the jungle. These are again mental illusions triggered by memories of the past.

In subsequent poems, Ortiz discusses death and martyrdom in "Hombre muerto" ("Dead Man") and "En San Pedro Alejandrino" ("In San Pedro Alejandrino"); the province of Esmeraldas in "Estela del Río Teaone" ("Trail

of the Teaone River"); and his destiny in "Desvelo" ("Wakefulness").
Although "Wakefulness" suggests alertness, the protagonist is presented as
if he were caught up in the dreamlike world of surrealism in which the
dividing line between life and death is not clearly delineated. He is merely
participating in a larger plan designed by forces over which he has no
control. The journey continues through a

> Y hay un lago profundo al pie de ese camino,
> pero por más que me sumerja en sus aguas
> no me mojo,
> ni tampoco me quema el fuego imaginado.

> (profound lake at the end of that road,
> but as much as I submerge myself in its waters
> I do not get wet,
> neither does the imaginary flame burn me.)

The uncertainty expressed in the first stanza is reiterated in the second, as it
becomes clear that the road about which he speaks is the path of life. The
water and the fire from which he escapes unscathed are nothing more than
the experiences of daily existence.

The oral tradition plays an important part in the psychological makeup of
this protagonist, and much of it comes from a particular source:

> un pescador de piel oscura
> navega hacia la costa en su canoa,
> navega, o canta en la espesura,
> para que otro recoja su pescado y su folklore;

> (a fisherman of dark skin
> navigates toward the coast in his canoe,
> navigates, or sings in the thicket,
> so that another might gather his fish and his folklore.)

Juxtaposed here are two basic types of existence experienced by the protagonist, city and country. In the urban setting, mechanization predominates as revealed in the surreal description of the panting pile driver and the
shout of the factories. In contrast to the hustle and bustle is the tranquil life of
black fishermen from the coast who are close to their cultural roots and who
do not face the dehumanizing urban scene. The coastal setting is where the
protagonist has his origins, but he realizes that he is a better person for
having participated in the two extremes of Ecuadorian life. Progress, it
seems, has not divested him of the most basic cultural concerns.

As revealed in this brief analysis, *Earth, Rhythm and Drum* is basically a
poetic assessment of Afro-Ecuadorian culture. In spite of Ortiz's knowledge
of Afro-Ecuadorian history, culture, and social dynamics prevalent in the
Esmeraldas community, one does not find the degree of social protest that is
so prevalent in Uruguayan and Peruvian black poetry written during the
same historical period. Ortiz recognizes but does not completely reject
adverse past experiences. Instead, he transforms them into positive aspects

of poetic creativity in keeping with his conception of *negritud* in Afro-Ecuadorian literature. This tendency continues in his later poetry.

Formulas: Poems "Without Poetry" (1973) also contains the fourth edition of *The Unburied Watchman* and the fifth edition of *Earth, Rhythm and Drum*. *Earth, Rhythm and Drum* is not divided into two parts in this edition, but it has four additional poems: "Invocación" ("Invocation"), "Consuelo" ("Consolation"), "Arrullo" ("Lullaby"), and "Negritud con bembosidades" ("*Negritud* with Thick Lips"). There is also an important declaration by the poet concerning his ethnic background. This precedes the poem "Almost Colored":

> I am a mulatto, the son of mulattos. As a result it can be easily understood that all my literary work is, to a certain degree, fragmented or fragmentary, because it corresponds to an intention of a personality not very well identified or united.[22]

Ortiz sees the schism in his work as reflective of his black and white backgrounds. His poetic variety, he tells us, is a result of his mulatto heritage. As a result of his dual ethnic perspective, Ortiz is able to lend a bi-ethnic perspective to his craft. As a mulatto, he stands upon a unique cultural divide, with the possibility of viewing the world as both black and white.

The four additional ethnic poems in this section treat the Afro-Ecuadorian experience in terms of rhythm, song, dance, the past, and Pan-Africanism. "Invocation" is a plea for cultural relativity and recognition in an insensitive setting. The initial appeal is to a higher being, as blacks are presented in the first stanza as an isolated people on the verge of disappearing phenotypically because "only an indelible stain of us remains" ("Solo una mancha indeleble nos queda"). Yet this attitude reflects the predominance of blackness in miscegenation. The present situation is, of course, rooted in the past—inglorious years referred to as

> de aquellos años sepultados
> en los viejos mares sin luceros.
>
> (those years buried
> in the old seas without stars.)

The African past is implored in a recurring motif:

> Goza tu danza eyengué
> negro bacongo-lebú
> negro bubú, negra malinké.
>
> (Enjoy your dance Eyengué
> black *bacongo*—Lebú
> black *bubu*, negra Malinké.)

These references are to different tribesmen engaged in a ritual dance of cultural affirmation among colonial Bantu slaves (*bacongo, bubu*). The enemy responsible for the plight of blacks is referred to in the familiar "you," suggesting that the two opposing groups are close. Nevertheless, blacks have been victimized by history, which they cannot forget. What is doubly depressing is that the Almighty has remained indifferent to past atrocities. The final hope is that this will change in the future. Throughout "Invocation," the protagonists are at home within their physical environment, but they remain as estranged spiritually as ever.

"*Negritud* with Thick Lips" advances some of Ortiz's central concepts concerning *negritud* and the African presence in America. Early in the poem, he speaks of

> Muntu del Congo Katanga,
> hasta América llegó
> y con su ritmo marimba tirimba
> y en nuestra sangre prendió.
>
> (Muntu from the Congo Katanga
> arrived in America
> And with his marimba rhythm
> and in our blood took root.)

The concept of Muntu is derived from Bantu philosophy, and Janheinz Jahn elaborates upon this system of viewing the cosmos:

> So we get in simplified form four basic
> concepts which are to be explained in what follows:
>   I Muntu = 'human being' (plural: Bantu);
>   II Kintu = 'thing' (plural: Bintu);
>   III Hantu = 'place and tune';
>   IV Kuntu = 'modality'.
> Muntu, Kintu, Hantu and Kuntu are the four categories of African philosophy.
> All being, all essence, in whatever form it is conceived, can be conceived
> outside them.[23]

Jahn devotes a chapter, "NTU: African Philosophy," to a discussion of these four categories. He clarifies ideas surrounding Muntu by stating, "The concepts Muntu and human beings are not coterminous since Muntu includes the living and the dead, orishas, loas and Bon Dieu. Muntu is therefore a force endowed with intelligence, or better: Muntu is an entity which is a force which has control over Nommo (water and heat)."[24] Ortiz has obviously integrated these concepts into his poetic creations. His statements concerning Bantu philosophy are outlined in the article "*Negritud* in Latin American Culture."

"*Negritud* with Thick Lips" begins with a bongo crescendo, invoking images of deities of the African past who successfully made the transition to America, thereby maintaining cultural continuity. Through rhythm—"vibrate the *Cumbia*, the *Bamba*, the *Rhumba*" ("vibran la cumbia, la bamba, la rumba")—and the drum, associations are made between historical leaders (Patricio Lumumba, a Congo leader) and religious myths (Shangó, Yoruba god of lightning and thunder). As the poem relates to Muntu, it is apparent that the poet is attempting to emphasize that "Muntu includes the living and the dead, orishas [Yoruba god], loas [voodoo gods] and Bon Dieu [God]." *"Negritud* with Thick Lips" assumes the global approach, embracing humans "from Nigeria to Panama" ("de Nigeria a Panamá"), "from Cameroon to San Juan" ("de Camerún a San Juan"), but always within the frameworks of rhythm and struggle.

Formulas continues the abstract trends begun in earlier pure poetry. Ortiz is not so concerned with presenting readily available images to the reader as he is with being more undecipherable and conscious of the depth of experience treated. "Inquisición romántica" ("Romantic Inquisition") discusses an old theme within a new context:

> ¿Dónde están las que bajan
> a las orillas de los ríos
> y moldeaban tenues esferas con el agua?
> ¿Dónde están las que cantaban
> a la luz de los candiles
> una línea melódica olividada
> en la noche de los orígenes?
>
> (Where are those who go down
> to the bank of the rivers
> and cast tenuous spheres upon the water?
> Where are those who sang
> to the light of lamps
> in a melodious forgotten line
> on the night of origins?)

The principal motif in this poem is the *ubi sunt*, or where are they now? The reference throughout is to "them," the original African arrivals to Ecuador. Ancient rites and practices are elaborated in the first stanzas in the form of many rhetorical questions, with the physical universe predominating. The most dramatic contrast occurs in the last question and answer in which formerly the people danced "to the beat of the rumblings of the wind" ("al compás de los rumores de los vientos"), but now they are

> en el corazón de penumbrosas discotecas
> oliendo y sacudiendo el esqueleto.
>
> (in the heart of darkened discotheques
> smelling and shaking the skeleton.)

The poet is decrying the loss of cultural heritage. Some of the same sentiments are carried over into "El sitio de la fama" ("The Site of Fame"):

> Todo el ruidoso mar
> se filtraría por la cabeza
> del velero carcomido del pescador.
>
> Toda la selva rumorosa
> estaría en el vientre de una guitarra
> y en el hachazo seco del leñador.

Todo el rencor de los esclavos se chorrea
por el abismo que los separa
de sus amos muertos.

(All the noisy sea
would filter through the head
of the moth-eaten sailboat of the fisherman.

All the noisy jungle
would be in the stomach of a guitar
and the dry chop of the woodsman.

All the rancor of the slaves spurts
through the breach that separates them
from their dead owners.)

This poem commences with an archetypal setting on the beach, harking back, perhaps, to the arrival of blacks on Ecuadorian shores. The immensity of the scene as well as its overpowering impact causes the protagonist to seek refuge within himself. Anaphora with "All" reiterates the enormity of the natural world in contrast to his own fragility. The first three stanzas are instrumental in setting the scene that recounts traditional occupations of blacks in rural Ecuador as well as their turbulent arrival upon the continent and the struggle for liberation.

Then the poet focuses upon the minute elements of the universe that are, nevertheless, so important in the order of things, the extraordinary image of sunset, for example:

Toda la luz de la mañana se condensa
en el último chispazo de la tarde.

(All the light of the morning is condensed
in the last spark of the afternoon.)

The spider and the ant, too, carry out their roles in the balance of nature. Inevitably, though, all things

se consumen
en el tubo apasionado del gusano.

(are consumed
in the passionate tube of the worm.)

This final, disturbing image presents death as the equalizer.

Because of the human nature of these poems, a great deal of the action occurs in the mental realm, often in a dreamlike state. The experience in "Inquietud" ("Uneasiness") is purely vicarious because a woman is unobtainable for the male protagonist; she is a figment of his imagination. Nevertheless, he can still dream of what might have been. Most of these poems do transpire in a world that can only be described as being beyond reality, a world of nightmares, beliefs, and other times. In poems such as "Fórmulas" ("Formulas"), "Donde la noche empieza" ("Where Night Begins"), "Camino" ("Path"), "Exodo" ("Exodus"), and others, Ortiz continues his flight from the concrete, objective world to cloak his poetry in surreal discourse.

The tension between two stated world views in the poetry of Adalberto Ortiz is apparent. Temporally this is evident in the dialectic between the cyclic time of myth (Afro-Ecuadorian) and the linear time of history (Ecuadorian). In *Earth, Rhythm and Drum*, Ortiz creates from the perspective of his own cultural and ethnic interval of passage. *Formulas*, on the other hand, represents the poet's transition to more Western concerns. Only by viewing Ortiz in this manner is it possible to appreciate the complexity of his poetic trajectory as well as his importance in Afro-Ecuadorian cultural affirmation.

Nelson Estupiñán Bass: Black Song for Light

Estupiñán Bass has published half a dozen good novels and three volumes of poetry: *Canto negro por la luz* (*Black Song for Light*, 1954); *Timarán y Cuabú: Cuaderno de poesía para el pueblo* (*Timarán and Cuabú: Poetry Notebook for the People*, 1956); and *Las huellas digitales* (*The Digital Trails*, 1971). He also has to his credit *Las tres carabelas* (*The Three Caravels*, 1975), a collection of poetry, stories, and drama. Like the other Ecuadorian poets being discussed, Estupiñán Bass forms a part of the literary mainstream. Also, the trajectory of Estupiñán Bass is similar to theirs; he commences by writing ethnic poetry and progresses to what Adalberto Ortiz calls more Western works.

Black Song for Light, subtitled *Poemas para negros y blancos* (*Poems for Blacks and Whites*), contains twenty-six poems and is divided into two parts, "Los puertos apagados" ("The Calm Ports") and "La esperanza" ("Hope"). Of the dozen poems that compose the first section, the majority treat the black woman and love. There is a progression in his interpretation from exterior physical descriptions to internalizations of her presence through memories and fantasies. In poems of the first kind, Estupiñán Bass successfully relates the woman to her physical and natural environments while creating an image of human vitality.

"La gualanga" ("The Gualanga"), for instance, deals with the impact of the physical environment, as well as a woman, upon the protagonist:

> Ayer de la manana entré
> de afuera de Quinindé
> y a la subida del guayco
> la gualanga me picó.
>
> La gualanga, la gualanga,
> la gualanga me picó.
>
> (Yesterday morning I entered
> the outskirts of Quinindé
> and at the top of the hill
> the Gualanga bit me.

The Gualanga, the Gualanga,
the Gualanga bit me.)

The refrain is repeated on several occasions throughout the poem as an association is made between the impact of plant and woman. In this instance, "Gualanga" is an indigenous specimen of the area, as are the others mentioned in the poem.[25] After this unpleasant encounter with a natural obstacle, his attention turns to more pleasant surroundings in the form of a woman, the beautiful Anselma, her

Cuerpo oloroso a piñuela
con labios de pepepán.

(body smelling of cypress nut
with lips of fruit.)

Anselma, the object of his adoration, is a physical delight. Even the mighty wind desires to partake of her favors as her salient characteristics are accentuated by the corresponding objects in nature. The senses of smell and taste especially are stimulated in this encounter. Anselma's movement is so effortless that she is described "as a tree . . . before the afternoon wind" ("como guadúa . . . ante el viento de la tarde").

The presence of this enchanting woman has a disconcerting impact upon the protagonist, but he is not certain whether to attribute his actions to her or to the Gualanga. Toward the poem's end, confusion reigns due to the protagonist's inability to disassociate the woman from the plant and the lack of clarity in his own mind concerning physical actions. Metaphorically, the dilemma is resolved because he has been touched by the love bug.

The idea of a woman being defined positively in relation to the natural world through sound and rhythm is also the thrust of "Lola Matamba." "Negra bullanguera" ("Fun-Loving Black Woman"), on the other hand, places emphasis on her physical being:

Negra, negra bullanguera,
negra, juyunga, cuscunga,
tu boca anoche me supo
a un mate de agua surumba.

Negra, negra bullanguera,
negra, juyunga, cuscunga,
hacé callá tu cadera
dejá tranquila mi vida.

(Black woman, fun-loving black woman,
black woman, monkey, owl,
your mouth last night tasted to me
like a drink of sweet water.

Black woman, fun-loving black woman,
black woman, monkey, owl,
quiet down your hips
leave my life in peace.)

The motif of the "fun-loving black woman," through anaphora in subsequent stanzas, characterizes her as an uninhibited, desirable person. The image cluster "woman, monkey, owl" detracts, on the surface, from her positive presentation, however, because these terms are pejorative when applied to black people in Ecuador. Moreover, the black woman is a hip-swaying enchantress whose nonhuman qualities make her appear wild and exotic. The positive impact, though, lies in the area of rhythmic sound and the tone of voice used in speaking. As is evident in the first stanza, this portrait is in retrospect as the man remembers the physical encounter. She is totally positive in his mind, and she is related to *surumba*, a sweet, fragrant drink common to the natives of the region. The protagonist apparently has honorable intentions; he mentions marriage and a family. Even though the description of the woman as a sexual animal continues, augmented by the image of her as having "hips of a panther" ("caderas de pantera"), the poetic voice terminates on a note of ethnic harmony. Their future son with "fists the color of tar" ("puños color de brea") presents an attitude for the future of black survival. In this poem, Estupiñán Bass is guilty of stereotyping the black woman as a hot-blooded sensuous animal with nonhuman qualities, albeit from a perspective friendly enough to guarantee a generally positive reading.

The poet's fascination with the physical being of the black woman continues in "Canto a la negra quinceañera" ("Song to a Black Fifteen Year Old"), which describes the coming of age of a young girl. The constant analogies between the black woman and similar natural objects continue: "Your body must be juicy like a rubber tree" ("tu cuerpo ha de estar jugoso, como un árbol de caucho"). So does the poet's fascination with hips, and her body comes alive before the reader with vibrant, happy breasts that are also characterized by a simile of nature—"like a bunch of fruit preserved in a refrigerator" ("como un gajo de frutas conservado en una refrigeradora"). Abruptly, the emphasis changes to the future in an effort to go beyond the physical and to delineate some human problems that this young woman must face on an intellectual level. These include global preoccupations such as the functions of the universe as well as the more immediate specter of hunger. As an adult, there are legitimate responsibilities to be handled that cannot be resolved by a beautiful body alone. The stated purpose of the second half of the poem is to bridge the gap between the child and adult worlds without too much emphasis on the negative aspects of life. It is necessary, as he advises in an analogy with blackbirds, always to take a sane, practical approach to earthly situations.

In "Tú sabías" ("You Knew"), the poet's fascination with the female body reaches its culmination. It is a transitional poem that represents the passage from the exterior to the interior worlds in terms of the narrator's perceptions. The poem begins and terminates with images of passion and physical communication. The entire experience is related in past tense:

Tú sabías
que día y noche

mi sangre insomne te acechaba.
Que mis brazos anhelantes
te perseguían sin tregua por todos los caminos.

(You knew
that day and night
my restless blood watched you.
That my longing arms
pursued you without rest over all the roads.)

The initial scene presents a great deal of pent-up emotion on the part of the male protagonist. Tense, emotionally charged verbs and adjectives accentuate this attitude. These repressed desires are at the point of bursting, and he describes them, ironically, in religious terms:

Que mi sangre
que había profanado los templos
se había alzado tumultuosa
por sobre los miserables mandamientos de las esclusas.

(That my blood
which had profaned the temples
had settled tumultuously
upon the miserable commandments of the floodgates.)

Direct address with "You knew," which borders on apostrophe, lends an accusatory tone to the poem in an effort to blame the female for his suffering. In the second stanza, the poet draws a fitting analogy between physical love and death, and he casts blame upon the woman in an image of body, plant, and night. Furthermore, he continues in subsequent stanzas with fascination for her body, "elastic," "hard," and "sonorous" ("elástico," "duro," and "sonoro"). The descriptions vary from harsh to suave, but always within the context of nature as he looks for explanations of his passion in order to clarify the mental confusion.

The phrase "Perhaps the fault was" ("Tal vez la culpa estuvo") begins a series of anaphora that prefaces five of the remaining seven stanzas. As the climax of the poem nears, the object of his desires—"your body" ("su cuerpo")—is placed in an archetypal, harmonious setting with nature, emphasized by a powerful description:

Tal vez la culpa estuvo, negra,
en tu cintura deleznable,
que un día mis manos temblorosas allanaron,
y echando al fuego las veneradas imágenes del templo
hicieron estremecer hasta tus más íntimos goznes.

(Perhaps the fault was, black woman,
in your slender waist,
that one day my trembling hands subdued
and throwing into the fire the venerated images of the temple
they made tremble even your most intimate hinges.)

A sense of quiet pervades the poem in spite of the joy at final conquest. In the fifth stanza, there is the reference to desecrating the temple; later the seven deadly sins; and, finally, the image of burning the worshipped images of the temple. Allegorically, this temple is the body, Christ's abode, an idea borne out within the poem's context. So for the protagonist, the physical conquest of the black woman's body is the violation of a sacred object, in keeping with Christianity. The overriding eroticism of the poem is demonstrated in this last stanza as the verb *subdue,* meaning also to *level* or *flatten,* is central. The impact of the man's body atop the woman's elicits an orgiastic response from her. So whereas "The Gualanga" describes vicarious physical relationships, Estupiñán Bass has charted a poetic process of progression to sexual conquest in "You Knew."

When the emotional impact of amorous relationships is examined, Estupiñán Bass is at his lyrical best. "Canto a los ojos de la mujer del sur" ("Song to the Eyes of a Sea Woman"), for example, is a surrealistic ode to a woman, the archetypal Mother Earth, and to love. "Domingo de lluvia y tu recuerdo" ("Rainy Sunday and Your Memory") juxtaposes the past joyful situation with the present depressed state of a man whose lover is absent. Because of her loss he can remember her appropriately only through poetry. In the process of trying to externalize his sentiments, he succeeds only in amplifying the state of depression:

> quise llenarlas de alegría,
> mas yo mismo las siento
> salpicadas de pena

> (I wished to fill them with happiness
> but I myself feel them
> Bespattered with pain.)

A retrospective account of their happiness together ensues, with the rain personifying most of his unhappiness. The most intimate details of their relationship are reconstructed but always from the point of view of suffering. Rain, in the end, is viewed metaphorically as disillusionment, a fact that is accentuated in the last confessional stanza.

The poet has managed to create a metaphoric environment in which the interior sentiments of the protagonist reciprocate the external physical surroundings. Rain for him is a negative force that compounds his suffering, a feeling that he can only express through meaningless, unstable words. There is a series of affirmations and negations throughout "Rainy Sunday and Your Memory," as implied in the title. It is raining sadness because of their separation.

"La partida" ("The Departure") continues the idea of absence of a loved one and remembrances. The poet employs images of a ship at sea to describe the sense of abandonment; this time the male has taken the initiative in their separation. He is operating from a perspective of power and suggests ways in which she can encounter him, prefixing the alternatives with "perhaps," "maybe," or "possibly" ("tal vez," "acaso," "o quizas"). Their irreconcilability is conveyed in nautical terms:

> Mi sur es tu norte,
> pero mi norte no eres tú
>
> (My south is your north
> but my north is not you.)

Throughout, the woman is referred to as the sea, another female archetype with life-giving properties. This analogy with maritime imagery is maintained to the last stanza, in which the sense of separation from the woman, "raising anchor" ("levar ancla"), is amplified by the analogy with love, "sea vertigo" ("vértigo de mares"). Emotions are such that they are as sands before a strong wind. However, the tearful memory of her is still conserved within his heart.

"Los puertos apagados" ("The Calm Ports") closes the cycle of disillusionment expressed in these four poems. The setting is a night filled with negative memories. The first quartets of the sonnet decry his situation, which consists of "cloudy roads" ("caminos nublados"), "destroyed dreams" ("sueños destrozados"), and "small destiny" ("destino pequeño"). If he can survive the negativism that terminates in an allusion to death, then there is hope in the figure of a female:

> Mujer, tú tal vez seas el faro que persigo
> en esta larga noche, en que solo consigo
> ver, desde mar afuera, los puertos apagados.
>
> (Woman, you perhaps are the lantern I pursue
> in this long night, in which I only manage
> to see, from out at sea, the calm ports.)

He sees his salvation and ultimate rescue from the throes of depression in the person of a woman. Presently, though, an uncertain haven beckons. The uncertainty is appropriate, because "Song to the Eyes of a Sea Woman," "Rainy Sunday and Your Memory," "The Departure," and "The Calm Ports" all, to a degree, demonstrate a vacillating relationship between male and female. They are poems populated with memories of longing, rejection, ecstasy, and separation with the two being unable to exist peacefully apart.

The remaining poems in "The Calm Ports" treat a variety of topics. "Venganza" ("Vengeance") deals with an assault upon a white woman by a black man who resents his inferior position in society. The incident is narrated first from the third-person perspective but ends on a confessional note. "Comparación de nuestro verde" ("Comparison of Our Green") extols the life-giving, vibrant physical environment of Esmeraldas and the function of the people there. "Exploración a la infancia" ("Exploration of Infancy") stresses positive values associated with family life such as closeness, daily activities, and the idea of working together for the common good.

The passage of time is the motif that prevails in "Exploration of Infancy," the poem being narrated by a mature person in retrospect. In the initial stanza, the reader is advised of the temporal shift. The point of view changes to the past in the fourth stanza. Unfortunately, childhood and youth can only be captured through memories, which is disappointing to a protagonist who expected more. He cannot answer the call for resurgence and is disturbed by the aging process. His futility is expressed as he realizes that he is facing an irreversible process of aging with which he cannot cope. He is torn emotionally between the desire to escape to a simpler existence and the realization that he is on the path toward death, "the external secret of darkness" ("el secreto eterno de la sombra"). Although this poem expresses a pessimistic outlook toward the future, hope is evident in some of the remaining poems in the volume.

Indeed, "La Esperanza" ("Hope") is the title of a section consisting of fourteen poems that treat anti-imperialism, hope, historical figures, the black experience, and other themes of human existence. The lead poem, "Hope," is a sonnet that pleas for salvation for humankind against oppression. Pedro, the poem's protagonist, is a cabinetmaker who has been brutalized by the police for his political activities among workers. His promise is that "Hope will flourish some day" ("la Esperanza florecerá algún día"). The images of planting, blooming, and flourishing persist throughout the poem. Pedro hopes to see his sacrifice and the fruit of his labors reflected in better treatment of the workers who "can here on Earth enjoy springtime" ("puedan aquí en la Tierra gozar la primavera"). Concern for the working classes is evident throughout much of the poetry of Estupiñán Bass; in this case, however, hope without positive actions will not change the present social system.

The idea of people of the same social class destroying each other for the sake of the rich is also one of his recurring motifs, as evidenced in "Carta al soldado" ("Letter to the Soldier"), in which the poet offers advice to a fighting man, imploring,

> nunca alces tu fusil contra los pobres,
> . . . .
>
> Tu puesto está entre los indios, negros y mulatos
> y los trabajadores de las fábricas.
>
> (never raise your weapon against the poor,
> . . . .
>
> Your place is among the Indigenous, Blacks and Mulattos
> and the workers in the factories.)

Since the origin of most foot soldiers is the working poor, an attack upon them is an act of repression against the soldier's own kind. Ethnic and economic lines are clearly drawn here between those who have and the less fortunate. When the revolution occurs, the rich will use the poor to destroy the powerless. The soldier fights

a defender algo que no es tuyo,
que jamás será tuyo,
ni de tu mujer ni de tus hijos.

(To defend something that is not yours,
that will never be yours
nor your wife's nor your children's.)

Because wars, civil or otherwise, are so divisive and take such a tremendous
toll upon the people who fight them, "Letter to the Soldier" questions blind
devotion to duty and military discipline.

"La batalla" ("The Battle") scrutinizes the archetypal battle of Good and
Evil and the perpetual contest between God and Satan to dominate human
desires. The narrator views himself as victim of the process in which each
force alternates in gaining the upper hand; he does so without caring who
ultimately prevails. The problem here is that the individual does not wish to
confront the contradictions inherent in human nature. Rather, he wants a
simplified existence, but that is not what life is all about. The same type of
idealism is expressed in "Tarjeta postal de la tarde" ("Postal Card of the
Afternoon") in which the poet strives for a peaceful environment filled with
happiness. Unfortunately, the degree of harmony he seeks is absent in a
society in which so much emphasis is placed upon economics and color.

"Rabia" ("Rage"), "Canción del niño negro y del incendio" ("Song of the
Black Child and the Burning"), "Mensaje negro para el indio cayapa"
("Black Message for the Cayapa Indian"), and "Canto negro por la luz"
("Black Song for Light") all examine the Afro-Ecuadorian situation, varying
between expressions of anger and a call for ethnic harmony. "Rage" repre-
sents emotions pent up for centuries:

La más hermosa herencia legada por mis padres
fué su rabia,
esta rabia que de repente me sube jadeante
por la escalera de la sangre;
esta rabia que día a día
más y más
voy acariciándola
incrementándola
canalizándola
y que algún día la entregaré a un machete o a un hijo.

(The most beautiful inheritance bequeathed by my parents
was their rage,
this rage that suddenly rises panting in me
by the stairway of blood;
this rage which day by day
more and more
I go about caressing it
increasing it
channeling it
and some day I will pass it along to a machete or to a son.)

"Rage" describes an awakening, a social coming of age of somebody who was apparently oblivious to the social situation. Couched within legalistic jargon, the rage is internal and inherited but threatens to manifest itself in exterior acts of violence. Tension and urgency are apparent in repetition and in the highly expressive verbs ("caressing," "increasing," "channeling") that outline the program for action in the incubatory, growth, and action stages of militancy.

The poet's rage is directed toward the miserable human condition brought on by oppressive governments locally and internationally. The specter of fascism manifests itself in the second stanza with many of the negative connotations associated with this doctrine intact. There is some hope because of the human capacity for struggle, but the present suffering is unbearable. The poet, who has remained estranged from social activities, begins to view the present as a prolongation of the past, prompting his negative reaction. The present hopelessness arises from historical events that have stripped men and women of their will and dignity. Slavery bears no small responsibility for their plight, as we see in the final image of repression:

> ecos de barcos de perfiles borrosos,
> de látigos desgarrando espaldas doblegadas
> y de un tumulto de gritos apagado a punta de patadas.

> (echoes of ships with blurred profiles
> of whips tearing bent backs
> and a tumult of shouts silenced by kicks.)

Blacks have never been able to overcome the stigmas attached to slavery. He is disturbed because of his link through heredity to those who suffered most. But the channeling of revolutionary energy creates ambivalence for the poet; in the final stanza,

> me horrorizo y me alegro al mismo tiempo
> cuando pienso en el estallido de nuestra rabia.

> (it horrifies me and I'm happy at the same time
> when I think of the outburst of our rage.)

He realizes that social progress depends on violence and destruction, that without it nothing will ever change the existing social order. The poet's inner rage will probably be with him for some time to come; there is no correspondence between poetic sentiment and social change in Ecuador.

"Song of the Black Child and the Burning" examines attitudes in the black Esmeraldas barrio of Caliente. The poem begins on an intended insult directed toward a black individual, an insult that he quickly transforms to reaffirm his identity:

> Negro he sido, negro soy,
> negro vengo, negro voy
> negro bien negro nací,

negro negro he de vivir
y como negro morir.

(I have been Black, I am Black,
I come Black, I go Black
A good Black Black I was born
black black I have to live
and as a Black I will die.)

This initial positive stance is followed by an incident involving a fire in Barrio Caliente that the poet recounts. Pepe, the poet's white friend, has a mother who perpetuates discrimination by not allowing her son to play with blacks. As Barrio Caliente burns, she asks,

—¿Por qué no se quemó, Dios mío
todo ese Barrio Caliente?

(—Why hasn't it burned, my God
all of that Barrio Caliente?)

Amid the tragedy of losing loved ones and possessions, there is no human compassion on the part of this woman.

The poet, however, projects a time of harmony and improved ethnic relations. This generation is lost, so he must look to the future to break down the barriers of color, of hate, and consequently appeals to children for unity in both spirit and action:

mano a mano se unirán
corazón con corazón

(hand to hand they will join
heart to heart.)

The possibility of this happening in his lifetime is nil, but the poet nevertheless will view these harmonious relationships from a cosmic perspective. The important element for him is not to compromise his sense of blackness, self-worth, and dignity, an attitude that he reiterates in the final stanza.

The desire to improve ethnic relations is the thrust behind "Black Message for the Cayapa Indian." The distance between blacks and Indians in Ecuador has existed for centuries due to a number of historical and cultural reasons. The animosity between these two groups is a constant preoccupation for the poet:

Mil veces te he preguntado
sin tener contestación:
¿Por qué me aborreces, indio,
si de ambos es la nación?

(A thousand times I have asked you
without having an answer:
Why do you hate me, Indian,
if the Nation is both of ours?)

In spite of both groups being Ecuadorian and sharing many cultural similarities and patterns, the lack of interethnic communication persists. Anaphora with "a thousand times" ("Mil veces") emphasizes the lack of dialogue in work situations or in cultural activities. "Hate," "enemy," "despise," and "pain" ("aborreces," "enemigo," "despreciado," and "pena") are words used to describe the perceived attitude of Indians toward blacks.

In determining the true meaning of these perceptions, the poet is presented with a number of historical incongruities from the perspective of The Truth:

> Me dijo: —Siempre te he odiado
> porque estuvo en el error
> de suponer que illegabas
> también de conquistador.
>
> El no supo el sufrimiento
> que en las minas te diezmaba,
> ni vio que una misma cruz
> a los dos crucificaba.
>
> (It told me:—I've always hated you
> because you were in error
> believing you arrived
> also as a conqueror.
>
> He did not know about the suffering
> that decimated you in the mines,
> nor saw that the same cross
> crucified both of you.)

The problem is one of communication. Both blacks and Indians were victims of the Spanish conquest, but from the fight for dominance over the region with maroons and freed slaves years ago, the Indians' animosity has persisted to the present. Moreover, because human nature often leads people to want to assert their dominance—in this case blacks—the ethnic situation treated in this poem, just as the one in the preceding selections, is not likely to change for the better. Because Indians once viewed blacks as being no different from the conquering Spaniards, a cultural and historical gap still exists between them.

"Black Song for Light," the final poem in "Hope," raises the question of ethnicity but within the context of the origin and destiny of the human race. It begins on a harmonious, almost apologetic note:

> Hombres blancos, rojos, mestizos, amarillos,
> para todos vosotros abro mis palabras como brazos,
> fraternales,
> a pesar de ser negras.
>
> (Whites, Reds, Mixed, Yellow men,
> for all of you I open my words like arms
> brotherly
> in spite of their being black.)

The same self-effacing attitude flows into the second stanza and becomes even more pronounced when the poet exclaims,

> este canto es claro y blanco
> a pesar de ser negro.

> (this song is clear and white
> in spite of being black.)

This process of affirmation and negation based upon color is a dialectic that tempers the ethnic poetry of Estupiñán Bass just as it does that of Ortiz. He is reacting to unfounded theories concerning the intellectual capacity of blacks. Therefore, he uses the qualifier "in spite of being black" to justify his present attitude. What follows in ensuing stanzas is a surrealist, poetic re-creation of man and the universe. The ascending spiral begins with the first appearance of primitive life forms on earth and continues through the creation of Man. The plea for understanding among men in the first two stanzas is ironically juxtaposed to the destructive actions that lead to the demise of the human race, brought on by the "wind of hate" ("viento del odio"). Images associated with the obliteration of humans are the smoke and fire of destruction. Although human beings are capable of recovering from the ultimate disaster, as shown in the evolution from insect to man, the absurdity of a reenactment of this theory is behind the repetition of "How much time" ("Cuánto tiempo"). Humans would be better served by minimizing destructive conflicts and living in peace. The same type of understanding necessary for solving ethnic division is necessary to avoid worldwide tensions. Because of his verbal and intellectual capacity, even a humble person can contribute to human understanding:

> Miradme:
> yo mismo soy ahora
> una blanca bandera
> a pesar de ser negro.

> (Look at me:
> I myself am now
> a white flag
> in spite of being Black.)

The color paradox between black and white, shadow and light, persists throughout the poem. It has the positive effect, though, of pointing out some of the ridiculous implications of unjustified discrimination. There is finally a fusion of opposites as the white flag of hope will be borne by a black person, which symbolically represents cultural assimilation and biologically represents miscegenation in the mulatto persona of the poet.

Ethnicity is not Estupiñán Bass's sole concern in this volume, however. "Evocaciones de Estéban Cabezas" ("Evocations of Esteban Cabezas"), "Ante la tumba de Vargas Torres" ("Before the Tomb of Vargas Torres"), and "Epístola censurada a Gaitán" ("Censured Epistle to Gaítan") are homages to Ecuadorians and Colombians whom the poet respected. "Postal Card of the Afternoon," mentioned earlier, treats the discrepancy between appearance and reality. The beautiful, peaceful, natural environment is placed in ironic juxtaposition to the human subjects who must struggle daily to make ends meet. In his postal card, the poet does not wish to document the processes of nature. Rather, he intends to record the struggle for survival eked out by the poor; the dock workers; the sawmill hands; the rubber, hemp, and ivory nut laborers who are often overcome by urban or outside forces. The question is, if God can be so positive in his exposition of Nature, how can he be so indifferent to the plight of Man?

The idea of the presence of an omnipotent, indifferent being is the theme of "Ahora" ("Now"). In the poem's first of three divisions, a series of rhetorical questions is raised, one of the more significant being,

> ¿Eres otro dios desalmado,
> tú, que debes dialogar con el alma del hombre?
>
> (Are you another soulless god
> you who must dialogue with the soul of man?)

The vital communication between Man and God is absent in all of the poems that treat religious topics. The poet paints a sad picture of human existence throughout the three segments and in the final stanza implores God to return and help the suffering masses. Both "Postal Card of the Afternoon" and "Now" end on notes of wishful thinking. If the past is any indication of the future, however, then the plight of the dispossessed is not likely to change due to divine intervention.

The last two poems from *Black Song for Light* to be discussed are "Canto al hombre maldito" ("Song to the Accursed Man") and "El hombre en la luna" ("The Man on the Moon"). The first is an indictment of war and fascism in which the author condemns the German invasion of Russia as a setback for all peoples.

> Por ti, hombre maldito, Anticristo, Caín,
> Atila, peste, tigre, tiniebla, tempestad,
> el mundo hoy vive preso dentro de una caverna.
>
> (Because of you, accursed man, Antichrist, Cain,
> Attila, disease, tiger, cloud, storm,
> the world today lives imprisoned within a cave.)

The final attitude expressed is that this, too, shall be overcome by human resiliency. The same antifascist, anti-imperialist posture characterizes "The Man on the Moon." The poem is ironic in perspective and tone, as being on the moon is synonymous with remaining aloof from everyday social concerns. "What does it matter" ("Qué importan") recurs on numerous occasions throughout the poem to stress a lack of earthly human commitment. The poet views America as a battleground of good and evil forces, with the latter gaining the upper hand. Historical allusions to the Colombian battalion in Korea and the murder of Sandino in Nicaragua are combined with everyday acts of physical and mental violence and exploitation, as well as with a denial of human rights to project an ominous future for a Latin America filled with pain and suffering. The situation has not changed substantially since the independence era of Simón Bolívar.

Antonio Preciado Bedoya: Merriment

Antonio Preciado Bedoya has published two volumes of poetry, *Jolgorio: Poemas (Merriment: Poems,* 1961) and *Tal como somos (Just as We Are,* 1969). Like Adalberto Ortiz and Nelson Estupiñán Bass, Antonio Preciado has been incorporated into the Ecuadorian literary mainstream. Indeed, Rodrigo Pesántez Rodas, a noted Ecuadorian critic, speaks of Preciado's poetry in the following terms: "In spite of the great poetic power of his work, the attitude and the sincere social compromise of the author is not a secondary step. At the same time he sings, he denounces."[26] From Pesántez Rodas's point of view, Preciado fulfills the criteria of what a good poet should be. He is able to combine his "art for art's sake" with a keen social awareness. Like many other black poets in South America, Preciado begins his poetic trajectory by interpreting his most immediate experiences—the lives of black people in his community in Ecuador. But as with most concerned artists, Preciado seeks to transcend his immediate local circumstances and enter into the poetic mainstream of his culture.

The poetic development of Antonio Preciado is remarkably similar to that of Adalberto Ortiz. In their early works, both poets are preoccupied with identity, culture, heritage, and ethnicity. In their later volumes, however, the focus turns more inward, dwelling upon the subjective manifestations of emotional states. *Merriment* and *Just as We Are* are examples of the polarization of Preciado's poetry. *Merriment* is divided into two sections, "Bom bom bom" and "Dawn," both of which stress positive values in the black experience by concentrating on *negritud* and physical liberation. In the first part, Preciado dwells upon questions of blacks' culture, their dynamics and vitality, and their physical and spiritual well-being. The second has a stronger motif of social protest throughout the poems.

"Yo soy de aquí" ("I Am from Here"), from "Bom bom bom," treats the African heritage and the black presence in the Americas:

> Yo soy de aquí,
> de esta tierra de mar,
> de esta tierra de sol.
>
> Negro soy,
> negros, papá y mamá.
>
> (I am from here,
> from this land of sea,
> from this land of sun.

> I am Black,
> Blacks, papa and mama.)

In these first stanzas, a sense of belonging is established as the poet strongly emphasizes his physical roots and his black ethnic identity. Next, repetition of "I am from here" establishes the black as a hard-working individual who is close to nature, as exemplified in the images of back-breaking toil and the expressed love for the earth. The narrator is presented as a person in tune with the spiritual and physical realities of the region, its flora, fauna, folklore, and movement. The proverbial black rhythm plays an integral part in the poet's perception of himself:

> Soy de carbón,
> y mis pies zapatean por liberarse de la candela de una rumba.
> Soy de carbón
> y el fósforo del bombo enciende mi cintura.

> (I am of charcoal
> and my feet tap to liberate them from the fire of a rhumba.
> I am of charcoal
> and the match of the drum ignites my waist.)

Reiterated in this stanza is the emphasis upon blackness, as reflected in the descriptive adjectives "black," "tar" ("alquitrán"), and "charcoal." In "I Am from Here," a sense of euphoria is generated through an awareness of positive ethnic identity. There is no vacillation by Preciado as occurs in some of the poems by Ortiz and Estupiñán Bass.

The image of the barrio is the concern of "Barrio Caliente" ("Hot Barrio") with its physical aspects stressed in the first stanzas. The people, the sights, sounds, smells, and impressions are cataloged with recurring motifs of drum, dance, and rhythm. However, Barrio Caliente is a spiritual as well as a physical reality, so Preciado places emphasis upon this former dimension in the final stanzas:

> Barrio de los negros,
> de calles oscuras
> preñadas de espantos,
> que llevan, que asustan,
> que paran los pelos
> en noches sin luna.

> Barrio encendido,
> de noche y de día,
> infierno moreno,
> envuelto en las llamas
> de son y alegría.

> (Barrio of Blacks
> of dark streets
> bursting with spooks
> that carry off, that frighten,
> that make hairs stand
> on moonless nights.

Inflamed barrio
by night and by day,
black hell
enveloped in the flames
of rhythm and happiness.)

In spite of the outward manifestations of joy and enthusiasm, Barrio Caliente is no paradise by any means. The last stanza, cloaked in fiery imagery of destruction, reveals the dynamic opposition between appearance and reality that underscores the real tension in this environment; the barrio is consuming itself, wasting human potential, by engaging in unimportant activities. On the positive side, though, all of these festive activities strengthen the barrio as a place where the dynamics of culture are defined and distilled.

Negritud and the African connection are the thematic concerns of "Bom bom bom," the title poem of the section. "Bom," of course, is the onomatopoetic drum sound that is so vital to the rhythms and musicality of Preciado's poetry:

Bom bom bom del Africa,
¡de la tierra negra!
Bom bom bom del bombo,
¡de la raza ebria!

(Bom bom bom from Africa
from the black land!
Bom bom bom of the drum,
of the inebriated race.)

The poem begins as an exotic ritual, an atavistic attitude, designed to appeal to the most superficial of human instincts, "warlike dances" ("danzas guerreras"), "eating human flesh" ("cenas de humanos"), and "inflamed parties" ("encendidas fiestas"). The image of the drum as an ancestral element, underscoring ties with Africa, supersedes the level of superficiality in this poem. Rather, this instrument connects black cultures throughout the New World diaspora:

¡Bom!, resuena aquí,
¡Bom!, resuena allá.
¡Bom!, dice Brasil,
en zamba brutal.
¡Bom!, contesta Haití.
También Panamá.

(Bom! it resounds over here
Bom! it resounds over there
Bom! speaks Brazil,
in brutal samba language.
Bom! answers Haiti.
Also Panama.)

In spite of linguistic diversity, Portuguese, French, and Spanish cultures share a common Old World cultural bond in the presence of the African drum. As pointed out by Ortiz, this ancestral element is one of the essential characteristics of *negritud*. Thus, Preciado uses both drum and marimba in his poetry to show their importance in the Afro-Hispanic context. In "El llanto del cununo" ("The Cry of the Cununo"), the drum is portrayed as reflecting human sentiments surrounding death. "Marimba amiga" ("Marimba Friend") offers encouragement to the marimba, while in "Marimba" music permeates all. The poem captures the tone of the rhythmic activity from its bustling beginning, through the hard-driving climax, to its abrupt ending. Images of sweat are the most prevalent—"pores are spurting water," "the shirts are not dry," "they are perspiring"—but the amount of physical activity is subordinated to the attitude of an audience:

> Los poros agua están chorreando,
> ya las camisas no están secas,
> los bailarines van sudando,
> . . . .
>
> ¡Venid, hermanos, vamos todos,
> oigan, la cosa está candela!
>
> (Come on, brothers, let's all go,
> listen, the thing is hot.)

The final two verses are repeated five times in the poem's seven stanzas to dramatize an activity about to take place. Here we see a total physical description, from head to toe, with all of the accompanying sights and sounds involved in the dance.

Life in Barrio Caliente is not all dancing and singing, however. "Embarque" ("Shipment") describes the physical activity of toiling on the docks. "América la buena" ("America the Good") is a positive portrait of a seamstress who is unperturbed that others profit from her labors. "Lavandera" ("Washerwoman") captures the rhythm surrounding cleaning activities.

"Allá en el monte" ("Out There in the Forest"), a poem from a similar perspective, portrays a provider, a hunter and fisherman. Written in the first person, it shows that a great deal of reciprocal respect is evident between vegetation, humans, and other animals. "Out there in the forest" is a chant repeated at the beginning of each of the nine quartets as a prefiguration of lived experiences. The forest comes alive under the protagonist's scrutiny, as we see in the stanza dedicated to the trees:

> Allá en el monte, el quebracho
> y el guayacán varonil.
> Llantas la sangre del caucho,
> música el negro pambil.
>
> (Out there in the forest, the breakax

and the manly *guayacán*
tires the blood of the rubber tree
music the black palm.)

The use of anthropomorphism reflects the protagonist's identification with and love of nature. These sentiments are revealed in the adjective "manly" to describe the vegetation, the transformation of the rubber tree into tires as the sap is being drained away—an occasion for crying—and the music of the palm tree that lends harmony to the environment. The protagonist respects his physical surroundings as well as the folklore of the region associated with La Tunda. In a related poem, "Río viejo" ("Old River"), the river comes alive to engage in dialogue and to reminisce, demonstrating further that anthropormorphism is an essential ingredient in Preciado's nature poems.

"Out There in the Forest" is a reflective poem in the sense that there is a spatial separation between the protagonist and the natural surroundings with which he is so familiar. The scene changes as his thoughts roam, and they are not limited to the pleasant experiences in his daily activities. The tough physical environment contrasts with the interior sentiments of the protagonist who is shown to be an individual of several dimensions. There is a sharp disparity, for instance, between the implicit violence in his work and in his final impression of family life. The violent imagery of machete, shotgun, traps, and snake is juxtaposed with the scene of happiness and warmth provided by his woman and home. The fire image, "the heat of my black woman" ("el incendio de mi negra"), is dual in projecting a vision of both the hearth and his woman's impact upon him.

"Rumbera" ("Rhumba Dancer") also captures the sense of rhythm, life, and vitality that permeates the woman's perceived role in black culture. This poem is "generic" because it addresses the dancer's different degrees of blackness, *morena*, *negra*, *zamba*, and *mulata*, in the emphasis upon ethnicity and motion. As portrayed by other writers in this study, the concern is movement and different body postures of the dancer in relation to her natural environment. She is compared in her rhythmic dimension to an unleashed storm ("la tormenta se desata") and a rough sea ("la mar agitada"). With its attendant onomatopoetic quality, accentuated by drumbeat sounds and verbal exclamations, "Rhumba Dancer" brings alive a scene in which the woman strives for new rhythmic heights.

The image of the black woman, usually *mulata*, *morena*, *negra*, or *zamba*, is evident throughout the "Bom bom bom" section of *Merriment*. She is there not only as the sensual and sexually attractive rhumba dancer but also in her capacity as partner, spiritual and physical supporter of the black man. In "Marimba," for example, the poet speaks of "each black man and his black woman" ("cada negro con su negra"). "Out There in the Forest" also reveals this dimension:

y en mi rancho, mi alegría:
¡el íncendio de mi negra!

(and in my house, my happiness
the warmth of my black woman!)

Because the black woman is characterized as the total woman, the black man views her as a highly desirable partner. Preciado shows this attitude in "Creole," in which the protagonist is willing to risk numerous physical obstacles in order to satisfy his machismo tendencies. Neither wind, nor sun, nor floods, nor the Devil himself can deter this man from seeing his woman. Apparently, she is worth the risks involved. Not all is positive in these amorous relationships, though, as is evident in "Chimbo," a title that characterizes a sweet dish. The man rationalizes his inexplicable behavior, blaming it on witchcraft and other acts of domination. What is interesting about his allegations is that they are products of Esmeraldas, where, according to popular belief, the use of snakes, cat entrails, and candles are all common ways of enchanting an individual. The remedy is also in keeping with tradition; the hex can be washed away by bathing in rue, firewater, and verbena. The effectiveness of "Chimbo" lies in the fact that it is written in popular language and manages to capture the sincerity of this man's concerns within their folkloric dimension. The octosyllabic verse has been for many decades the principal vehicle of expression of popular poetry in Ecuador. Therefore, style, rhythm, vocabulary, and feelings combine to capture an emotionally charged experience.

In the first section of *Merriment*, Antonio Preciado views black people in both a serious and a light-hearted manner. They are shown to be hardworking individuals who live life to its fullest. Within the confines of the barrio and the community, there appears to be very little tension. We are presented with a people who have some positive sense of their past, their culture, and who are capable of coping in the present through their own resourcefulness. Yet Preciado expands this culturalist dimension beyond regional and national borders to link the Afro-Ecuadorian struggle with world liberation movements.

It is in the second half of *Merriment* that Preciado's perspective changes from cultural to historical-dialectical. This transformation involves an assessment not only of slavery and historical determinism but also of issues such as economics and labor exploitation, class and ethnicity, and prevailing societal values that make for a stratified human structure. These issues are prevalent in "Bom bom bom," but they are drawn into direct focus in "Dawn" along with their attendant impact upon Afro-Ecuadorians. This section comprises five poems, which expose a vein of social protest: "Banano" ("Banana"), "Caucho" ("Rubber"), "Amanecer" ("Dawn"), "Un poema a Guillén" ("A Poem to Guillén"), "Tierra madre" ("Mother Earth"), and "Canto a Cuba amanecida" ("Song to Awakened Cuba").

In "Banana," sweetness turning to bitter is a motif that encases two quatrains decrying the exploitation of blacks in the banana industry. There is a tragic sense of loss by the caretakers who are referred to as "midwife" ("partero") and "nursemaid" ("niñero"). But the process continues:

Este banano tan nuestro no es nuestro nada:
se va volando y volando, como con alas.
Se ve el banano en un barco, pa'l otro lado,
con el banano viajero van nuestras manos.

(This banana so much ours is nothing of ours;
it goes away flying and flying, as with wings.
The banana is seen on a boat, for the other side,
with the traveling banana go our hands.)

Although the workers feel that the banana is theirs due to the time and effort spent nurturing it, such is not the case. The contradiction is evident in the first verse, in which "ours" is placed in paradoxical opposition. The sense of movement and marketing of the fruit is captured in subsequent lines with "go" and "flying." Regardless of the mode of transportation, a part of the worker goes in the form of his labor, symbolizing the intrusion occasioned by capitalist investment and exploitation.

"And the rubber so generous knows nothing" ("y el caucho tan generoso no sabe nada") sets the tone for "Rubber," in which, again, the theme is exploitation and insensitivity. The rubber tree is robbed of its precious sap and the black of his physical being. Neither can do anything to change the circumstances.

Se va la sangre del caucho,
se va muy baja,
y vuelve de mil colores,
pero muy alta:
P'al negro del monte adentro,
¡cero pelotas!
P'al negro de los tormentos,
¡dura la goma!

(The blood of the rubber tree goes,
it goes very cheap
and returns in a thousand colors,
but very high
For the Black in the forest
zero soccer balls
For the Black with so much anguish
the rubber is cruel!)

This segment in particular conveys a sense of loss and hopelessness. On the one hand, the tree is being drained; on the other, the black cannot profit from his labors. As with bananas, rubber products are cheap to produce but expensive to buy. A paradoxical situation involving economic impotency and human degradation underlies the composition of these poems, both of which imply that a change is overdue for the present worker-product-compensation system.

"Dawn" is the key poem in this section and perhaps in the entire book. It interprets a spiritual awakening that the poet hopes will lead to physical liberation for blacks. The poem begins by chronicling the past but later projects into the future.

> Nosotros atravesamos nuestra noche,
> descalzos,
> con un ¡ay! ensangrentado entre los labios,
> con un sol encendido en las entrañas,
> como un diablo indeciso.
> Y estas manos tan nuestras no eran nuestras,
> clausuraron la voz, la encadenaron.
> ¡Ay!, ¡qué duro tormento!,
> más duro que la muerte:
> ser hombre y no ser hombre,
> vivir y no vivir,
> ser como el cielo,
> realidad y mentira.
>
> (We crossed our night,
> barefooted,
> with a bloody ay! between our lips,
> with a fiery sun in our entrails,
> like an indecisive devil.
> And these hands so much ours were not ours,
> they closed down our voice, they chained it.
> Ay! what cruel punishment!
> more cruel than death:
> to be a man and not to be a man,
> to live and not live,
> to be like heaven,
> reality and lie.)

The night referred to initially is the dark metaphor associated with slavery, an experience that brought out the worst and the best in humans. Associations and images, in a negative light, move from the physical to the mental realm. Overshadowing the entire experience is the loss of personhood and humanity—"these hands so much ours were not ours"—the loss of free will in the state of zombification as a slave. Unbearable physical pressure led to a sense of total self-alienation: "to be a man and not to be a man / to live and not live." These images point to one of the basic contradictions of slavery, that a human being should be incapable of acting independently by being denied the essentials of humanity.

The dehumanization continues in "Dawn" through the loss of many cultural attributes, including free speech, song, and dance; condemnation to wander in the American diaspora is akin to expulsion from the mythic Garden. Slowly, however, the internal fiery sun has been converted to boiling lava, awaiting eruption. The catalog of historical atrocities continues, and exclamations of outrage amplify not just because of cultural loss but also from the lack of a future, exemplified through the image of darkness:

> Y despertar, al otro día,
> con la noche perenne ante los ojos,

y un cementerio de sonrisas,
agrio en las entrañas.

(and to awaken, another day
with never-ending night before our eyes
and a graveyard of smiles
sour in our entrails.)

The wasted, bitter smiles compound the "bitter sadness" ("triste armargura") that has been the trademark of this ignoble existence. But the change has taken place:

Ahora que Africa despierta,
como un gran sol, que quema y que contagia,
como una llama inmensa,
iremos hacia el pan, hacia el trabajo,
iremos a la tierra repartida,
a la igualdad total de los humanos,
porque somos iguales para el sol y la brisa,
para la madre tierra.

(Now that Africa awakens,
like a great sun, that burns and infects,
like an immense flame,
we shall go toward food, toward work,
we shall go to redistributed land,
toward the total equality of all humans,
because we are equal in the eyes of the sun and the breeze,
in the eyes of Mother Earth.)

"Now that" accentuates the transition from slavery to freedom, and the poet's emphasis is not upon what blacks were but instead upon what they are. The focus of power appears to be changing with the recognition of Africa and the descendants of Africa as potential forces of equality throughout the world. The last five stanzas project into the future, a future filled with nourishment, work, just rewards for all—including equality. "Dawn," the awakening, becomes a metaphor for psychical and physical liberation for black people worldwide, with warranted emphasis upon the capacity for survival and progress.

Two of the poems in this section assess events in Cuba since Castro's revolution. "A Poem to Guillén" praises the Cuban poet for his revolutionary work toward the liberation of Cuba. "Song to Awakened Cuba" extols the revolution for returning Cuba to its rightful owners, the Cuban people:

Guajiro, ya tienes tierra,
guajiro, tu tierra es tuya.
Siembra y coge tu cosecha,
¡linda cosecha de Cuba!

(*Guajiro*, now you have land
Guajiro, your land is yours

Plant and gather your harvest
beautiful harvest of Cuba.)

In the poem dedicated to Guillén, Preciado is concerned about the role of the poet in the revolutionary process. The awakening metaphor appears in stanzas one—"your Cuba already awakened" ("tu Cuba ya amaneció")—and four—"it is your awakened homeland" ("es tu patria amanecida"). The overriding tone is euphoria at the accomplishments of a triumphant revolution and its ability to restructure life for the betterment of the majority. Cuban ownership of the modes of production diminishes the flow of cash from Cuba and helps to alleviate the rampant poverty on the island. "Cuban pesos that remain!" ("Pesos cubanos que quedan!") is an appropriate manner of describing the reversal of a prerevolutionary situation that saw a great deal of Cuban capital being invested in foreign banks instead of being utilized as an economic stimulus for the island and its people.

Then, in direct discourse, the poet praises Guillén:

Tu estuviste en la pelea,
antes que Fidel llegara;
tú comenzaste la guerra
con tu lírica metralla.

(You were in the struggle
before Fidel arrived;
you began the war,
with your lyric burst.)

Guillén, since converting to Marxism in 1937, has remained at the forefront of the struggle. Here he is credited with fomenting revolutionary ideology through verses denouncing discrimination, racism, exploitation, and inequality. Consequently, he is the poet of the revolution and currently poet laureate of Cuba. Preciado is careful, however, not to give Guillén more credit than Fidel Castro; in the end they are shown side by side, fighting for liberation.

In "Tierra Madre" ("Mother Earth"), the last poem to consider, the immensity of the earth and the bonds of fragile humans to this all-sustaining force are portrayed. The vulnerability of humanity is contrasted to the power of the archetypal Mother:

¡inmensa madre!
Y es que aquí estamos todos,
con el hambre en la lengua,
con dolor,
con sudor,
¡con frío, madre infinita!

(immense mother!
It is that we are all here
with hunger on our tongue,
with pain, with sweat,
with cold, infinite mother!)

This is an anguished, existential plea on the part of the poet, one that goes beyond mere physical existence to embrace the deeper meaning of life. The question of why understanding is achieved only after such sacrifice is not resolved in the poem. However, in spite of the suffering and deprivation of people, one thing remains constant: Mother Earth, who does not show favoritism to anybody. Instead, she provides sustenance to all.

*   *   *

Of these three Afro-Ecuadorian poets, Adalberto Ortiz, Nelson Estupiñán Bass, and Antonio Preciado, Preciado seems to be the most comfortable with his identity. His work represents the product of a long process of poetic self-assessment begun by Ortiz and continued by Estupiñán Bass. Like his countrymen, Preciado commences with the concrete world of Esmeraldas upon which he constructs an autonomous verbal creation. The ultimate objective of all three, however, is a poetry that has no reference to a reality beyond the poem.

In a recent assessment of black poetry, entitled "La Lira Negra" ("The Black Lyre"), Nelson Estupiñán Bass uses the Ecuadorian context as a point of departure for evaluating the whole of Afro-Hispanic poetry. He discusses black poets from the perspectives of picturesque ingenuousness, romantic sentimentalism, affirmation, irony and sarcasm, protest, and universal brotherhood.[27] Estupiñán Bass closes with an assertion: "The black man, on a world level, desires authentic brotherhood, without any racial discrimination."[28] To a degree, Ortiz, Estupiñán Bass, and Preciado all reflect these thematic tendencies and strive toward the stated social goals of Estupiñán Bass, which may never be attainable.

4

In Search of Blackness:
The Afro-Colombian Poet

The Social Context

In the concluding introductory remarks to his recent study *El hombre colombiano (Colombian Man,* 1974), Manuel Zapata Olivella, an Afro-Colombian novelist and intellectual, makes the following assertions concerning ethnic dynamics in Colombia: "Very little would we contribute to achieving a true racial and cultural equilibrium, if we persist in ignoring that we make up a hybrid people with social inequalities based upon the colonial heritage. . . . it is necessary to recognize the creative participation of Indians, Hispanics and Blacks in our culture."[1] Zapata Olivella tackles the problem of defining contemporary Colombian culture by meticulously examining the contributions of Indians, Spaniards, and blacks to the national ethos. The past has left a legacy of inequality and discrimination that the future can possibly rectify. In Zapata Olivella's estimation, however, the present does not represent an era of change for the betterment of the unfortunate members of Colombian society.

Statistically, blacks represent 6 percent of the Colombian population, compared with 2.2 percent Indian, 47.8 percent mestizo, 24 percent mulatto, and 20 percent white.[2] Colombian social structure has not changed significantly since the colonial era when blacks and Indians occupied the lowest strata of the social ladder. Indeed, two Colombian sociologists contend, "Industrialization in Colombia has not changed, in principle, social stratification."[3]

Throughout the centuries, blacks have been subjected to the same types of negative stereotyping in Colombia as in other countries with similar ethnic compositions. The images include a belief in blacks' innate mental inferiority, their laziness, their orientation to the present, and their being overly sensuous. It is an accepted fact, moreover, that color is the most important factor in class division in Colombia. In his discussion of "The Afro-Colombian in the National Culture," Leslie B. Rout, Jr., summarizes Colombian attitudes (most of them negative) toward blacks as advanced by Mejía Córdoba, Franco, Price, Solaún and Kronus, Sayres, and Sanders. He concludes, not surprisingly, "From the evidence accumulated, it should be obvious that racial prejudice and color discrimination were not eradicated root and branch with the abolition of slavery in 1852."[4] Nevertheless, of the four countries under discussion in my study, Colombia is the only one in which blacks presently demonstrate the desire to improve their collective social situation. The Black Power movement in the United States during the 1960s and Third World liberation movements had lasting repercussions on Afro-Colombian self-assertion and awareness during the 1970s.

In *Historia del negro en Colombia* (*History of the Black in Colombia*, 1980), Ildefonso Gutiérrez Azopardo summarizes recent black-oriented activities under the subheading "The Awakening of the Black and *Negritud*." He lists the following significant activities:

> 1) 1975: Entrance as a candidate for the presidency of the Republic for the period 1978–82 of a black doctor/writer from Cartagena. 2) 1975–77: Birth of the movements "Black Population," "Negritudes," and "Black Culture." In Buenaventura appeared the groups "The Black Panthers," and "The Kettle"; in Popayán the group "Maroon," made up of black students; in Tunja the study group "Tabala," made up of university students; in Pereira the "Circle of Studies of the Problematics of the Black Communities of Soweto." 3) 1976: Meeting in Cartagena of North American anthropologists and sociologists to discuss the contributions of Blacks to American culture. 4) 1977: First meeting on black culture of the Americas convened in Cali. The Center for the Investigation of Black Culture which edits the journal *Negritud* was created.[5]

Gutiérrez Azopardo is impressed with neither the direction nor the sincerity of these movements, which is a typical majority viewpoint. In his summary remarks, he poses the question, "playing with the future of the Black?"— suggesting that black leaders are taking the masses who adhere to their philosophy of militancy and separatism down a frustrating road of disappointment. However, any positive gains by Afro-Colombians are welcomed by blacks to break the cycles of discrimination, marginality, and exploitation.

Colombian black intellectuals and creative writers long ago made the connections between race, class, and caste. Their attitudes justify Rout's conclusion: "In their works, many have long insisted that, although the Afro-Colombian accepts his position and tells himself that the issue is class, in reality, he is tagged by whites on the basis of race and/or color."[6] While Manuel Zapata Olivella is seeking a true racial and cultural equilibrium, the lessons of history demonstrate its impossibility in Colombia, at least in the foreseeable future.

How is the Afro-Colombian author, then, supposed to react to the transition from a society that acknowledges historical injustices to blacks to one committed to ethnic harmony? Like most black writers in South America, Colombians first come to grips with their own identity and only then begin the search for a solution that incorporates personal, national, and universal concerns into their literary production.

Jorge Artel: Drums in the Night

Parallel to the situation in Ecuador, some black writers in Colombia form part of the literary mainstream. It is possible to find references to exponents of black literature such as Candelario Obeso, Jorge Artel, Helcías Martán

Góngora, Manuel and Juan Zapata Olivella, Hugo Salazar Valdés, Arnoldo Palacios, and others in the *Bibliografía de la poesía colombiana (Bibliography of Colombian Poetry)* by Héctor Orjuela, the *Antología crítica de la poesía colombiana (Critical Anthology of Colombian Poetry)* by Andrés Holguín, and other major historical and critical works devoted to Colombian letters. In the United States, novelist Manuel Zapata Olivella and poet Helcías Martán Góngora have had doctoral dissertations written on their literary production in addition to the usual articles and chapters in scholarly publications.

For the most part, however, North American critical attention has focused upon fiction. Indeed, aside from the dissertation on Martán Góngora by Moses Harris, little has been written about Afro-Colombian poetry. While Jorge Artel is mentioned in several critical articles, Hugo Salazar Valdés has yet to be recognized as a first-rate poet. Artel's publishing career spans a forty-year period that reveals constant development. Although three solid volumes of his poetry have been published, his work has yet to be treated in its entirety. "Artel," writes Juvenal Herrera Torres, "is not a poet limited to circumstantial factors of bygone towns and times. Artel is universal and effective. He is a poet from Colombia for the world."[7] In his poetic dimensions, Artel follows the same pattern of most Afro-Hispanic writers. That is, he uses his personal ethnic experience to build upon in order to convey both national and international messages. Within this poetic conception of Artel, Herrera is of the opinion that "a universal and classist dimension" predominates, that "the problem is not of color but of class."[8] Only a close examination of Artel's poetry will determine to what degree racism and classism affect his poetic interpretations, since it is generally assumed in Colombia that class is more important than color in determining social position. Herrera believes that Artel operates under this very assumption.

The editor of the *Diccionario de escritores colombianos (Dictionary of Colombian Writers)* describes Jorge Artel in the following manner:

> He was born in Cartagena on April 27, 1909. His true name is Agapito de Arcos. Lawyer and poet. Bard of color and poet of his race; singer of happy sadness in popular and human verses; poet of color and of protest.[9]

The poetry of Jorge Artel certainly contains these elements, all of which have shown a maturation parallel to the author's own artistic development. Artel has published three volumes of poetry: *Tambores en la noche (Drums in the Night,* 1940); *Poemas con botas y banderas (Poems with Boots and Flags,* 1972); and *Antología poética (Poetry Anthology,* 1979), the latter a compilation of most of the socially critical poems of the former books along with some new material.

Drums in the Night consists of forty-six poems divided into two sections, "Drums in the Night" and "Other Poems." The fifteen poems of "Drums in the Night" are devoted to the Afro-Colombian experience, with three major preoccupations expressed thematically by Artel: the importance of dance, music, and rhythm in folklore and culture; past and present relationships with Africa; and the continuing search for identity and respect. Nearly half of "Drums in the Night" represents the first thematic trend outlined above, and "La Cumbia" ("The Cumbia") does so perhaps better than any others. The cumbia is a dance born of miscegenation and cultural amalgamation that occurred among blacks and Indians during the initial clash between peoples of divergent world views. The indigenous flute and the African drum were and still are essential instruments in the development of the cumbia. In her perceptive analysis of the dance, *The Cumbia*, Delia Zapata Olivella has written:

> The continuous contact between Indians and Blacks during Colonial servitude, and their intercourse under the imposed circumstances by their common submission to the slave owners, must have produced, among its consequences, the approaching and the partial fusion of their musical expressions: the melancholy *gaita* or indigenous flute, in close contrast with the happy and impetuous resonance of the African drum. Thus emerged this rhythm that we call cumbia and which today incarnates the feeling of a large portion of the Colombian people.[10]

Artel's poem "The Cumbia" begins,

> Hay un llanto de gaitas
> diluído en la noche.

> (There is a cry of flutes
> diluted in the night.)

Artel captures the intense mood of this dance through both a personification of natural forces and a vivid description of night and earth:

> Y la noche, metida en ron costeño,
> bate sus alas frías
>
> . . . .
>
> Y la tierra,
> como una axila cálida de negra,
> su agrio vaho levanta, denso de temblor,
>
> (and the night, abundant in coastal rum
> flaps its cold wings
>
> . . . .
>
> and the earth
> like the warm armpit of a black woman
> its agrarian aroma raises, dense with trembling.)

Whole-hearted participation of nature in the human dance suggests that the cumbia is more than a dance described as "frenetic" ("frenética") and "diabolic" ("diabólica").

> ¡Cumbia!—danza negra, danza de mi tierra!
> Toda una raza grita

en esos gestos eléctricos,
por la contorsionada pirueta
de los muslos epilécticos!

(Cumbia!—black dance, dance of my land!
An entire race cries out
in those electric gestures,
through the contortioned pirouette
of the epileptic thighs!)

The cumbia must be viewed in its mythic dimensions, as embodying the ancestral expression of Afro-Colombians. It grew out of the conflictive black experience in Colombia, but perhaps the expression "dance of my land" takes on a double meaning since the poet claims a dual heritage. His relationship to the past is maintained in subsequent stanzas, with the nighttime imagery of jungles, lighted bonfires, and ritualistic elements of the dance all an attempt to bridge the gap between past and present:

Late un recuerdo aborigen,
una africana aspereza,
sobre el cuero curtido donde los tamborileros,
—sonámbulos dioses nuevos que repican alegría,
aprendieron a hacer el trueno
con sus manos nudosas,
todopoderosas para la algarabía.

(An aborigine memory throbs,
an African harshness,
upon the sunburnt skin where drummers,
—sleepwalking new gods who ring out happiness,
learned to make thunder
with their callused hands,
all powerful for an uproar.)

In this stanza, there appears to be a conflict between old and new experiences as the "aborigine memory" stands juxtaposed to the "new gods." The latter have not succeeded completely in supplanting the African element that remains very much alive in the cumbia, danced by the poet's forefathers "at the seashore" ("a la orilla del mar"). The cultural dialectic is maintained between the African harshness of the drums and the happy resounding of the new gods. Artel's view of this dance, therefore, is as a transplanted element of African culture that has come to represent a vital element in the Colombian national synthesis.

In the first stanza of "¡Danza mulata!" ("Dance, Mulatta!"), reference is made to the "drum of the grandparents" ("tambor de los abuelos") and the "languishing rhythm of the race" ("Son languidescente de la raza"), which represents the typical atavistic view and links this poem to "The Cumbia" thematically. In subsequent stanzas, the mulatta is presented as an enigmatic figure:

Deja que el sol fustigue
tu belleza demente,
que corra por tus flancos inquietantes
el ritmo que tus senos estremece.

Aprisiona en tu talle atormentado
esa música bruja
que acompasa la voz de la canción.

¡Danza, mulata, danza!
En tus piernas veloces y en el son
que ha empapado tus lúbricas caderas
doscientos siglos se agazapan.

(Let the sun lash
your demented beauty,
let it pass across your disquieting flanks
the rhythm that your breasts shakes.

Capture in your tormented figure
that bewitching music
that tempers the voice of the song.

Dance, Mulatta, dance!
In your agile legs and in the rhythm
that has absorbed your lascivious thighs
two hundred centuries are hidden.)

Not only is the mulatta presented as a sensual and perhaps amoral being—
"disquieting flanks," "lascivious thighs"—but also there appears to be a
conflict within her physical being. To what are we to attribute her "demented beauty" and her "tormented figure"? Apparently it is the past, her
black African heritage, that causes the mulatta's unrest. Neither side of her
dual ethnic composition has been subdued by the other, so she has not been
assured of full participation in any social activities. As a historical figure with
two-thousand-year-old biological roots, the mulatta proves, in the poet's
view, that miscegenation is not a recent, American phenomenon. Artel
presents a similar characterization of the mulatta as a complicated figure in
"Romance mulato" ("Mulatto Ballad").

In "Barrio abajo" ("Barrio Below"), the poet is not so much concerned
with the far-reaching implications of the black woman's cultural heritage as
he is with her physical presence. The woman protagonist is in charge of her
physical surroundings and is an object of his desires. "Give me your
rhythm, black woman" ("dame tu ritmo negra") is his plea as the black
woman is presented in a positive light, as poetic inspiration for an admirer.
Through effective imagery there is a fusion of activities surrounding work,
activities in turn related to the sexual dimension of their encounter. "Bull-
erengue" ("Merriment") continues this positive attitude toward the black
woman in a composition written in popular language within a musical
context. The protagonist identifies with the drum ("tambor"), the maraca,
the flute, and the little drum ("tamborito") in order to gain her favors. La
Canción" ("The Song"), a realted poem, treats the spread of the oral tradi-

tion throughout the Americas and is another example of Artel's realization that there is a correlation between the present surface celebration of Afro-Colombian culture and its historical underpinnings.

"Ahora hablo de gaitas" ("Now I Speak of Flutes") is a poem of nostalgic longing for past experiences that only exist marginally in the present. The poet perceives the *gaitas*, indigenous flutes, as an integral internal force instead of as a physical reality.

> Gaitas lejanas la noche
> nos ha metido en el alma.
>
> (Far away flutes in the night
> have penetrated in our soul.)

The problem of understanding their significance then and now is the poet's major concern:

> —Llenen mi copa de ron,
> de ron blanco como el agua!
> yo quiero sentir lo mismo
> que sintieron mis abuelos
> cuando escuchaban las gaitas,
> colmando sus noches hondas
> con aguardiente de caña!
>
> (—Fill my cup with rum,
> with rum white as water!
> I wish to feel the same
> as my grandparents felt
> when they listened to the flutes
> filling their deep nights
> with firewater of cane!)

By viewing this act as ritual, as historical repetition, the poet can identify with his ancestors in a mythic sense; theoretically, each act is a representation of the original symbolic gesture. In most of the poems in "Drums in the Night," there is a degree of mythic-ritualistic interpretation of experiences in relating to dance, music, and rhythm, as well as to their impact upon Afro-Colombian culture. The volume *Drums in the Night* was written by Artel during his personal interval of passage, when he was attempting to assess both synchronic and diachronic time through an assertion of his Afro-Hispanic identity. His cultural affirmation becomes more pronounced in some of the poems treating the African presence.

Indeed, Africa provides one of Artel's prime literary sources, poems such as "Tambores en la noche" ("Drums in the Night"), "La voz de los ancestros" ("The Voice of the Ancestors"), "Velorio del boga ausente" ("Wake of the Missing Rower"), and "Dancing" being illustrative examples. In "Drums in the Night," the drum is established as a positive, permanent element of Afro-Colombian culture. Its omnipresence—it "seems as if it follows our steps" ("parece que siguieran nuestros pasos")—is inspiration-

al. Moreover, in the first stanza, Artel makes an association between man
and the sea that will prevail in most of the poems in the second half of the
volume. The drum triggers living images of the past in the poet's mind:

> Los tambores en la noche
> son como un grito humano.
> Trémulos de música les he oído gemir,
> cuando esos hombres que llevan
> la emoción en las manos
> les arrancan la angustia de una oscura saudade,
> de una íntima añoranza,
> donde vigila el alma dulcemente salvaje
> de mi vibrante raza,
> con sus siglos mojados en quejumbres de gaitas.

> (The drums in the night
> are like a human shout.
> Trembling with music I have heard them moan,
> when those men who carry
> emotion in their hands
> wrench from them the anguish of a dark body,
> give an intimate longing,
> where watches the sweetly savage soul
> of my vibrant race,
> with centuries drenched in moans of flutes.)

In this instance, the poet's African identity is an integral, latent part of his
personality, waiting to be summoned by the drum. The longing that the
ancestral instrument triggers points to a contradiction in the person's
psyche, which is exemplified paradoxically ("sweetly savage soul"). That
the poet recognized the drums' call is strong evidence that he has maintained a portion of his African identity. The drum speaks to him across the
centuries in a variety of positive ways, but the poet includes the indigenous
flute as a part of his heritage.

This nostalgic view of the past is maintained in "The Voice of the Ancestors." Voices are transmitted to the poet on the wind and the sea, forces on
which the transportation of blacks from Africa depended. The poet's vantage point is a quiet port:

> Oigo galopar los vientos.
> Sus voces desprendidas
> de lo más hondo del tiempo
> siembran en mí un eco
> de tamboriles muertos
> de quejumbres perdidas
> en no sé cuál tierra ignota,
> donde cesó la luz de las hogueras
> con las notas de la última lúbrica canción.

> (I hear the winds gallop.
> Their disinterested voices
> from the most remote of time

plant in me an echo
of dead drums
of lost moans
in I don't know which unknown land,
where the light of the bonfires ceased,
with the notes of the last lubricious song.)

The poet feels a great cultural loss in the "dead drums" and the "lost moans." He is aware of negative consequences of the black diaspora, of people destroyed in many different lands. His emotion reaches its peak in the last three stanzas when he identifies strongly with the past:

—Padres de la raza morena!—
Contemplo en sus pupilas caminos de nostalgias,
rutas de dulzura,
temblores de cadena y rebelión.

Almas anchurosas y libres
vigorizaban los pechos y las manos cautivas!
Una doliente humanidad se refugiaba
en su música oscura de vibrátiles fibras . . .
—Anclados a su dolor anciano
iban cantando por la herida . . .

(—Parents of the black race!—
I contemplate in your pupils roads of nostalgias,
routes of sweetness,
tremors of chain and rebellion.

Encompassing and free souls
invigorate your chests and your captive hands!
A suffering humanity takes refuge
in your dark music of vibrant strength . . .
—Anchored to your ancient pain
they go singing through the wound . . .)

A combination of synesthesia and visceral imagery demonstrates the relationship between the intimate, heartfelt source of music and its culture. Through apostrophe, Artel personally portrays the past suffering of blacks. His tendency is to juxtapose traumatic and pleasant experiences; in the first stanza, chains and rebellion result in freedom of spirit and body. Black music is an outgrowth of the period of captivity and enslavement, symbolized by the "captive hands" and "suffering humanity." This expression, though, comes from deep within, from the soul, and represents an externalization of years of struggle. In the final stanza, the poet agonizes over an experience that he cannot recapture. On a positive note, Artel draws a dichotomy between physical oppression and the inability of slavery to quell the spirit of blacks. Instead, the institution inspired different modes of expressing the most intimate feelings, perhaps even those not associated directly with Africa or slavery.

The *velorio*, or burial ritual, is the theme of "Wake of the Absent Rower," in which the body lies in state after being properly prepared. The death of one of the more physically gifted members of the community prompts sad responses from many of the group who remember his exploits. "Remember" ("Recordar") and "think" ("pensar") reinforce the idea that his activities took place in the past. Human and natural environments participate in this rite: "The women cry for him on the patio" ("las mujeres lo lloran en el patio") and "It even seems like the breeze has a slight cry of palms" ("Hasta parece que la brisa tien un leve llanto de palmeros"). The wake reflects burial practices in the Chocó region of Colombia, and the poem concentrates upon the intense emotional lelvel and reciprocal attitudes between humans and nature in the region of Artel's origin. In contrast, "Dancing" shows the superficial nature of the amalgamation of African and Anglo elements during a festive occasion sponsored by the majority culture. The music is by blacks; hence,

> Un pedazo de selva
> cayó en el salón!
>
> (A piece of jungle
> fell into the ballroom,)

and, in reference to Josefine Baker, the famous black dancer, "your legs playing with civilization." Yet despite the apparent cultural confusion, whites do accept black music and dance activities, one step, anyway, toward better human understanding, and it is a step aided by the ritual foundation of music and dance. So Artel clearly is very much engaged by ritual, both secular and religious, and its importance in Afro-Colombian culture. Many of these rituals originated on the African continent but persist today as reminders of the lasting strength of African culture in Colombia, which also both helps and haunts in the continuing search for identity and respect by Colombian blacks, the subject of several poems in *Drums in the Night*.

"El líder negro" ("The Black Leader") is written in popular language and describes the respect that the town has for Diego Lui because of his truthfulness. Even the whites take off their hats when he passes. In "Sensualidad negra" ("Black Sensuality"), Catana, whose beauty provokes envy on the part of other women, commands the admiration of men who view her not just as a sex object but also with honorable intentions. Catana, needless to say, is content with her blackness and beauty. "Mr. Davi" represents a nostalgic longing for the African homeland:

> Mr. Davi era negro
> y había nacido en tierras muy lejanas tal vez . . .
> Lo conocí en el puerto:
> llegó con su tristeza
> y su acordeón.
>
> (Mr. Davi was Black
> and had been born in faraway lands perhaps . . .
> I met him in the port:

> he arrived with his sadness
> and his accordion.)

The action in this poem transpires around a seaport and is tinged with irony. The sea, which is a metaphor for the slave trade in the Americas, now represents freedom, or the reverse passage. Mr. Davi's sadness is associated with a lack of direction in the present and the knowledge of an unhappy past. Subsequently he disappears.

Undoubtedly the most profound of these identity poems is "I Am Black," which involves self-affirmation and ethnic identity:

> Negro soy desde hace muchos siglos
> Poeta de mi raza, heredé su dolor.
> Y la emoción que digo ha de ser pura
> en el bronco son del grito
> y ei monorrítmico tambor.
>
> (I am black for many centuries.
> Poet of my race, I inherited your pain.
> And the emotion that I speak has to be pure
> in the rough sound of the cry
> and the monorhythmic drum.)

Recognition of his black heritage is of the utmost importance to the poet in this outward manifestation of identity. But the fact of being black carries with it a legacy of suffering that he is obligated to express poetically. This will involve capturing the rituals and modes of expression of his ancestors:

> El hondo, estremecido acento
> en que trisca la voz de los ancestros,
> es mi voz.
>
> La angustia humana que exalto
> no es decorativa joya
> para turistas.
> Yo no canto un dolor de exportación.
>
> (The deep, rendered accent,
> in which mingles the ancestral voices,
> is my voice.
>
> The human anguish that I display
> is not a decorative jewel
> for tourists.
> I do not chant pain for exportation.)

The poet's personal affirmation first entails an identification with his African past, internalizing years of experience and taking a positive approach to black culture. Going beyond the surface of experiences is necessary because even the uninitiated easily grasps the superficial ("decorative," "tourists"). Indeed, the narrator has to dig deep into his ancestral past in an attempt to bring into clearer focus the more meaningful expressions that explain his existence.

The second section of *Drums in the Night* highlights man's relationship to nature (the sea especially), the theme of love, and the idea of separation. "Other Poems" contains some of Artel's most successful lyrical poetry, with romantic love poems composing much of this section. In these fleeting, emotional moments, Artel manages to convey attitudes of intense longing.

In "Breve canción para Zoila" ("Brief Song for Zoila"), the poetic perspective is that of a seafaring person who, from the vantage point of the shore, expresses an emotional response to a loved one. His tender, gentle, loving attitude is conveyed in the first stanza through "to coo," "new born," "tender," and "in peace" ("arrullar," "recién nacido," "tiernos," and "en paz"). Her days, in this instance, are synonymous with the person's total make up. Stanza two commences by repeating the opening words of the first and with a quick flash to the past and a romantic, nostalgic remembrance conveyed by an abstraction. "To fish for bright stars" ("para pescar luceros") signifies that the protagonist is a bit out of touch with reality due to his amorous fantasizing. The abstract perception of the object of his desires continues into the third stanza, in which she becomes more transitory but at the same time more desirable. He is perceiving her as an extension of the sea, which becomes apparent in the first two stanzas and more concrete in the final ones. Indeed, the song "that I learned in the port" ("que aprendí en el puerto") is populated with "the musical gulls of my verse" ("las musicales gaviotas de mi verso"). "Brief Song for Zoila" reaches its romantic climax in stanza four in a dreamlike, nostalgic flight into the world of "smiling visions" ("visiones risueñas"), "moon song" ("canción de lunas"), and "perfumed words" ("perfumadas palabras"). The final simile represents the poet's attempt to envelop her into his private world of amorous symbolism.

The "cooing" image is bound closely with the motifs of love and separation. This is evident in "Versos para zarpar un día" ("Verses to Weigh a Day") in which a similar scene is played out:

> La insomne pupila del faro
> contemplará mi viaje . . .
> Y la pálida voz de la luna
> caerá sobre el mar, para arrullarme
> con su honda sonata de silencio.
>
> (The sleepless pupil of the lantern
> will contemplate my trip . . .
> and the pale voice of the moon
> will fall upon the sea, to lull me
> with its deep sonata of silence.)

An integral part of the life of a sailor is captured in these images of the lighthouse, departure, and the soothing impact of the sea. Three other poems, "Soborno emocional" ("Emotional Bribery"), "Canción para un ayer definitivo" ("Song for a Definitive Yesterday"), and "Silencio" ("Silence") reflect basically these same tendencies.

In "Other Poems" there is an apparent fusion of woman, the sea, and

other elements of nature, with marine life and water predominating thematically throughout the thirty poems. What begins as a romantic obsession
with the sea sometimes leads to a sense of alienation. These thematic
polarities are evident in "Canción para ser cantada desde un mástil" ("Song
to be Sung from a Mast") and "Poema incoherente con fondos de distancia"
("Incoherent Poem with Distant Depths").

The former poem is narrated from the perspective of someone who no
longer participates actively in seafaring enterprises but who nevertheless
conserves a rich memory. In fact, he is still externalizing his obsessions and
captures the sense of motion associated with maritime existence:

> Van mis velas hinchadas por el viento
> partiendo en dos la soledad.
> Van mis velas erguidas
> y yo en un mástil, rígido, cantando!
>
> (My sails go billowed by the wind
> parting solitude in two.
> My sails go swelled
> And I before a mast, rigid, singing!)

Since the protagonist's dreams are being transformed into reality, through
vicarious experiences there is the realization that most good things must
come to an end. Therefore, an analogy is drawn between the voyages at sea
and life's trajectory. There is a marked contrast between the first four stanzas
and the last four. The "billowed sails" and the "rigid, singing" mariner
stand in stark juxtaposition to the existential questions posed in the latter
stanzas:

> A dónde habrá de terminar mi viaje,
> este viaje turbulento y largo,
>
> (Where will my journey terminate
> this long and turbulent journey?)

As the protagonist confronts the specter of death, "without lanterns raised
in the night" ("sin faros erguidos en su la noche"), a more realistic view of
reality emerges. This does not negate, however, the joy and freedom of the
sea, which is the poem's major thrust. Estrangement from the sea, however,
is the theme of "Incoherent Poem," also from the perspective of an individual who questions the passage of time. The *ubi sunt* motif focuses the
protagonist upon past memories and heightens his present sense of loss.

The notion of departing permeates these poems associated with the sea
and reflects the protagonist's alienation from the physical world. Moreover,
the dynamics between man and the sea constitute the thematic basis of
fourteen additional poems, in several of which, Artel demonstrates that the
simple life associated with the water is preferable to the urban life of Cartagena, for example, or other cities.

The poet, however, is more concerned with forging a harmonious relationship between man and all elements of nature, as evidenced in "Añoranza de la tierra nativa" ("Longing for the Native Land"), which develops a positive synthesis, and "Playa" ("Beach"), a poem of regeneration in which Artel is at his lyrical best:

> En los turbios ojos de pescadores
> despertó la mañana,
> colmando el fragante paréntesis de playa
> con su muda algarabía de colores.
>
> . . . .
> Por los bordes del monte
> se derrama un sol
> que inunda la ciudad.
> Y en la orilla festoneada de atarrayas
> se siente caer el día como agua bautismal.
>
> (In the drowsy eyes of the fishermen
> awakened the morning,
> filling the fragrant parenthesis of beach
> with its gibberish of colors.
>
> . . . .
> Through the fringes of the forest
> spills a sun
> that inundates the city.
> And on the shore covered with nets
> one feels the day fall like baptismal water.)

Daybreak is humanized in all of its splendor and is defined in relationship to humans. It permeates all of the surrounding physical environment as if sketched from a painter's brush. The image of night retreating before day enhances the evocative nature of the poem begun with the morning awakening in the eyes of the fishermen. This life-giving process is presented as having a positive impact upon the beach, the city, and its inhabitants who all receive their stimulation from archetypal functions of the universe. Thus, humans are inextricably linked to the dictates of nature.

Throughout these poems, it becomes evident that the poet defines himself and his physical environment in relation to the sea, a tendency even more observable toward the end of *Drums in the Night* in a fusion of ethnic identity, the sea, and personal identity. This process of self-definition is evident in "Mi canción" ("My Song") and "Canción imposible" ("Impossible Song").

In "My Song," the poet speaks of his poetic inspiration:

> Un tono cálido
> amasado de gritos y de sol.
> Una estrofa negra
> borracha de gaitas vagabundas
> y golpes dementes de tambor.
> Un oleaje frenético
> erizado de calor.

Una playa foeteada
como espaldas morenas,
por las fustas ardientes,
y un pedazo de mar—hermano mayor
que me enseñó a ser rebelde—,
me dieron la canción.

 (A hot tone
kneaded from shouts and sun.
A black strophe
drunk with wandering flutes
and demented drum beats.

 A frenetic rough sea
bristled with heat.
A filled beach
like black backs
by the burning twigs
and a piece of sea—older brother—
who taught me to be a rebel—,
they gave me the song.)

As revealed in "My Song," Artel's artistic creation is a product of Afro-Colombian culture and the physical environment of the seaport of Cartagena. Images conjured up, perhaps, from his ancestral memory dominate this poem and much of his early poetry. Here, the narrator is overcome by a combination of physical and mental realities that reflect the people ("a black strophe"), the sea ("A frenetic rough sea"), and the land ("A filled beach"). All three ingredients are reinforced throughout the remainder of "My Song," showing that the poet has discovered the motivational forces behind his literary production.

Related to the issue of inspiration are the questions of identity and self-definition that are addressed in "Impossible Song," the volume's last selection. In the first stanzas, the poet portrays his initial unrest at being unable to pin down the source of his discontent but suspects that it arises from ethnic factors:

 Ignoro aún si es negra o blanca,
si ha de cantar en ella
el indio adormecido que llora en mis entrañas
o el pendenciero ancestro del abuelo
que me dejó su ardiente
y sensual sangre mulata.
Si ha de llevar sabor de agua salada
o tambores al fondo
o claridades de sol de la mañana
o nebulosos fríos de montaña.

 (I still don't know if it is Black or White,
if it must sing in her
the sleeping Indian that cries in my entrails
or the quarrelsome ancestor of my grandfather

who left me his fiery
and sensual mulatto blood.
If it has to carry the flavor of salted water
or drums in the background
or clarities of the morning sun
or cloudy coldness of the mountain.)

What is it that the poet wishes to shout, to affirm? Does he wish to deny or to stress one particular element of his tripartite ethnic heritage? The amount of indecisiveness is demonstrated through the use of the conjunctions *if* and *or*, leaving the poet in a state of confusion in terms of both his background and his production. To deny one is to affirm the other in this dialectic of heritage.

The issue remains unsettled at the end of "Impossible Song," with the poet's promise that should he solve the dilemma concerning his identity, he "would write it with blood" ("la escribiría con sangre"). This is an appropriate note on which to end the volume, a point at which Artel begins to prefigure greater concerns for human destiny, concerns to be resolved in later volumes. *Drums in the Night* is not the poetry of social protest, but with its publication, Artel announced a rich and varied poetic trajectory. The merit of *Drums in the Night* is that it is one of the first volumes of contemporary poetry to place positive emphasis on being black in South America.

Poetry Anthology

Poetry Anthology is composed of poems from *Drums in the Night* and *Poems with Boats and Flags*. It is organized by Artel and consists of his best poems on social themes; his sea poems are not contained in this book. One salient characteristic of the *Anthology* is that it demonstrates how well versed Artel is in the black experience throughout the Americas instead of being limited to Colombia. Of the fifteen poems in the first section, twelve are contained in *Poems with Boats and Flags* and represent the best selections from that volume. "Volver" ("To Return"), "Este duro salitre que se extiende en mi pecho" ("This Hard Saltpeter that Extends to My Chest"), and "Poema para no ser olvidado" ("Poem Not to Be Forgotten") are the new additions.

The two latter poems concern the Chilean situation and express Artel's admiration for two cultural symbols, Salvador Allende and Pablo Neruda. "This Hard Saltpeter" is a pessimistic reconstruction of events surrounding Allende's death and its implications for revolutionary movements throughout the Americas. The saltpeter in the poet's chest is a metaphor for disgust and inarticulateness over the

delirantes aceros
y monstruosos engendros
cuyos picos de plomo
abatieron a Allende.

(delirious steel
and monstrous offsprings

whose lead beaks
shot down Allende.)

The poet desires that the image of Allende remain etched upon the continental psyche. Even from his vantage point, analogies can be drawn with the
Chilean experience:

Yo estoy aquí, hundido
en cualquier ciudad de Colombia,
viendo golpear y asesinar los estudiantes,
masacrar indígenas inermes
tenderles celadas a las guerrillas,
mientras la policía marina y el ejército
nos sacan de las bibliotecas y los claustros
porque hay que oponer a la cátedra,
al libro, a nuestros poemas,
el planteamiento imperialista,
la culata, el garrote y la bala.

(I am here, buried
in any city of Colombia,
seeing the students being beaten and assassinated,
the massacre of unarmed indigenous people
laying out corpses of guerrillas,
while the police and the army
expel us from the libraries and the faculty
because one must oppose the professor,
the book, our poems,
imperialist planning,
the gunbutt, the club, the bullet.)

As far as the poet is concerned, what transpired in Chile to overthrow
Allende was not an isolated incident. Rather, it represents a repressive trend
that is plaguing many American countries, Colombia in particular. Reaction-
ary violence takes its toll upon all rebellious and defenseless segments of
society. A significant contrast is drawn in the last verses cited here in which
scholarly activities are juxtaposed to repressive tactics. Thus, a dichotomy is
established between democratic and militaristic aspects of culture.

The poet continues his lament for Chile throughout the final stanzas and
introduces the *ubi sunt* motif, evoking the names of Neruda, Hughes, Lorca,
and others who through their poetry have sought to effect social change.
Allende, he maintains, lives on as a symbol of resistance,

frente a la historia,
frente al odio de la reacción—sirviente del Pentágono—
con su metralleta humeante iluminándole las manos,
alumbrando a nuestros pueblos el camino.

(facing history
facing the hate of the servant reaction of the Pentagon
with his smoking machine gun illuminating his hands
brightening the road for our people.)

Artel views the Chilean reaction to dependency as an archetypal battle between Good and Evil: in this case Evil triumphs. Upon this defeat, though, Good is able to construct a sustaining myth in the person of Allende.

"Pequeña oración a Neruda" ("Small Prayer to Neruda") is a portrait of the Pablo Neruda of the *Canto general*, his culturalist interpretation of the Americas, and expresses similar attitudes of rebellion toward injustices; even in death, Neruda contemplates the historical atrocities. And, because of his ability to forge a poetic vision representing centuries of Chilean existence, Neruda occupies a special place in Chilean social mythology. But from the grave, he remains a silent witness to the atrocities of a nation. Just as the ideology of Allende persists as a resistance to the fascist order, so does much of the poetry of Neruda live on as testimony of a turbulent historical period. Throughout the poem there is a juxtapositioning of incongruous images to create an unsettling view of a country betrayed.

Constructing a plethora of experiences upon a metaphor of returning, the poet, in the poem "To Return," juxtaposes past and present in a rambling surrealistic style. It is a complex poem, embracing local and international functions that combine the trivial and the important. Most important, "To Return" is concerned with the destiny of humankind:

> Solo, en fin, el que regresa puede
> construir ataúdes de ceniza
> para sepultar en ellos
> estrellas apagadas.

> (Only, finally he who returns can
> construct coffins of ashes
> to bury in them
> extinguished stars.)

"To Return," in essence, is a poem of spiritual and physical regeneration, a thematic perspective that it shares with "This Hard Saltpeter" and "Small Prayer to Neruda."

The images of the black experience etched in the second section of *Poetry Anthology* are amplifications upon and in some instances more profound than some of those presented in *Drums in the Night*. This is due to the apparent poetic and social maturation of the poet as well as his ideological stance. With the seventeen new poems of this part, Artel reestablishes himself as a black poet after being engaged in a great deal of historical, dialectical rhetoric in his second volume. The poems represent both a reaffirmation of *negritud* on his part and an exploration of the theme of Africa and its impact upon black culture in the Americas. Consequently, poems examine the physical environment of Africa, the confrontation and reaction of black cultures during adaptation throughout the Americas, and the specific milieu of black Colombians.

"Superstición" ("Superstition") relates a brutal, magical episode concerning the death of a drummer and his commitment to legend by a *griot*, an African oral historian, in whose mouth history is refashioned to reflect the aspirations of the community. This specific instance reveals that the drummer's hands were amputated as punishment for sending a false message. Here, however, the incident is elevated to mythic proportions because the drummer continues to function in the popular imagination. In time, the difference between fact and fiction will be difficult to fathom.

"La ruta dolorosa" ("The Painful Route") is an attempt to discover something positive, a common ground, in the experience of slavery, with emphasis upon the middle passage. The poem begins with a series of poetic incongruencies. First of all, there is vivid contrast between the "hot islands of alcohol and tobacco" ("cálidas islas de alcohol y de tabaco") and the "routes of terror" ("rutas de espanto")—where destiny united "the song with the whip" ("la canción con el latigo"). These types of inconsistencies from the beginning have constantly caused blacks to seek a common identity in the New World based upon the experiences that grew out of slavery. The poet questions:

> En qué salto de la sangre
> tú y yo nos encontramos
> o en qué canción yoruba nos mecimos
> juntos, como dos hermanos?
> Lo sabrán los mástiles remotos
> de la galera que nos trajo,
> el Congo impenetrable
> donde nuestros abuelos transitaron.
>
> (In which leap of blood
> did you and I meet
> or in which Yoruba song did
> we rock together like two brothers?
> The remote masts will know it
> of the ship that brought us,
> the unpassable Congo
> where our grandparents walked.)

Blacks on the American continents share much that they have yet to recognize, but history, symbolized through the ship metaphor, still bears witness to the events that transpired. On a human level, the process of recognition, of seeing oneself reflected in others on a large scale, remains a problem. A common black identity has to be forged out of many different yet similar national experiences. Since Artel's poems that deal with Africa out of necessity fall into the survival and rhetorical categories of literatures outlined by Brathwaite, it is fitting that Artel should evoke paradisiacal images of Africa in "The Painful Route." Hence, his physical proximity to the Niger River and its environs are a learning ground where

> junto a los cuales descifrábamos
> la ruda lección del viento
> y el itinerario de los pájaros.

> (We deciphered
> the rude lesson of the wind
> and the itinerary of the birds.)

Senegal, which is

> sonoro,
> sin bandera y sin amo,
>
> (sonorous
> without flag and without owner,)

is immediately

> estremecido por la demoníaca
> presencia del hombre blanco.
>
> (shaken by the demonic
> presence of the white man.)

Paradise, it seems, is once again invaded by the Devil. The poem continues with a rhetorical question:

> No ves en mis palabras
> el tatuaje de un látigo,
> no intuyes las cadenas
> y los tambores lejanos?
>
> (Don't you see in my words
> the tattoo of a whip
> don't you intuit the chains
> and the distant drums?)

The images are reiterated in an effort to construct a basis upon which to begin physical and psychical liberation. For Artel, the African image extends far beyond a glorious past to include motivation for the future struggle.

In this same vein, "Alto Congo" ("Congo") is a symbolic journey upstream to the African Source. The thought of such a trip extracts exaltation from the poet:

> ¡Qué grande es el alto Congo!
> Esta pudo ser mi patria
> y yo uno de estos remeros!
>
> (How large the Congo is!
> This could be my country
> And I one of those rowers.)

Within this African context, "Argeliana" ("Algerian Woman") is a sad poem in which a woman awaits the return of her absent fiancé. What is striking in this selection is the vivid contrast between the protagonist's mental state and her physical surroundings.

"Mapa de Africa" ("Map of Africa") is a statement calling for the liberation of Africa from her colonial status:

¿Cuándo podrán saltar estos colores,
tirar las letras—sus amarras—
que los clasifican como posesiones
y tomar su color, el único,
el verdadero color de Africa?

(When can they lower those colors,
throw away the letters—their support—
which classify them as possessions,
and take their color, the only one,
the true color of Africa?)

The verbs "lower" and "throw away" reinforce strong imagery associated with freeing the colonies. The tension is between belonging to somebody and asserting a personal identity. In an ironic reversal of fate, the

sin la terrible marca,
puesta como un hierro candente,

(terrible mark
placed like a hot iron,)

which is analogous to the brands put on slaves, will be removed. Only then will Africa be free. In "Map of Africa" the past glories of African countries are contemplated from a dreamlike point of view. Africa is portrayed unrealistically in an innocent state, but this attitude successfully juxtaposes her to the European intruder and his imposed values.

In the context of the New World, the African influence reaches far and wide, with several of Artel's poems being attempts to reconcile Old and New World existences. "Encuentro" ("Meeting"), for example, continues the search for the missing part of the poet's identity, his black persona. This time his counterpart is in the South, perhaps of the United States. The quest for meaning entails struggle and sacrifice but can be realized in spite of

la mirada larga y azul del hombre blanco
cayendo sobre mi carne
como un látigo.

(the long and blue look of the white man
falling upon my flesh
like a whip.)

Oppression notwithstanding, the search continues:

Ya puedo seguir mi viaje,
con la porción de angustia que me llevo
Hombre oscuro del Sur, hermano:
hoy en nuestro dolor sin límites te encuentro!

(Now I can continue my journey,
with the portion of anguish that carries me
Dark man of the South, brother:
today in our limitless pain I meet you!)

The common cultural basis of blacks in the Americas is slavery, a denominator that cannot be denied. The legacy of slavery is written in "festering tatoos" ("tatuajes lacerantes") and "folded lips" ("labios plegados"), circumstances that constantly deny to the black positive historical models. It is tragic that the author can only find commonality in suffering.

The same type of negativism pervades "El mismo hierro" ("The Same Brand"), which highlights discrimination against blacks in the United States and analogous situations throughout the Americas:

> un hierro idéntico, eslabona
> aquel dolor de siglos
> que asciende a nuestros labios.
>
> (an identical brand links
> that pain of centuries
> that rises to our lips.)

The metaphor of slavery reflects a situation that has condemned blacks to centuries of marginal social participation. Unfortunately, perceptions have not changed. America, which represents freedom and justice, has not delivered on her promises, at least not to those of African heritage.

In contrast, "Al drummer negro de un jazz session" ("To the Black Drummer of a Jazz Session") traces the enchanting presence of the drummer to his African heritage. "El lenguaje misteriosio" ("The Mysterious Language") attempts to interpret the secret messages of the liturgical drums, sentiments extended to "Soneto más negro" ("The Blackest Sonnet"), which examines the ancestral drum in its religious, ritualistic environment.

In an even more positive portrayal of a black, "Yanga" interprets the presence of an Afro-Mexican cultural hero who resisted slavery and domination in the seventeenth century. Yanga, uprooted from Africa, was one of the few who also enjoyed a leadership role in America. A symbol of freedom and resistance to slavery, he was able to recapture the manhood lost by so many:

> Varón insobornable,
> por quienes los tristes y perseguidos
> de tu raza recuperaron el sol y las canciones
> y pusieron a crecer la historia, como un árbol.
> Bajo su sombra circula la leyenda:
> "Una vez hubo un príncipe . . ."
>
> Tu nombre, oh, Yanga,
> siempre recordará que somos libres!
>
> (Uncorruptible man
> for whom the sad and persecuted
> of your race recaptured the sun and the songs
> and made history grow, like a tree.
> Beneath his shadow circulates a legend:
> "Once upon a time there was a prince . . ."

Your name, Oh, Yanga,
will always remind us that we are free!)

In the poetic imagination, Yanga is elevated to the level of myth. The best known Mexican maroon, a true flesh-and-blood character, Yanga is one of the black heroes for whom Artel has been searching.[11] He emerges as a larger-than-life figure who restored freedom and dignity, albeit briefly, to a segment of the black population in Mexico during the fight against Spanish domination.

"Poems without Hate or Drums" is the last of the selections that treats the larger Afro-American context. It begins by addressing the present-day Argentina in which the Argentine *candombes* (festive gatherings) and the Bantu descendants are alleged to be steadily "disappearing." But the poet offers a different interpretation of the situation:

aunque muchos te ignoren
yo sé que vives, y despierto
cantas aun las tonadas nativas,
ocultas en los ritmos disfrazados de blanco.

(Although many don't know you
I know that you live, and I awaken
you still sing native songs
hidden in the disguised rhythms of Whites.)

In Argentina, the paucity of blacks is due as much to the legitimization of a white Argentina, perhaps, as it is to natural factors. The intent of "Poems without Hate or Drums" is to expound upon the persistence of blacks in both the Argentine and the international gene pools. "We are a conscience in America" is his posture; he cannot deny his African heritage. The point is made several times that a "pure" race does not exist, especially not in the Spanish context. Because of the genetic exchange incurred in Spain as a result of successive historical dominations, the conquistador has no just claim to his supposed genetic superiority. But as a result of this process, white skin color assures him of a dominant position, a situation that prompts a sarcastic reaction by the poet. Yet the African past persists deep within the American psyche to a degree that it will never be denied:

Ellos están presentes,
se empinan para vernos,
gritan, claman, lloran, cantan.

(They are present,
they raise up to see us,
they shout, cry out, cry, sing.)

Artel reiterates the point that the black experience is indelibly etched upon the collective memory of America. Beginning with the concrete situation of blacks in Argentina, in "Poems without Hate or Drums," the poet constructs a literary metaphor of persistence and survival, a dynamism also present in Artel's vision of black Colombia.

The initial stanza of "Noche del Chocó" ("Night of the Chocó") demonstrates the importance of that persistence:

> En tus currulaos,
> tus velorios y tus cortejos fluviales,
> se prolongan los ritos,
> como voces perdidas,
> que hablan a mi raza
> del primitivo espanto frente a la eternidad.

> (In your *currulaos*
> your wakes and your watery processions
> rites are prolonged
> like lost voices,
> that speaks to my race
> of the primitive fright in front of eternity.)

Both secular and religious rites, dances and wakes, respectively, form an essential part of the Afro-Colombian mythology as passed down from generation to generation. The poet successfully captures the physical and spiritual environments of the Chocó by personifying night, a powerful force that historically has shared many secrets: it is both "secret key of the people" ("llave secreta de los pueblos") and "absolute owner of all abyss" ("propietaria absoluta de todos los abismos").

The climate and geography are also important in Artel's work. "Isla de Baru" ("Baru Island") is a brief poetic sketch that examines the impact of the tropics upon humans. "Barlovento" is more profound in that it combines the picturesque with the serious. It is the "hot land of the drum" ("tierra ardiente del tambó") and a place where

> El negro vive su vida.
> Pesca. Sufre. Canta.

> (The black man lives his life.
> He fishes. He suffers. He sings.)

The black does not have much to offset the cycles of work, misery, and moments of joy. His life is a series of high and low points that are clearly demonstrated in the excitement of these first two lines and the solemn reality of the last stanza.

"Palenque" is another poem commemorating an Afro-Colombian symbol of resistance to slavery and colonization:[12]

> ¿y quien ha de dudar que aquel abuelo
> no pudo ser un príncipe,
>
> . . . .
>
> Ultimo patriarca de Palenque:
> bien sabes
> que desde tus fogones crepitantes
> África envía sus mensajes!

(And who would doubt that that grandfather
couldn't be a prince,

. . . .

The last patriarch of Palenque:
You know well
that from the crackling bonfires
Africa sends its messages.)

Africa is very much a part of the old fellow's presence in Palenque, which
was established as a center of resistance for those slaves who dared to defy
the Spaniards. The past of the patriarch is indeed a glorious one since he
carries with him the knowledge that he was not always in a situation of not
being able to exercise power. In his contemplative mood, this possible
descendant of African royalty still, through natural forces, perceives continuous experiences with the Mother Country.

Taken as a whole, the poems of the second part of *Poetry Anthology*
chronicle the trajectory of blacks from their homeland in Africa to present-
day Colombia. "Map of Africa" and "Palenque" may be viewed as two
poles, the extremes within which Artel operates. The main point that he tries
to convey is that blacks form an integral part of the Colombian ethos and will
continue to do so for some time to come. The same is true from Argentina to
Canada.

Of the eleven poems in the last section, eight are new material. The salient
characteristic of these selections is their preoccupation with problems common to modern people, such as death, alienation, and a lack of communication among humans. "Aprende a comer mierda" ("Learn to Eat Shit") is
pessimistic advice given to a friend concerning his relationship to the world.
"Guitarra" ("Guitar") is a poem stressing the poet's ambivalent attitude
toward an instrument that at times has an impact upon human emotions.
"La tintorera del mar" ("The Sea Dyer"), written in a light vein, recalls the
poet's time with Palés Matos and their sharing of a tragedy and a sense of
loss. "A un guardia marino muerto" ("To a Dead Marine Guard") presents a
vivid, surreal image of dying. But the remaining four poems are the most
successful in the section.

"Canción en el extremo de un retorno" ("Song at the End of a Return") is a
poem in which the poet fantasizes a return to his native land. It is in fact a
recapitulation by the protagonist of his journeys to many countries:

Traigo los ojos ebrios de luz y de paisajes.
Mi alma, cargada de caminos.

(I bring my eyes drunk with light and landscapes
My soul, filled with roads.)

The poem is a mental return to faraway places populated by mountains,
rivers, and ships, but the poet finally arrives at his destination. He is
apparently operating in a fantasy world, viewing events as he wishes them

to be, not necessarily how they are. His tendency toward psychological projection is signaled by the abrupt change in the fifth stanza from past to future tense, which is maintained throughout the poem. In essence, "Song at the End of a Return" is a symbolic return to the poet's origins, to his roots. An air of triumph, of appreciation for his native culture, pervades the sentiments expressed here, signifying a spiritual rebirth:

> Lloverán tamboriles y gaitas nocheras
> como un canto de agua
> sobre mi vida nueva.

> (It will rain drums and nocturnal flutes
> like a song of water
> upon my new life.)

The physical environment will mirror his spiritual aspirations and achievements.

"Canción del hombre sin retorno" ("Song of the Man without Return") represents the opposite point of view; it is concerned with personal identity only insofar as it relates to a broader view of the human condition and expresses a desire for communion with humankind. The poem is a search for a lost relative on one level, but when extended to its maximum meaning, the quest embraces humankind's inability to reconcile with the Other, the second self.

Perhaps the answer to the question of identity and communication is to be found in the institution of the family, the theme of "Poemas del reencuentro" ("Poems of the Collision"), which is also prefaced by a return journey. The stability that the narrator is seeking seems to be at hand. The joy and security of home seem to offer the ideal repository for the tiredness and anxiety expressed by the poet throughout these latter poems. His "collision" appears to be with the basic values of life.

"Pesadilla del olvido" ("Nightmare of Oblivion"), the last poem in *Poetry Anthology*, points toward a total disintegration of the poetic world. The nightmare that the poet experiences is that of death, reiterated through the metaphor of oblivion. "When oblivion" ("Cuando el olvido") is the motif that prefaces each of the four stanzas, before the poem culminates in a negative crescendo. By cloaking the metaphor of death within floral imagery of destruction—"disturbing vine," "anemia of the dahlias," "gloomy gardens" ("turbia enredadera," "anemia de las dalias," "sombríos jardines")— the poet is able to convey a sense of unfulfillment. In an attempt to demonstrate that human destiny is so unpredictable, the constant return motif is repeated:

> volver—si es que volvemos—
> sin que sepamos quizás por qué hemos vuelto.

> (return—if it is that we return
> without knowing perhaps why we have returned.)

Any attempt to decipher the true meaning of existence is futile; in the end, death prevails. Life, the trajectory toward death, can indeed be a nightmare, the poet tells us, unless there is proper direction.

Hugo Salazar Valdés

Hugo Salazar Valdés has to his credit ten volumes of poetry, single volumes and compilations, varying in length from the eight pages of *Sal y illuvia* (*Salt and Rain*, 1948) to more than three hundred in *Toda la voz* (*All the Voice*, 1958). Individual poems by Salazar Valdés have appeared periodically in the *Revista Bolívar* and other Colombian periodicals. The view of Salazar Valdés offered by the *Dictionary of Colombian Writers* will serve as a brief introduction to his work:

> He was born in Condoto, Chocó, in 1926. An almost epic poet, singer of his race and cultivator of black poetry, with social thematics and good inspiration; his work is musical, human and lyrical.[13]

The brief description captures, succinctly, the essence of Salazar Valdés's literary production. While he is not unduly preoccupied with the Afro-Colombian experience, it is nonetheless an integral part of his poetry. The epic dimension of Salazar Valdés's poetry is evident in his broad-scale portrayal of the Chocó region and its inhabitants. In this regard, Jaime Mejía Duque has written in assessing *Dimensión de la tierra* (*Dimension of the Earth*, 1952), "With this work Salazar Valdés has lifted the Chocó from a mere geographic plane to give it esthetic force on the continent. Undoubtedly it represents a happy conception within contemporary Colombian poetry."[14] The strong emotional ties that Salazar Valdés feels for the land are channeled into a high level of musicality and lyricism throughout his verses.

His interpretation of the Chocó reaches its maximum level of expression in *Rostro iluminado del Chocó* (*Illuminated Face of the Chocó*, 1980). In this regard, Salazar Valdés is regional in his interpretation of a segment of Colombia and its relationship to the nation. But he is universal in his ability to begin with a concrete situation and expand it to embrace a wide range of human preoccupations. My analysis of Salazar Valdés's poetry will revolve around two books, *Carbones en el alba* (*Coals at Dawn*, 1951) and *Illuminated Face of the Chocó*.

Coals at Dawn

Three poems in this volume are devoted to night, which is presented as a creative, inspirational force. "Bajo la noche" ("Beneath the Night"), for example, is an unrhymed sonnet filled with allusions to nature, sounds, and contrasts. The first stanza vividly illustrates the interdynamics of the cosmos as clouds, water, stars, moon, and wind mesh to form a surreal image of darkness. Attention then turns to the earthly presence of the river, representing solitude and continuity of human experience. In the depths of night, however, the poet transcends the solitude to participate in creative activity:

la noche gira honda, honda, bajo la sangre
y unas manos antiguas el corazón recuerda.[15]

(the night spins deep, deep beneath the blood
and some ancient hands remember the heart.)

Night is presented as exercising a negative influence upon the poet, who is trapped in an archetypal cycle of timelessness and repetition. The protagonist's dilemma is personified by the recurrence of night, which to him represents total negation: "arrow without distance upon my being without time" ("saeta sin distancia sobre mi ser sin tiempo"). "Without" amplifies the lack of temporal and spatial mobility that causes the individual to react fearfully at the onslaught of yet another night. An ambivalent stance, between darkness and golden dawn, is revealed in the second tercet as fear and pain appear to be occasioned more by the approaching dawn than by the retreating night. But this is understandable since night is often viewed by the poet both as a period of intense creative activity and as a symbol of the passage of time.

The poet's relationship to night is further dramatized in the poem "Dolor" ("Pain"), in which his personal agony is associated with solitude and the creative process.

Acogédme en tus sombras, en tu lecho
de obscuridad y espinas que es el mío
y déjame que sangre de tu pecho
la soledad que colma mi vacío.

Tómame en la hondonada de tus golfos,
en tu ilesa verdad de fantasía.
Noche materna, realidad que nombro
hundido en mí como la Poesía!

(Capture me in your shadows, in your bed
of obscurity and thorns which is mine
and let me bleed from your chest
the solitude that fills my emptiness.

Take me in the ravine of your gulfs,
in your unscathed truth of fantasy.
Maternal night, reality that I name
buried in me like Poetry!)

Through personification of night, the narrator has managed to present a romantic conception of the poetic process. Night is an emotional buffer in which the poet can drown his solitude and creative fantasies as well as his other human agonies. Night is also the archetypal mother figure from which he can gain sustaining poetic force. The dynamics between inspiration and creativity are dramatized in his juxtaposing of fantasy and reality that results in "Poetry."

In "Nocturno" ("Nocturnal"), night, through metonymy, is a "tongue of ash" ("lengua de ceniza") related to the fleeting span of existence. A number of effective parallels are drawn to illustrate this point through the use of vivid similes and metaphors. The poem is a practical application of personal considerations to events common throughout the universe. Through a series of ephemeral analogies, the poet makes the point that love, for instance, is one of the least permanent of human emotions. But, like beauty, love will always provide a stimulus for the poet, even when he is trapped in the dark throes of depression.

Related to the night poems are those dealing with poetry and poetic inspiration, including "Yo soy el mar" ("I Am the Sea"), which presents the sea as a point of identification and a metaphor for freedom. Not only is it a source of inspiration but it is also related to the poet's origins and his physical being:

> ¡Yo soy el mar! Llevo sus lejanías
> en la pasión inmensa de mis sueños,
> sus olas son mis hondas agonías
> golpeando en las riberas de mi verso.

> (I carry its remoteness in the immense passion of my dreams
> its waves are my deep agonies
> pounding on the shores of my verse.)

In this poem, the archetypal dimension of the sea symbolizes both timelessness and eternity as well as the unconscious.

Much of the pent-up poetic energy bursts forth in "Elegía prematura" ("Premature Elegy"), which praises spring as a time of positive regeneration. The poem's future orientation reflects the hope that spring brings. Archetypally it is a season of creation, happiness, and love that lays to rest the gloomy powers of darkness, winter, and death. Ironically, the poem is a premature elegy presaging death.

> Sobre la soledad será la tarde
> negra copa de un vino que no había
> y en silencio de muerte, la esperanza
> callará su agonía.

> Y será la viudez de la doncella
> duelo del gozo y la melancolía,
> el caracol de sangre en mis arterias
> no tendrá sinfonía.

> (Upon solitude will be the evening
> a dark cup of a wine that was not
> and in silence of death, hope
> will quiet your agony.

> And it will be the widowhood of a maiden
> pain of enjoyment and melancholy,
> the trail of blood in my arteries
> will not have a symphony.)

The positive imagery of the first two stanzas is overshadowed by pessimism in the last two. "Solitude" initiates a series of negative images that dominate until the poem's end. The contrasts in the structure of "Premature Elegy" are striking. "Happiness" ("alegría") in the second verses of stanzas one and two becomes "was not ("no había") and "melancholy" ("melancolía") in three and four. In Spanish, a degree of parallel consonance is also maintained in the final verse of each stanza. The poem is narrated from the point of view of winter, from which the poet imagines the future and temporal repetition.

Christian symbolism dominates "Síntesis" ("Synthesis"), "Retrato" ("Portrait"), and "La cruz" ("The Cross"), three sonnets that present Christ and his martyrdom from basically the same perspectives. "Synthesis" describes Christ in his Christian mythic dimension. With anaphora the poet elaborates highlights in the life of Jesus, a process continued through "Portrait," in which the mythic dimension is fully realized:

> Miradlo allí clavado en la clausura
> de su voz, en la muerte derramada,
> y entre nudos de sangre, desgoznada
> como una flor de llanto, la figura.

> (Look at him there nailed in the confinement
> of his voice, in death spilled,
> and between bonds of blood, disconnected
> like a flower of tears, the figure.)

This image of a bloody, agonizing Christ is often used to encourage the masses to sacrifice and suffer in order to be better human beings. The symbol of these aspirations is the cross, portrayed here as an effective, powerful, religious symbol: in it, one can see that a human sacrifice has been turned into a positive model for the betterment of the race. Hence, people use the cross in a collective sense to reflect their religious aspirations because,

> y la herida del bálsamo florece
> en cicatriz de amor y de esperanza

> (the balsam wound grows
> in a scar of love and hope)

to overcome sufferings of the flesh.

Related to suffering, as well as longing and absence, is love, which manifests itself in several poems in *Coals at Dawn*. "Elegía del amor perdido" ("Elegy of Lost Love") and "Lamentacion por ella" ("Lamentation for Her") are intense poems of desire precipitated by remembrances of past experiences. The former poem begins with a series of attempts by the poet to gauge the magnitude of a woman's significance to him, a task that is immeasurable. In a rising level of intensity his praise continues, culminating in intense physical activity. The poetic climax is a scene of bitter-sweet sexual conquest-surrender. An atmosphere of fervent sexuality is filled with contrasts: "love leaves honey on the thorn" ("el amor deja la miel por el espino") and "blood changes the roses with the shout" ("la sangre cambia las rosas por el grito"). Ultimately, a tone of inherent violence underlies this apparent deflowering, "the hammer above the atrophy of meat" ("el martillo sobre la atrofia de la carne"), suggesting sexual abuse. Continuing its contrastive tendencies, the poem ends with an evocation of living, vibrant, sweet things. "Lamentation for Her" conjures up past experiences, with the phrase "I could have told her" ("Yo pudiera decirla") serving as an attempt to explain the protagonist's past inadequacies. Tone is the overriding factor in this poem, with the past subjunctive used throughout to accentuate effectively the poet's sense of doubt and hesitancy. "Fuego de poesía" ("Fire of Poetry") and "Casi blasfemia" ("Almost Blasphemy") make the same connection between love, anguish, and poetic inspiration.

In "Canción introspectiva" ("Introspective Song"), a poem of self-assessment that dramatizes an internal human conflict, the poet presents himself as a victim of ambivalent forces:

> Todos los hierros de la angustia
> tienen en mí su cara víctima;
> voy perseguido por las fauces
> de dos ancestros sin orilla:
> uno de fuego devorante,
> otro de piedra perseguida,
> que en el oleaje de mi sangre
> muerden su propia lejanía.
>
> (All the bonds of anguish
> have in me their dear victim;
> I go persecuted by the fauces
> of two ancestors without a shore:
> one of devouring flame,
> the other with stone persecuted,
> which in the surge of my blood
> they ridicule their own distance.)

This initial stanza draws a dichotomy that will be prevalent throughout the poem. The poet is agonizing over the fact that he is a product of a dual heritage that does not mesh in a coherent fashion—hence the "two ancestors without a shore." The ancestor of devouring fire is undoubtedly European; the one of "stone persecuted" is African. Within the resulting mulatto, each wishes to chart his own course, which is the central conflict elaborated here. This divided-self complex (a type of ethnic schizophrenia) leads, in this case, to alienation and despair. External contrasts that mirror the poet's internal sentiments dominate the other three stanzas of "Introspective Song." In the second, for example, they are morning and night, sun and shadows, rose and thorn. In the third, we see God and Lucifer and "light and shadow enemies" ("luz y tinieblas enemigas"). These tensions all lead to a confusing climax and to metaphysical questioning:

> ¿Cómo olvidarme destas cosa
> si son la cuna de mi lira?

(How can I forget these things
if they are the birthplace of my lyre?)

Such inherent incongruities persist between truth and lie, life and death. For the poet, these contradictions are a lifetime problem with which he must contend, and he is therefore a prisoner of his heritage and his psychological makeup.

In two poems that treat death abstractly and concretely, Salazar Valdés goes beyond personal questions. "Humana voz" ("Human Voice") focuses upon death as a human phenomenon. It is not a gratifying experience in which the reader is implored to

Oíd los clavos de la angustia
crucificándome en la muerte.

(Hear the nails of anguish
crucifying me in death.)

In "Canción con llanto por Aray" ("Song with a Cry for Aray"), the poetic attitude is one of embellishing the process of dying; in "Human Voice" the opposite is true. The poet experiences human fear, anguish, and alienation as normal reactions to death. The image conveyed is a Christian one of suffering elevated to an archetypal level through "nails" ("clavos"), "crucifying" ("crucificándome"), and "martyrdom" ("martirios"). Death has "cruel twisted hands" ("torvadas manos crueles") that evoke a "poisoned song" ("canción envenenada"). The poet speaks as if he deserves this type of death because of original sin. In these two poems, then, the author gives us both a lyrical and a practical interpretation of death in his continuing exploration of basic human concerns.

Illuminated Face of the Chocó

Illuminated Face of the Chocó is similar to *Dimension of the Earth*, published nearly thirty years earlier, in its assessment of the physical environment and the culture of the Chocó. In this book, Salazar Valdés also considers bodies of water, ports, cities, animals, fruits, and religious and secular ceremonies, while devoting much of his attention to the Afro-Colombian segment of the population. In fact, *Illuminated Face of the Chocó* contains the greatest number of poems treating the black experience of any publication by Salazar Valdés.

Black identity has always been a part of Salazar Valdés's literary production, from "Introspective Song" in *Coals at Dawn* to the present. *Pleamar (High Tide*, 1975), for example, contains several poems on African origins and presence, including "Raya" ("Line") and "Canción" ("Song"). The latter poem will demonstrate the author's approach to this vital human issue:

Un sol de uvas,
unas uvas solares
es la piel donde el vino de mi raza

palpita. Una noche sencilla,
imaginable, pero noche de altares
maduros de utopías.
las que vienen conmigo de los antiguos ríos
del Africa, descalzas y danzantes,
son el vaso de amor
sin labios y sin límites,
inmortal en el oro de los sueños.

(A sun of grapes,
some ancestral grapes
is the skin where the wine of my race
palpitates. A simple night,
imaginable, but a night of mature
altars of utopias.
Those which come with me from the ancient rivers
of Africa, barefooted and dancing,
are the vessel of love
without lips and without boundaries
immortal in the gold of dreams.)

The initial metaphor in "Song"—which is constructed around sun, grapes, and wine—is an imaginative way of posing the question of heritage. *Grapes* is a term often used by Salazar Valdés as a euphemism for black. The atavistic nature is accentuated by both the physical environment and the biological composition of the protagonist. In this instance, the poet conveys a paradisiacal view of Africa but as biological Source. The image of a non-problematic existence in Africa is projected into subsequent verses when the poet admits that this type of world is imaginary. In "Song," the poet is intent upon demonstrating that both his personal background and his physical environment are instrumental in determining his poetic output. This assumption is evident in the last three stanzas, in which humans and nature mesh in a surreal outpouring of sentiment.

"Mulata" ("Mulatta") and "El mulato" ("Mulatto") from *Illuminated Face of the Chocó* express an ambivalent idea toward the reality of miscegenation, an important aspect of identity. The mulatta is situated, first of all, within a setting of positive plant imagery, where she gives the impression that she is bearing a heavy burden. She is, nevertheless, an attractive physical specimen for men in spite of her symbolic lack of direction. The poem is limited, however; it never transcends the level of ethnic heritage and exotic desires as its companion piece does.

The duality of the mulatto's personality and its impact upon him is the theme of the parallel poem. Two lines,

Duda hasta por dónde va,
si por las nubes o el río,

(You doubt even which way your're going
Whether by air or water,)

establish a leitmotif that prefigures the poet's assessment of the mulatto's dilemma, which he views as essentially a search for identity. The poet constructs a series of opposing earth and sky images that he believes to be analogous to the mulatto's ethnic heritage. This parallel reaches its climax in the third of five stanzas:

> como cuando el hombre solo
> se busca y no se halla, sino
> en dos mitades del todo
> que son uno dividido.

> (as when man alone
> looks for himself and does not find it, rather
> in two halves of the whole
> that are one divided.)

Just as the physical universe is divided into two dimensions, represented by river and sky, the halves are inextricably bound as a part of the same whole. This is exemplified in the image of the cloud being a creation of the river. In the human dimension, the verses above illustrate the same process. The poet, in this instance, views the process of miscegenation as incongruous but nevertheless reflective of the biological composition of many nations. Hence, the mulatto should not be despondent about his heritage because,

> que ser mulato es hermoso
> hasta en el desequilibrio
> y en la bifronte beldad
> de caminar dos caminos.

> (to be a mulatto is pretty
> even in the unbalance
> and in the double-faced beauty
> of walking two roads.)

Such ambivalence leads to the conclusion that, miscegenation aside, an individual must forge his own destiny.

With "Baile negro" ("Black Dance") and "La negra María Teresa" ("Black María Teresa"), Salazar Valdés captures the rhythm and the black woman of Afro-Colombian culture. The poems were originally published in *Revista Bolívar* and are included also in *Toda la voz (All the Voice,* 1958).

"Black Dance" is filled with the auditory and visual imagery surrounding a dancer during a night of celebration:

> Tin tan, tin tan, tin tan,
> suena el timbal.
> Porongo, bolongo, morongo,
> canta el bongo.
> Gime la flauta,
> ruge el tambor,
> y entre los "chaquis" de las maracas
> va el lagrimón.

(Tin tan, tin tan, tin tan,
sounds the kettle drum.
Porongo, bolongo, morongo,
sings the bongo.
Trills the flute,
roars the drum,
and in between the *chaquis* of the maraca
the accordion moans.)

The rhythm section, consisting of percussion (timbal, marimba, bongo, drum, maracas), woodwind (flute), and keyboard (accordion) instruments, paints an initial scene of harmony and joyful festivities. Scene two focuses upon the stimulating presence of the black woman who is the star attraction:

la negra da media vuelta,
sube los brazos
y en la epilepsia
de las caderas,
hay fogonazos
y batatazos,
y entre los senos
boas perversas,
como en los ojos
de borrachera,
laten los perros
de los ancestros
y de los ritos
de Africa negra.

(The black woman does a half turn,
raises her arms
and in the frenzy
of her hips,
there are bumps
and grinds
and between her breasts
wicked boas,
as in the eyes
of drunkenness,
throb the obsessions
of ancestors
and of rites
of Black Africa.)

In a mythic sense the dance goes beyond its present physical limitations. True, the black woman is stereotyped in her physical and rhythmic dimensions, but the obsessions of ancestral Africa persist in this dance, the rhumba, which is viewed as a secular ritual and thereby transcends mere sexuality. Therefore, her movements repeat patterns performed by many who have gone before her as well as those who will come later. The erotic nature of the dance is revealed in the third scene with the appearance of a black man who is in turn described as

salaz y ansioso
. . .

rítmico, loco,
carbón de ébano
betún vigilia,
noche su vida,
gritos sus miembros.

(lustful and anxious
. . .

rhythmic, crazy
jet black
pitch, he watches
dark is his life
his limbs cry out.)

"Black Dance" reaches its climactic heights in this suggestive scene in which there is a fusion of black rhythm and music. Even the sweat of the dancers, "the Blacks sweat crude oil" ("sudan petróleo los negros") bursts forth in the vivid evocation of sights, sounds, and smells in an activity that allows blacks to celebrate while putting aside many preoccupations: "they kill their agony" ("matan su agonía"). "Oh, my race!" ("ah, raza mía!) is the poet's final identificatory comment in recognizing that he shares in cultural expressions and patterns that have somehow spanned the centuries.

María Teresa is a volatile presence who is physically imposing to say the least. The poet is concerned mostly with her external appendages in his head-to-toe description of her. His impressions are centered once again on dancing (the cumbia), and she is a carbon copy of the woman in "Black Dance." María Teresa is "dark as China ink" ("oscura de tinta China") and "a black woman of African stock" ("negra de Africana estirpe") with full breasts and hips. In both poems, moreover, the association is made between protagonists and their African heritage. The poet goes one step further in "María Teresa" by injecting popular speech into the next to the last stanza, from the protagonist's voice, lending authenticity to the scene. In both cases, too, the woman's sensuality-sexuality is presented as a disturbing factor in the dance proceedings.

In "Black Dance" and "María Teresa," Salazar Valdés equates sexuality with the African ancestral heritage, in stereotypical fashion. The characterization in the poems is not all negative, however, since on several occasions the author attempts to make the connection between ritual and ancestry. Nevertheless, the specter of black woman as sex object remains consistent. Although to his credit, Salazar Valdés does present this character within her cultural context.

Another dimension of the black experience in Colombia is presented in "Las fiestas" ("Celebrations"), "San Pacho," and "El velorio" ("The Wake"). "Celebrations" is a general discussion of regional festivities while "The Wake" portrays the tragic results of a case of snake bite. "San Pacho" recounts specific activities in Quibdó surrounding the celebrations devoted to San Francisco de Asis. The poet classifies his reaction to religious and secular ritual as "vernacular and spontaneous" ("vernacular y espontáneo") before launching into a description of religious processions (Virgen de las Mercedes), dance (the rhumba), tasting (silver firewater), and disagreements (the slash of a razor). All form part of the anonymous popular history of the Chocó region.

Rituals devoted to San Pacho (Francisco) are viewed by the poet as an opportunity to reestablish both religious and secular ties. The celebrations provide a time for one to hear collective and communal myths and legends that have been transformed by time to meet present realities. "San Pacho" is an imaginative, firsthand portrayal by the poet. He witnesses a spontaneous physical and emotional outpouring, a true "orgy of rhythms" ("orgía de ritmos"), both Spanish and African. In addition, material culture such as modes of dress, food, and living conditions form an integral part of the poetic narrative. The principal theme throughout "San Pacho," however, is unification, as evidenced in the last stanza, in which Indians, mulattos, mestizos, blacks, and whites come together in an ethnic synthesis. In spite of the different ethnic backgrounds involved, the poet views the birthday of San Pacho as one of cultural fusion. The different entities are implored to respect each other for the common good. The atmosphere of joy and cooperation prompted by these festivities should, idealistically, carry over into everyday life. The poem is a fitting end to a discussion of Salazar Valdés, whose trajectory is different from that of the other poets in this study, except for Zapata Olivella. Salazar Valdés's process of poetic self-identification evolves gradually instead of being established in a first book of ethnic poetry. His epic bent, which persists throughout his volumes, is essential to his attempt to present a total view of Colombia, which he accomplishes through a lyrical fusion of the social and the aesthetic.

Juan Zapata Olivella: Liberated Poetry

In the 1970s, Juan Zapata Olivella published five volumes of poetry, books that demonstrate a thematic complexity consistent with the interests and experiences of their author. His poems deal with the multifaceted dimensions of the human condition, addressing questions of love, time, ethnicity, metaphysical anxieties, and societal interactions. The Afro-Colombian experience, moreover, is a thematic constant in Zapata Olivella's poetic evolution from *Albedrío total (Total Pleasure*, 1970) to *Panacea: Poesía liberada (Panacea: Liberated Poetry*, 1976). The predominating motif in *Total Pleasure*, however, is love, a theme that Zapata Olivella treats in a compelling manner, resulting in some of the best amorous expression in contemporary Spanish American poetry. The social situation, history, the sea, and folklore are also weaved into the artistic fabric to present an uneven but well-written volume of verse.

Total Pleasure is divided into four sections, "Espartaco" ("Spartacus"), "Del Propio patio" ("From the Same Patio"), "Amor se escribe con lírica" ("Love Is Written with Lyrics"), and "Dilatation" ("Dilatation"). "From the Same Patio" interprets the black experience, while "Love Is Written with Lyrics" forms the book's thematic core. In the former section, "Todos somos America" ("We Are All America") scrutinizes from a historical perspective the importance of blacks in the construction of industries on two continents. "Meridiano sin lágrimas" ("Meridian without Tears"), "Mulata" ("Mulatta"), and "Negrita claridad" ("Black Claridad") treat ethnic concepts that recur in Zapata Olivella's poetry. On the positive side, there is considerable development in his women, from physical objects to a sophisticated poetic presence and ideal of beauty in *Panacea* and *The Dreamy Hammock*.

In "Mulatta," Zapata Olivella views miscegenation in its spiritual and physical dimensions. The perspective is that of the international gene pool, a theory that discounts purity of blood and instead recognizes the importance of multiple ethnic groups in the composition of the human race. A woman is addressed:

> Toda la hibridez de tu boca
> es fruta sensual de todo trópico,
> hay achiote en tus labios de Guinea
> y esa audaz malicia en tu mirada
> denuncia el temple del ancestro indígena.
> Si miramos el mapa de tu cuerpo desnudo,
> se asomarían todos los pueblos del mundo,
> apurar un cocktail sería una dicha
> servido en tus senos de ánforas de Grecia.
>
> Qué silueta maciza,
> qué fina inteligencia,
> y qué tierna mirada,
> de mujer cuajada.
>
> (All the hybridness of your mouth
> is sensual fruit of all tropics,
> there is annatto on your lips from Guinea
> and that malicious boldness in your stare
> reveals the haughtiness of your indigenous ancestry.
> If we look at the map of your naked body,
> there would appear all the peoples of the world,
> to finish a cocktail would be a pleasure
> served on your breasts like urns from Greece.
>
> What a solid profile,
> what keen intelligence,
> and what a tender look,
> for a successful woman.)

Ancient cultures (Guinea, Greece) are instrumental in the formation of the mulatta; therefore, she is not limited to the immediate biological exchange that occurs in the Americas. Rather, the poet amplifies her cultural base to include two of the most important cultures of world civilization. In addition to her physical attractiveness, Zapata Olivella attributes intelligence and success to the mulatta without negating her sensuality. In a related context, the same type of sensual imagery is present in "Negros senos" ("Black Breasts") from the volume *Amor en azul transparente (Love in Transparent Blue)*. The narrative voice maintains,

> son los senos míos cual cicatrices
> de una raza del Africa lejana.
>
> Anforas negras ceñidas a mi pecho
> como proas de barcos errabundos.
>
> (My breasts are like scars
> of a race from far away Africa.
>
> Black vases sewn to my chest
> like masts of wandering ships.)

Dialectically, the white substance produced by these black breasts has served to nurture much of humanity. The poem treats the subject matter within more of a romantic, amorous context than the strict culturalist focus of "Mulatta," however.

"Meridian without Tears" defines suffering as one of the continual experiences of blacks in the Americas and discusses the historical contrast between appearance and reality:

> El negro sufre
> disimulando su dolor
> con una cara de fiesta
> maquillada.
>
> (The black man suffers
> disimulating his pain
> with a face made up
> for partying.)

The initial image of deception is amplified in subsequent verses as the protagonist "hides" and "guards" pain that subsequently "extinguishes itself" and "goes away in the rhythm of dance" ("Se va / en la cadencia de la gaita"). Anaphora in the first five stanzas—"the black man suffers"—culminates with the same depressing imagery:

> El negro se ha tragado
> su tristeza.
> El negro mastica su dolor
> El dolor de la raza
> está en el tambor.
>
> (The black man has swallowed
> his sadness
> the black man meditates on his pain
> the pain of the race
> is in the drum.)

Far from simple expressions of joy, many outward manifestations of festivities overshadow the true feelings of a people whose history is one of toil and struggle. Pain and suffering are a "song of the earth," a type of blues that grew out of slavery. Musical syncretism as an expression of this experience is evident in the drums, maracas, and the flute, instruments so apparent in "Meridian without Tears." Since an applicable definition of *meridian* is "the highest point of power," the ironic title amplifies a bleak portrayal of Afro-American reality.

Bullanguero: Poesía popular (Turbulence: Popular Poetry, 1974) is a compilation of poems from Zapata Olivella's earlier volumes with some new poems as well, all written from the perspective of the common people, many in the popular idiom. "Eugenesia" ("Eugenics"), "Envidia" ("Envy"), and "Aristocracia criolla" ("Creole Aristocracy") are three of the new poems that address the Afro-Colombian situation. The first two scrutinize the adverse impact of racism upon the black psyche, which leads to the questioning of ethnicity and negative emphasis upon blackness, resulting in self-hate. "Creole Aristocracy" discusses the historical tendency of the oligarchy to set itself apart from the masses with ideas based upon pureness of blood and intellectual superiority. In reality, the poet tells us, the privileged position is based upon exploitation of the poor.

These issues are given expanded treatment in *Panacea: Liberated Poetry*, a volume divided into five sections: "Libérrima" ("Very Free"); "Negritudes" ("Blackness"); "Amorosas" ("Love"); "Púrpura" ("Purple"); and "Marineras" ("Marine"). *Panacea*, like *Turbulence*, is an anthology containing both old and new materials. The poems vary from an elegy to Neruda to an ode to Portugal. As with most of Zapata Olivella's poetry, his main interest is the human condition, the joys and frustrations encountered in being alive. Love, the sea, personal identity, and the black experience together form the thematic basis of *Liberated Poetry*.

In this collection, as differentiated from Zapata Olivella's other volumes, there is a central core, "Blackness," devoted to the Afro-Hispanic experience. Thirteen of the fifteen poems in this section are new. The ideological context of several of the pieces displays a preference for revolution, a complete change in the existing social order. "Alegría negra" ("Black Happiness"), "Romance de los pueblos negros" ("Ballad of Black People"), "El Negro sale a votá" ("The Black Goes out to Vote"), and "Los Negros tienen candidato" ("The Blacks Have a Candidate") all reflect this political belief. The joy of "Black Happiness," for example, will be assured only when blacks are allowed to participate fully in the national culture. The attitude expressed in this poem is that in spite of ancestral pain and suffering, a positive self-image will facilitate the recapturing of lost honor, will, and sense of self, all of which have been constantly denied throughout Colombian history. That dialectical tension between past and present time, popular and official idioms is underscored in "Ballad of Black People." The initial metaphor is of freedom and hope, a situation

en que se soltaron
gruesos eslabones
de duras cadenas.

(in which were broken
heavy links
of strong chains.)

Juxtaposed are images of rhetorical, mythic Africa, the legacy of slavery, the process of integration into national culture, and a demand for the liberation of Afro-Colombians from the stifling restrictions of the archaic oligarchical social structure. Given the opportunity, blacks are capable of controlling their own destiny:

Libertá, libertá
a sembrá la tierra
pa recogé el grano
de verdá, verdá.

(Freedom, freedom
to sow the earth
to gather the grain
truly, truly.)

"The Black Goes out to Vote" and "Blacks Have a Candidate" both encompass political ideals set forth in the platform of Juan Zapata Olivella in his unsuccessful bid for the presidency of Colombia for the term 1978–1982. The basic necessities of schools, health, shelter, and food are addressed from a popular perspective, from the point of view of people who have been repeatedly deceived by the electoral process. The difference now is that the people have a candidate who is black and who has some understanding of their needs. This political occasion is celebrated within the popular cultural tradition in "Blacks Have a Candidate," in which the gathering is described as

de todas las razas,
morenos, mulatos,
mestizos y zambos,
y también los blancos.

(of all races
blacks, mulattos
mestizos and *zambos* and also whites.)

If the popular energy were transformed into solidarity among peoples of the same socioeconomic status, then, perhaps, a black would be a viable candidate. But history and culture dictate otherwise and the poet can only dream:

¡Y al llegar la aurora habrá patria nueva
para muchos años, y no para rato,
pues al fin el pueblo tiene candidato!

(And when the new dawn arrives there will be a new homeland
for many years, and not for a short while
well at last the people have a candidate!)

Interestingly enough, the last two stanzas are in the future, demonstrating
the paradoxical clash between political expectation and realization. These
poems elaborate Zapata Olivella's commitment to social change, an area in
which poetic diction and political action coalesce. While he is identified as
the black candidate, Zapata Olivella's aim is not to divide the country but to
form a progressive political coalition.

Similarly, in portraying the black woman positively—in "La negrita Cla-
ridá," "La negra Catalina," and "Negra modelo" ("Black Claridad," "Black
Catalina," and "Black Model")—he creates a new feminine ideal; she is
defined from a physical, folkloric perspective within her natural context, the
image "black" predominating. "Dark skin" ("Piel oscura"), "jet-black
warmth" ("azabache tibio"), "body of tar" ("cuerpo de alquitrán"), "of
carbon" ("de carbón"), and "truly black" ("negra de verdad") are the poetic
signs employed to capture the rhythmic beauty of Claridad. Catalina, too, is
presented as a provocative physical specimen, honorable but pleasure seeking. In the third poem, the poet's maximum positive expression is paid to the
black model who, from head to toe, is the maximum expression of beauty:

¡Pelo de negro azabache,
cuello de gaviota en vuelo,
y unos senos redondos
como bolas de billar!

(Jet black hair,
neck like a sea gull in flight,
and those round breasts
like billiard balls!)

The poet begins with a classic image of beauty and transfers its meaning to
the black woman. The traditional swan is now a sea gull; the description
does not end but extends from head to neck, to breast, to navel, to thighs, to
feet. Rhetorically, the very elements that created such human beauty are
called to question. Zapata Olivella's presentation of the black woman is
totally positive and for a very important reason. After centuries of denigra-
tion and denial, the time has arrived to lend positive meaning to a figure who
has been so essential in the perpetuation of Colombian society.

The essential difference between this black model and the other women
portrayed in this study is that she has a profession, commercial talent, and a
future. The poet visualizes her in pinups, serials, and calendars due to her
physical qualities. No longer is the black woman merely a strong body with
agile feet, but rather she also has brains (university student) and, in this
instance, has channeled these attributes toward making an economic impact.

Ancestral heritage is also an important factor in *Liberated Poetry*. "Tambores Caribeños" ("Caribbean Drums") and "America es una Sola" ("America is One") represent an attempt to synthesize divergent world views in the difficult crucible that is America. Significantly, the sea is the archetypal setting of a rhythmic attempt to communicate across time and space in the first poem:

>Tambor africano,
>tambor antillano,
>danza de mar incontenible,
>cadencia y ritmo insustituible.
>
>. . . . .
>
>Brazos ágiles
>piernas eléctricas,
>los abuelos reclaman
>los ecos ancestrales.
>
>(African drum,
>Antillean drum,
>dance of the irrepressible sea
>unsubstitutable cadence and rhythm
>
>. . . . .
>
>Agile arms
>electric legs,
>grandparents cry out
>ancestral echoes.)

The image of the ancestral drum persists throughout the poem. More than a festive activity, the scene represents, symbolically and ritualistically, an attempt to engage in dialogue with the collective memory of Africa through sacred time. "America is One" represents a synthesis of Old and New World cultures with the black as a vital link in the two experiences. The poem is a chapter of Afro-American oral history from the perspective of Dorotea, an elderly person who draws upon a wealth of information. She narrates from the seashore:

>Tus abuelos vinieron de más allá,
>y la negra Dorotea
>con su cabeza tizná,
>muestra orgullosa
>la orilla larga del mar.
>
>(Your grandparents came from way over there
>and black Dorotea
>with her sooty head
>proudly shows
>the long shore of the sea.)

"America is One" proceeds to document the importance of blacks in the building of the Colombian nation and others as well. Physical toil associated with slavery in the mines and fields was only part of a larger struggle to overcome.

Although the social situation has not changed significantly, black strategy for dealing with it has:

> los negros saben ahora estudiá
> y cada día saben má, cada día saben má.

> (Blacks now know how to study
> and each day they know more, each day they know more.)

Viewing Afro-Colombian history in its national context, the poet juxtaposes more radical modes of behavior to the acquisition of knowledge.

> Ni la evasión, ni la insurrección,
> ni la astucia del cimarrón
> sirvió pá ná,

> (Neither escape, nor insurrection
> nor the daring of the cimarron
> served for anything.)

The ability to sustain and to endure provided the basis for today's positive outlook. Struggle has always been the key to black progress in the Americas, a situation not likely to change.

Throughout his poetry concerning the Afro-Colombian, Juan Zapata Olivella defines struggle as a metaphor for the historical presence of his people. Despite his heartfelt optimism for the future, progress is painfully slow. In *La hamaca soñadora: Poemario infantil* (*The Dreamy Hammock: Infant Verse*, 1979), the author's most sensitive poems address a young, black college student, who studies despite physical odds, and a black child. "Negra universitaria" ("Black University Student") criticizes the obstacles confronting her as well as the fact that because of her color people "continue treating her like a nobody" ("la siga tratando como a una cualquiera"). In "El niño negro" ("The Black Child"), this dissatisfaction is even more explicit:

> caminarás sobre una montaña de prejuicios,
> amarás y sufrirás en negro,
> reirás en negro, llorarás en negro,
> y cuando mires el horizonte
> a la hora del crepúsculo
> verás blancas nubes flotando transparentes
> sobre la densidad de un cielo negro africano.

> (You will walk upon a mountain of prejudice
> You will love and suffer in black,
> You will laugh in black, you will cry in black,
> and when you look at the horizon
> at the hour of twilight
> you will see white transparent clouds floating
> above the density of a black African sky.)

The poet is enumerating a legacy of truth. Change in the social order does not appear to be imminent, as evidenced in the ironic juxtapositioning of white clouds over the black African sky. Symbolically and realistically, the oppression will continue. The poet's message to the black child, then, is to know himself and his society and to seek fulfillment within those limitations. At the beginning of "The Black Child," the important point is made that blacks "always will be" ("siempre serás"), meaning a permanent presence on this earth, with Colombia no exception.

*   *   *

Viewing their poetic productions as a whole, it is apparent that Jorge Artel, Hugo Salazar Valdés, and Juan Zapata Olivella are striving for the type of "racial and cultural equilibrium" stressed by Manuel Zapata Olivella at the beginning of this chapter. Each views problems inherent in the Afro-Colombian social situation from both economic and ethnic perspectives. While Artel, Salazar Valdés, and Zapata Olivella realize that past inequities weigh heavily upon present realities, the three are content with presenting a set of *poetic* circumstances and leaving their interpretation to the audience. There is no question, however, concerning their discontent with the social status quo in Colombia.

Conclusion:
Africa, South America, Negritud

After analyzing the poetry of these nine writers, one can clearly see the meaning of the Afro-Hispanic dichotomy. In language, style, and technique, most of these poets follow Hispanic tradition, employing *décimas*, *romances*, *liras*, *sonetos*, and other European forms. Yet the poetry is Afro in its conception of *negritud* and its interpretation of the black dimension of South American culture. As the poetry expresses socially critical attitudes and is elegiac in treating the demise of blacks and their traditions, it fuses the pains of slavery and the oppression of contemporary prejudice. In so doing, the poetry shows that if there is a central thread unifying the writers of Afro-Hispanic poetry, it is *negritud* and its attendant ramifications. By taking a stand, by venting anger and frustration through creative means, blacks in South America have been able to transform their bitter experience into a statement of hope, a positive development toward a black identity.

The key to the process is the attitude that these writers and blacks in general have toward Africa, which for the poets discussed in this study is a common creative ground. Africa represents more than an escape; it symbolizes a type of spiritual and psychical liberation that cannot be achieved in the poet's present, concrete situation. Indeed, the poeticizing of Africa represents an attempt to reconcile mythic and profane time in the search for a positive ancestral model. This literary return to the Source is an attempt to encounter past positive values in a set of present negative circumstances.

Within the scope of this study, the problem of black identity, an issue during the early decades of the twentieth century in the writings of Uruguayans Brindis de Salas and Barrios, still commands the attention of the other seven poets. Significantly, in their call for equality and justice, Colombian blacks, at the other end of South America, are now repeating the same process of self-affirmation undertaken by their Uruguayan counterparts fifty years ago. Time and space have not significantly changed the manner in which blacks perceive themselves and are in turn perceived by society. There is, then, a continuity of vision among writers in terms of their interpretation of the Afro-Hispanic experience; their creations transcend geographic, temporal, and national boundaries. The human issues raised in the epigraph by Afro-Uruguayan Timoteo Olivera are crucial concerns today for Antonio Preciado and his cohorts.

Miscegenation, of course, is a key factor in human relations in many South American countries, and it raises an insoluble identity question that is passionately grappled with by Santa Cruz, Ortiz, and Estupiñán Bass primarily, in an effort to arrive at an ethnic balance. Interested persons in the United States are often accused of not understanding ethnic dynamics in Latin American societies due to a lack of perspective and the desire to apply their own foreign standards to South America. Indeed, in a review of his landmark study *The Black Image in Latin American Literature*, Richard Jackson is accused by Efraín Barradas of misinterpreting *mestizaje* (miscegenation) because he fails to recognize the dual nature of this blackening-whitening process. Based on my readings, experiences, and observation in South America, *mestizaje* is fine—so long as you come out at the lighter end of the spectrum. The writers discussed in this study make it clear that miscegenation has not solved their color problem. Moreover, the nonliterary sources that I cite at the beginning of each chapter support the fact that racism and discrimination are social practices confronted daily by most blacks in South America in spite of official versions to the contrary.

Given the treatment and present status of most blacks in South America, it is no surprise that the ideological bent of most of these writers is socialist. To a person they see, hear, speak, and write from the perspective of a dependent, minority culture. They view the combination of capitalism and oligarchy as oppressing all members of the lower classes in general and blacks in particular. While Brindis de Salas, Barrios, Santa Cruz, Ortiz, Estupiñán Bass, Preciado, Artel, Zapata Olivella, and Salazar Valdés all matured in societies where the official version of social dynamics is that class is more significant than race, all in one form or another have questioned that assumption. It is ironic that, so far, the poets who come from countries with the smallest number of blacks (Uruguay and Peru) are the ones who register the most vehement protests against racism and discrimination. Ecuadorians and Colombians recognize that it exists and reluctantly treat inequality as a normal part of societal functions.

If racism is part of American life, then what course do blacks have but to return to Africa—even if it is a mythic continent, hidden in legends and the past—for their dreams and for their inspiration? As a group, these nine writers perceive Africa as being the most important factor in creating and sustaining black cultural expression in South America. Although most of them have never seen Africa, they still sense its power within them as a source of inspiration for their understanding and poetic expression of the historical and ethnological presence of blacks in the Americas.

Notes

Notes to Introduction: Toward a Definition of Afro-Hispanic Poetry

1. Rosa E. Valdés Cruz, *La poesía negroide en America*, 11. *Negroide* meaning characteristic of blackness or similar to it is often used to describe features such as lips and hair in a derogatory sense.

2. Oscar Fernández de la Vega and Alberto N. Pamies, *Iniciación a la poesía afroamericana*, 72.

3. Enrique Noble, "Ethnic and Social Aspects of Negro Poetry of Latin America," 392.

4. Ibid., 393.

5. Ibid.

6. José Luis González and Mónica Mansour, *Poesía negra de América: Antología*, 27. I was unable to locate the term *negrista* in several dictionaries.

7. Mónica Mansour, *La poesía negrista*.

8. Leopoldo Zea, "Negritud e indigenismo," 17.

9. Adalberto Ortiz, "La negritud en la cultura latinoamericana," 10.

10. Janheinz Jahn, *Muntu: An Outline of the New African Culture*, 207.

11. René Depestre, "Saludo y Despedida a la Negritud," in *Africa en América Latina*, ed. Manuel Moreno Fraginals (Mexico: Siglo XXI, 1977), 346.

12. Martha Cobb, *Harlem, Haiti, and Havana: A Comparative Critical Study of Langston Hughes, Jacques Roumain, and Nicolás Guillén*, 53. Jackson's comments are in the conclusion of his article "Racial Identity and the Terminology of Literary Blackness in Spanish America," *Revista Chicano Riqueña* (Autumn 1978): 43–48.

13. Jackson, "Racial Identity," 48.

14. Edward Kamau Brathwaite, "The African Presence in Caribbean Literature," *Daedalus* 103, no. 2 (1974): 80–81.

15. Bonnie J. Barthold, *Black Time: Fiction of Africa, the Caribbean, and the United States*, 6.

16. Ibid., 7.

17. Ibid., 16.

18. Catherine Belsey, *Critical Practice*, 2.

19. Expressive realism is the theory that "literature reflects the *reality* of the experience as it is perceived by one individual, who *expresses* it in a discourse which enables other individuals to recognize it as true." Ibid., 7.

Notes to 1 Our Race: Modern Afro-Uruguayan Poetry

1. Leslie B. Rout, Jr., *The African Experience in Spanish America: 1502 to the Present Day*, 204.

2. Carlos M. Rama, *Los afro-uruguayos*, 79–80.

3. Ildefonso Pereda Valdés, *El negro en el Uruguay: Pasado y presente*, 192.

4. Ibid., 204.

5. Ibid., 213.

6. Alicia Behrens, *Marcha*, 4 May 1956, 10.

7. Ibid., 15 June 1956, 9.

8. This information is based upon my research in the Biblioteca Nacional in Montevideo during January 1981. See also Richard L. Jackson, *Black Writers in Latin America*, 93–111, for an excellent discussion of this period.

9. Letter to author from Alberto Britos, 29 December 1982.

10. Translations of Spanish throughout are my own, unless otherwise indicated.

11. Nestor Ortiz Oderigo, *Aspectos de la cultura africana en el Río de la Plata* (Buenos Aires: Editorial Plus Ultra, 1974), 122–23.

12. Ibid., 71.

13. Paulo de Carvalho-Neto, "The Candombe, A Dramatic Dance from the Afro-Uruguayan Folklore," *Ethnomusicology* 6, no. 3 (1962): 166.

14. Ibid., 168.

15. Rubén Carámbula, *Negro y tambor: Poemas, pregones, danzas y leyendas sobre motivos del folklore afrorioplatense*, 61.

16. *Nuestra Raza* 4, no. 44 (1937): 2.

17. Ibid., 11.

18. *Nuestra Raza* 5, no. 56 (1938): 1.

19. *Nuestra Raza* 5, no. 55 (1938): 9.

20. *Nuestra Raza* 5, no. 56 (1938): 4.

21. Ceferino Nieres, "El poeta Pilar E. Barrios, autor de *Piel negra* habla para Uruguay," 2.

> R.—¿En la lucha por nuestros problemas Ud. cree que se puede llegar a algo?
>
> B.—Siempre hay la posibilidad de llegar cuando se parte, amigo mío, aun cuando se toman caminos equivocados. Lo que no es posible, es realizar un viaje sin

antes emprenderlo . . . soy optimista a pesar de los desacuerdos y pesimismos reinantes.

Notes to 2
From Cañete to Tombuctú:
The Peruvian Poetry of Nicomedes Santa Cruz

1. Leslie B. Rout, Jr., *The African Experience in Spanish America: 1502 to the Present Day*, 226.

2. J. M. Valega, *Historia general de los peruanos*, 3:288. Two other recent histories that do not devote any attention to the blacks are Rubén Vargas Ugarte, S.J., *Historia general del Perú: La república 1879–1884*, 10 vols. (Lima: Milla Batres, 1971); and the *Nueva historia general del Perú: Un compendio* (Lima: Mosca Azul Editores, 1979), a collection of general essays.

3. Jorge Basadre, *Historia de la republica del Peru: 1822–1933*, 6th ed., 16:237.

4. See, for example, Héctor Centurión Vallejo, *Esclavitud y manumisión de negroes en Trujillo* (Trujillo: Universidad de Trujillo, 1954).

5. Denys Cuché, *Poder blanco y resistencia negra en el Perú*, 11.

6. Ibid., 164.

7. Luis Millones, *Tugurio: La cultura de los marginados* (Lima: Instituto Nacional de Cultura, 1978), 42–43.

8. Ibid., 61.

9. Ibid.

10. Luis Alberto Sánchez, *Introducción crítica a la literatura peruana*, 165.

11. Nicomedes Santa Cruz, personal interview with author, 8 June 1979.

12. They are "Si tú eres cantor completo," "Eres de carpintería," "De tu joven corazón," "El jilguero que bien canta," "A la muerte no le temas," "Nada en este mundo dura," "Muerte, si otra muerte hubiera," and "Muerte que tanto te ensayas."

13. Quotations from *Décimas* are from the Juan Mejía Baca edition, 1960; translations throughout chapter are mine.

14. Nestor Ortiz Oderigo, *Aspectos de la cultura africana en el Río de la Plata* (Buenos Aires: Editorial Plus Ultra, 1974), 106. The *minnesinger* were German lyric poets and musicians of the twelfth to the fourteenth centuries; the *troubadors, trovadores*, were lyric poets-musicians from the eleventh through thirteenth centuries in France, Italy, and Spain; the *minstrels* were musical performers and comedians of the nineteenth century in the United States; and the *jilli keas* were African popular poets-musicians of the

eighteenth and nineteenth centuries. These performers have in common their adherence to the oral tradition and their emphasis upon perpetuating popular culture.

15. Ortiz Oderigo, *Aspectos de la cultura*, 106.

16. "Nicomedes Santa Cruz y la poesía de su conciencia de negritud," *Cuadernos Americanos* 5 (1975) : 182–99.

17. Leonard Harris, "Philosophy in the Black World." The author maintains, "Negritude conceived of black cultural values as a unit, rather than strictly a national or local cultural phenomenon. The aesthetic and moral values endemic to traditional Africa carried worldwide in the cultural germ of the African diaspora, were considered just values upon which a progressive society could be built" (838). In principle these ideas sound great, but for practical purposes they are not strictly applicable in Latin America due to national and cultural distinctions that *negritud* sought to unify.

18. René Depestre, "Saludo y despedida a la negritud" in *Africa en América Latina*, ed. Manuel Moreno Fraginals (Mexico: Siglo XXI, 1977), 337–62.

19. Ibid., 344.

20. Ibid., 347.

21. Ibid., 355.

22. Pedro M. Benvenutto Murrieta, *El lenguaje peruano*, 103. Santa Cruz gives a list of black contributions to the "Replana" in "Replana y jerga" in *Estampa*, 14 June 1964, and "Jerga y replana," *Estampa*, 21 June 1964.

23. Cuché, *Poder blanco y resistencia*, 181.

24. *La Crónica*, 6 January 1957.

25. Nicomedes Santa Cruz, personal interview with author, 31 July 1979.

26. Raúl Banchero Castellano, *La verdadera historia del Señor de los Milagros* (Lima: Inti-Sol, 1976), 10.

27. Luis Millones, *Minorías étnicas en el Perú* (Lima: Pontifica Universidad Católica, 1973), 19.

28. Clorinda Pachas Torres, *Paisaje geográfico de Chincha* (Chincha: N.p., 1978), 52.

29. Jaime Marroquín, et al., *Documental del Perú: Ica*, 51.

30. *La Prensa*, 13 February 1953.

31. This poem is included in an interview with Roberto Remo, "Afroamérica: las raíces de la unidad."

32. Depestre, "Saludo y despedida a la negritud," 361–62.

33. *Cuadernos del Tercer Mundo* 2, no. 12 (1977): 102.

34. Ibid.

35. Ibid.

36. Ibid., 104.

Notes to 3
From Esmeraldas to Eternity:
Afro-Ecuadorian Poetry

1. Alfredo Espinosa Tamayo, *Psicología y sociología del pueblo ecuatoriano*, 38–39.
2. Alfredo Fuentes Roldán, "San Lorenzo: Puerto marítimo de población negra," 372.
3. Leslie B. Rout, Jr., "The Afro-Ecuadorean in the National Culture," in *The African Experience in Spanish America: 1502 to the Present Day*, 230–32.
4. Thomas E. Weil, et al., *Area Handbook for Ecuador*, 80–81.
5. Norman E. Whitten, Jr., *Black Frontiersmen: A South American Case*, 199.
6. Wistting Fierro Ruiz, *Los ecuatorianos despreciados y humillados*, 36.
7. Violeta Luna, *La lírica ecuatoriana actual*, 20.
8. Rodrigo Pesántez Rodas, *Poesía de un tiempo*, 11–12.
9. Luna, 16.
10. Wilfred Cartey, *Black Images*, 45.
11. Adalberto Ortiz, "La negritud en la cultura latinoamericana," 10.
12. Ibid., 18.
13. G. R. Coulthard, "Antecedentes de la negritud en la literatura hispanoamericana," 76–77.
14. Ibid., 77.
15. The 1945 edition does not contain the poems "Lo verán y lo veremos," "La despedida," and "Desvelo." Quoted passages are from the 1953 edition; translations throughout are mine.
16. Tomás García Pérez, "Leyenda Canción de la Tunda," in Julio Estupiñán Tello, *El negro en Esmeraldas: Apuntes para su estudio*, 158.
17. Ibid., 159.
18. Benjamin Núñez, *Dictionary of Afro-Latin American Civilization*, 81.
19. In a relevant discussion of "nominal realism," J. Bekunuru Kubayanda explains, "In African oral traditions, nominal realism . . . encompasses the various realms of discourse (including poetic formulae) in divination and ritual sacrifices, libation ceremonies, mortuary and birth rites, and other similar oral practices. In the New World context, nominal realism comes to the surface in the verbal art, that is, the incantations and songs of the obeah men, *macumberos, santeros,* and other priests and priestesses of the African-derived religions." *Afro-Hispanic Review* 1, no. 3 (1982):25.

20. Núñez, 286.
21. Ibid., 366.
22. Adalberto Ortiz, *Fórmulas: Poemario "sin poesía,"* 83.
23. Janheinz Jahn, *Muntu: An Outline of the New African Culture*, 100.
24. Ibid., 101–2.
25. M. Acosta Solís, *Nuevas contribuciones al conocimiento de la Provincia de Esmeraldas*, 1:493.
26. Rodas, *Poesía de un tiempo*, 60.
27. Nelson Estupiñán Bass, "La lira negra," 6–14.
28. Ibid., 14.

Notes to 4
In Search of Blackness:
The Afro-Colombian Poet

1. Manuel Zapata Olivella, *El hombre colombiano*, 17.
2. Aquiles Escalante, *El negro en Colombia*, 5. It is estimated that 30 percent of the population has some African blood. Most blacks occupy the Pacific lowlands that extend into Panama and Ecuador.
3. Juan Luis de Lannoy and Gustavo Pérez, *Estructuras democráticas y sociales de Colombia*, 112.
4. Leslie B. Rout, Jr., *The African Experience in Spanish America: 1502 to the Present Day*, 247.
5. Ildefonso Gutiérrez Azopardo, *Historia del negro en Colombia*, 88–89.
6. Rout, *The African Experience*, 248.
7. Juvenal Herrera Torres, "Prólogo," *Jorge Artel: antología poética*, vii.
8. Ibid., ix.
9. Luis María Sánchez López, *Diccionario de escritores colombianos*, 50.
10. Delia Zapata Olivella, "La Cumbia: síntesis musical de la nación colombiana," 190–91.
11. For a discussion of the exploits of this historical figure, see Rout, *The African Experience*, 106.
12. See ibid., 109–10, for an explanation of Afro-Colombian resistance to slavery.
13. Sánchez López, *Diccionario de escritores colombianos*, 434.
14. Jaime Mejía Duque, "El Chocó en la nueva poesía americana: a propósito de un libro," 736.
15. Hugo Salazar Valdés, *Casi la luz*. This volume also contains *Coals at Dawn* and *Dimension on Earth*. Citations are from this edition. Translations are my own throughout.

Bibliography

General

Arnold, James A. *Modernism and Negritude: The Poetry and Poetics of Aimé Césaire.* Cambridge: Harvard University Press, 1981.

Ballagas, Emilio. *Mapa de la poesía americana.* Buenos Aires: Pleamar, 1946.

Barthold, Bonnie J. *Black Time: Fiction of Africa, the Caribbean, and the United States.* New Haven: Yale University Press, 1981.

Belsey, Catherine. *Critical Practice.* New York: Methuen, 1980.

Bueno, Salvador, ed. *Introducción a la cultura africana en América Latina (1970).* 2d ed. Paris: UNESCO, 1979.

Carter, Shelia, ed. *Poetry of the Spanish Speaking Caribbean.* Mona, Jamaica: University of the West Indies, 1980.

Cartey, Wilfred. *Black Images.* New York: Teacher's College Press, 1970.

Carvalho-Neto, Paulo de. *El folklore de las luchas sociales.* Mexico: Siglo XXI, 1973.

Castro de Lee, Cecilia. "El niño en la poesía negroide hispano-americana." *Boletín Cultural y Bibliográfico* 16 (1979): 57–73.

Cobb, Martha. *Harlem, Haiti, and Havana: A Comparative Critical Study of Langston Hughes, Jacques Roumain, and Nicolás Guillén.* Washington: Three Continents Press, 1979.

Coulthard, G. R. "Antecedentes de la negritud en la literatura hispanoamericana." *Mundo Nuevo* 11 (1967): 73–77.

Cunard, Nancy. *Negro Anthology (1931–32).* 1934. Reprint. New York: Negro Universities Press, 1969.

Dathorne, O. R. *Dark Ancestor: The Literature of the Black Man in the Caribbean.* Baton Rouge: Louisiana State University Press, 1981.

Domíngez, Ivo. "En torno a la poesía afro-hispanoamericana." *Cuadernos Hispanoamericanos* 319 (1977): 125–31.

Dzidzienyo, Anani. "Activity and Inactivity in the Politics of Afro-Latin America." *Secolas Annals* 9 (1978): 48–61.

Esquenazi-Mayo, Roberto. "Impacto de África en la literatura hispanoamericana." In *Expression, Communication and Experience in Literature and Language,* edited by Ronald G. Popperwell, 135–37. London: Modern Humanities Research Association, 1973.

Fernández de la Vega, Oscar, and Alberto N. Pamies. *Iniciación a la poesía afroamericana.* Miami: Universal, 1973.

Fontaine, Pierre-Michel. "Research in the Political Economy of Afro-Latin America." *Latin American Research Review* 15 (1980): 111–41.

González, José Luis, and Mónica Mansour. *Poesía negra de América: Antología.* Mexico: Ediciones Era, 1976.

González Cruz, Luis F. "Nature and the Black Reality in Three Caribbean Poets: A New Look at the Concept of Negritude." *Perspectives on Contemporary Literature* 5 (1979): 138–46.

González-Pérez, Armando. *Antología clave de la poesía negra afroamericana.* Madrid: Ediciones Alcalá, 1976.

Jackson, Richard. "Canción negra sin color: la experiencia negra y la negritud de síntesis en la poesía afrohispanoamericana contemporánea." *Instituto Internacional de Literatura Iberoamericana* 2 (1978): 921–30.

———. *The Black Image in Latin American Literature.* Albuquerque: University of New Mexico Press, 1976.

————. *Black Writers in Latin America*. Albuquerque: University of New Mexico Press, 1979.

Jahn, Janheinz. *Bibliography of Neo-African Literature from Africa, America and the Caribbean*. New York: Praeger, 1965.

————. *Muntu: An Outline of the New African Culture*. Trans. Marjorie Grene. New York: Grove Press, 1961.

————. "Poetry in Rumba Rhythms." In *Introduction to African Literature*, edited by Ulli Beier, 139–50. London: Longmans, 1967.

Kennedy, Ellen Conroy, ed. *The Negritude Poets*. New York: Viking, 1975.

Kubayanda, J. Bekunuru. "The Linguistic Core of Afro-Hispanic Poetry: An African Reading." *Afro-Hispanic Review* 3 (1982): 21–26.

Latino, Simón, ed. *Antología de la poesía negra latinoamericana*. Buenos Aires: N.p., 1963.

Levine, Robert M. *Race and Ethnic Relations in Latin America and the Caribbean: A Bibliography*. Metuchen, N.J.: Scarecrow Press, 1980.

Mamonton, Stephen. "A presenca da África na poesía latino american do sec XX." *Africa* 4 (1979): 420–26.

Mansour, Mónica. *La poesía negrista*. Mexico: Era, 1973.

Megenney, William. "Common Words of African Origin Used in Latin America." *Hispania* 66 (1983): 1–10.

Moreno Fraginals, Manuel, ed. *Africa en América Latina*. Mexico: Siglo XXI, 1977.

Morner, Magnus. *Race Mixture in the History of Latin America*. Boston: Little, Brown and Co., 1967.

Nascimiento, Elisa. *Pan-Africanism and South America*. Buffalo: Afrodiaspora, 1980.

Noble, Enrique. "Ethnic and Social Aspects of Negro Poetry of Latin America." *The Phylon Quarterly* 4 (1958): 391–401.

Nuñez, Benjamín. *Dictionary of Afro-Latin American Civilization*. Westport, Conn.: Greenwood Press, 1980.

Ortiz, Adalberto. "La negritud en la cultura latinoamericana: Poemas negristas." *Expresiones Culturales del Ecuador* 1 (1972): 10–18.

Pereda Valdés, Ildefonso. *Antología de la poesía negra americana*. Santiago, Chile: Ediciones Ercilla, 1936.

————. *Antología de la poesía negra americana*. 2d ed. Montevideo: Organización Medina, 1953.

Rout, Leslie B., Jr. *The African Experience in Spanish America: 1502 to the Present Day*. New York: Cambridge University Press, 1976.

Sanz y Díaz, José. *Lira negra: selecciones afroamericanas y españoles*. Madrid: Aguilar, 1945.

Szwed, John F., and Roger D. Abrahams. *The West Indies, Central and South America*. Part 2 of *Afro-American Folk Culture: An Annotated Bibliography*. Philadelphia: ISHI, 1978.

Toruño, Juan Felipe. *Poesía negra: ensayo y antología*. Mexico: Colección Obsidiana, 1953.

Ullrich, Polly. "Gwendolyn Brooks: The Bard of Blackness." *Chicago Sun-Times*, 1 October 1980, 55.

Valdés Cruz, Rosa E. *La poesía negroide en América*. New York: Las Américas, 1970.

Williams, Lorna V. *Self and Society in the Poetry of Nicolás Guillén*. Baltimore: Johns Hopkins University Press, 1982.

Wilson, Leslie N. *La poesía afroantillana*. Miami: Universal, 1979.

Zea, Leopoldo. "Negritud e indigenismo." *Cuadernos Americanos* 6 (November–December 1974): 16–30.

Uruguay

Authors

Barrios, Pilar. *Piel negra: poesías (1917–1947)*. Montevideo: Nuestra Raza, 1947.
————. *Mis cantos*. Montevideo: Comité Amigos del Poeta, 1949.
————. *Campo afuera: poemas*. Montevideo: Publicaciones Minerva, 1959.
Brindis de Salas, Virginia. *Pregón de Marimorena: poemas*. Montevideo: Sociedad Cultural Editora Indoamericana, 1946.
————. *Cien cárceles de amor*. Montevideo: Compañía Impresora, 1949.

Other Works Consulted

Ayestarán, Lauro. *El folklore musical uruguayo*. Montevideo: Arca, 1967.
Barrios Pintos, Anibal. "Negros esclavos y libres." *El Día: Suplemento Dominical* (Montevideo), 18 June 1978, 1–3; 25 June 1978, 3–4.
Becco, Horacio Jorge. *Negros y morenos en el cancionero rioplatense*. Buenos Aires: Sociedad Argentina de Americanistas, 1953.
Britos, Alberto. "El libro que la raza espera." *Nuestra Raza* 167 (1947): 8.
Carámbula, Rubén. *Negro y tambor: poemas, pregones, danzas y leyendas sobre motivos del folklore afro-rioplatense*. Buenos Aires: Editorial Folklórica Americana, 1952.
Carvalho-Neto, Paulo de. "The Candombe, a Dramatic Dance from Afro-Uruguayan Folklore." *Ethnomusicology* 3 (1962): 164–74.
————. *El carnaval de Montevideo: folklore, historia, sociología*. Seville: Universidad de Sevilla, 1967.
————. *El negro uruguayo: hasta la abolición*. Quito: Editorial Universitaria, 1965.
————. *Estudios afros: Brasil-Paraguay-Uruguay-Ecuador*. Caracas: Universidad Central de Venezuela, 1971.
Diggs, Irene. "The Negro in the Viceroyalty of the Río de la Plata." *The Journal of Negro History* 3 (1951): 281–301.
Flores, El Pardo. "Palermo tiene ya su poeta de color en Juan J. Arrascaeta." *La Razón*, 12 March 1947, 16.
"Fue homenajeada la autora de *Pregón de Marimorena*." *Nuestra Raza* 154 (1946): 9.
Ganón, Issac. *Estructura social del Uruguay*. Montevideo: Editorial As, 1966.
Garganico, John F. "El perfil del negro en la narrativa rioplatense." *Historiografía y Bibliografía Americanistas* 21 (1977): 71–109.
Guadalupe, Julio. *Canto para la noche grande de Ramón Pereyra*. Montevideo: Imprenta Metro, 1959.
Ibarburú, Alba. "El negro en el Uruguay." *Revista Bahía Hulan-Jack* 7 (1962): 25–27.
Isola, Ema. *La esclavitud en el Uruguay: desde sus comienzos hasta su extinción (1743–1852)*. Montevideo: Instituto de Investigaciones Históricas, 1975.
Lanuza, José Luis. *Morenada*. Buenos Aires: Emecé, 1946.
Nieres, Ceferino. "El poeta Pilar Barrios, autor de *Piel negra*, habla para Uruguay." *Revista Uruguay* 3, no. 36 (1948): 2–3.
Pereda Valdés, Ildefonso. *Antología de la Poesía negra americana*. 2d ed. Montevideo: Medina, 1953.
————. *El negro en el uruguay: Pasado y presente*. Montevideo: Revista del Instituto Histórico y Geográfico del Uruguay, 1965.
————. *El negro en la epopeya artiguista*. Montevideo: Barreiro y Ramos, 1964.
————. *El negro rioplatense y otros ensayos*. Montevideo: Claudio García, 1937.
————. *Toda la poesía negra de Ildefonso Pereda Valdés*. Montevideo: Indice Mimeográfica-Offset, 1979.
"Pregón de Marimorena." *Nuestra Raza* 153 (1946): 9–10.
Prince, Blake. "Virginia Brindis de Salas, poetisa de rara concepción lírica." *Nuestra Raza* 149 (1946): 6–8.

Rama, Carlos M. *Los afro-uruguayos.* Montevideo: El Siglo Ilustrado, 1967.
Suárez Peña, Lino. *La raza negra en el Uruguay: novela histórica de su paso por la esclavitud.* Montevideo: Talleres Gráficas Moderna, 1983.
Wilson, Leslie N. *La poesía afroantillana.* Miami: Universal, 1979.

Peru

Author

Santa Cruz, Nicomedes. *Décimas.* Edición no venal. Lima: Juan Mejía Baca, 1959.
————. *Décimas.* Lima: Juan Mejía Baca, 1960.
————. *Décimas.* 2d ed. Lima: Librería Studium, 1966.
————. *Cumanana: décimas de pie forzado y poemas.* Lima: Juan Mejía Baca, 1964.
————. *Canto a mi Perú.* Lima: Librería Studium, 1966.
————. *Ritmos negros del Perú.* Buenos Aires: Losada, 1971.
————. *Décimas y poemas: antología.* Lima: Campodónico, 1971.

Other Works Consulted

Alarco, Rosa. "Danza de los negritos de Huánuco." *Revista de la Universidad Nacional Mayor de San Marcos* 13 (1975): 55–96.
Angeles Caballero, César. "El folklore negro del Perú." *La Crónica,* 6 January 1957, 8.
Banchero Castellano, Raul. *La verdadera historia del Señor de los Milagros.* Lima: Inti-Sol, 1976.
Basadre, Jorge. *Historia de la República del Perú, 1822–1933.* Vol. 16. Lima: Editorial Universitaria, 1970.
Bendezu Neyra, Guillermo. *Argot limeño o jerga criolla del Perú.* Lima: Editora Lima, 1977.
Benvenutto Murrieta, Pedro M. "El lenguaje peruano." Ph.D. diss., Universidad Católica, 1936.
Boisset, Felipe M. *El problema racial en el Perú.* Lima: Imprenta Unión, 1919.
Bustamente, Carlos Inga, Calixto. *El lazarillo de ciegos caminantes.* 1773. Reprint. Lima: Peisa, 1974.
Castañeda, Jorge. "El negro en el Perú." *Mercurio Peruano* 490 (1972): 92–95.
Castro Arenas, Mario. "Cumanana." *Correo,* 7 February 1965, 17.
Cuché, Denys. *Poder blanco y resistencia negra en el Perú.* Lima: Instituto Nacional de Cultura, 1975.
Donaire Vizarreta, Juan. *Campiña iqueña: aspectos folklóricos.* 2d ed. Lima: Talleres Gráficos Mercagraph, 1959.
Donayre, Jorge. "Nicomedes: un permanente diálogo de amor con el pueblo." *Expreso,* 4 June 1964, 12.
Espinar, Rodolfo. "Nicomedes Santa Cruz: el intelectual del pelo." *Expreso, Estampa,* 6 November 1966, 18–19.
Fajardo de Marin, Luz Girao. *Monografía del distrito de Ica.* Lima: N.p., 1965.
Fuentes, Manuel Atanasio. *Lima: apuntes históricos, descriptivos, estadísticos y de costumbres.* Paris: Imprenta E. Moreno, 1925.
Handy, Otis. "The Spanish American Décima and Nicomedes Santa Cruz." Ph.D. diss., University of California, Berkeley, 1979.
Harris, Leonard. "Philosophy in the Black World." *Negro History Bulletin* 41 (1978): 836–40.
Hildebrandt, Martha. *Peruanismos.* Lima: Moncloa-Campodónico, 1969.
Ibarra, Begoña. "Nicomedes, él de las décimas." *La Prensa, 7 días del Perú y del mundo,* 24 July 1966, 34.
Kattar, Jeannette. "Nicomedes Santa Cruz, Poete Noir du Peru." Université de Dakar, *Annales de la Faculté des lettres et Sciences Humaines* 7 (1977): 184–208.

Larraburre y Unánue, Eugenio. *Cañete: apuntes geográficos, históricos, estadísticas y arqueológicos.* Lima: Imprenta del Estado, 1874.

Laschober, Paula Jeanne. "Socio-Economic Aspects of Juan del Valle y Caviedes' Satire of Colonial Afro-Peruvians." Ph.D. diss., University of Washington, 1979.

León García, Enrique. "Las razas en Lima: estudio demográfico." Ph.D. diss., Universidad de San Marcos, 1909.

Mac-Lean y Estenós, Roberto. *Negros en el Perú.* Lima: Editorial D. M. Miranda, 1947.

Marroquín, Jaime, et al. *Documental del Perú: Ica.* 2d ed. Lima: N.p., 1970.

Matos Mar, José, and Jorge A. Carbajal H., eds. *Erasmo: Yanacón del Valle de Chancay.* Lima: Instituto de Estudios Peruanos, 1974.

Miranda Tarrillo, Ricardo. "Nico Cumanana: Arte popular negroide costeño." *La Prensa, 7 días del Perú y del mundo,* 7 February 1965, 19.

Neira Samanez, Hugo. "A lo universal por lo negro: otra sorpresa en Nicomedes." *Expreso,* 6 April 1964, 10.

"Nicomedes um rapsodo peruano." *Jornal de Letras* 169 (1963): 1–6.

Nueva historia general del Perú: un compendio. Lima: Mosca Azul, 1979.

Pachas Torres, Clorinda. *Paisaje geográfico de Chincha.* Chincha: N.p., 1978.

Palma, Clemente. *El porvenir de las razas en el Perú.* Lima: Imprenta Torres Aguirre, 1897.

Pavletich, Esteven, Javier Pulgar Vidal, and Nicolás Viscaya. *Antología de los negritos.* Huánuco: Editorial Santa María, 1973.

Poniatowska, Elena. "Habla el peruano Nicomedes Santa Cruz." *Siempre* 1103 (1974): 39–41, 70.

Radiguet, Max. *Lima y la sociedad peruana.* 1856. Reprint. Lima: Biblioteca Nacional, 1971.

Remo, Roberto. "Afroamérica: las raices de la unidad." *Cuadernos del Tercer Mundo* 2, 12 (1977): 96–104.

Rojas Alva, Alberto. "Los Santa Cruz: herederos conservan la tradicional fama del apellido." *La Prensa, 7 días del Perú y del mundo,* 3 April 1960, 14–15.

Romero, Emilio. *El santo de la escoba: Fray Martín de Porras.* Lima: Juan Mejía Baca, 1959.

Romero, Fernando. "La evolución de la marinera." *Organo del Instituto Cultural Peruano Norteamericano* 6 (1946): 11–21; 8 (1947): 12–20.

Salas, Teresa C., and Henry J. Richards. "Nicomedes Santa Cruz y la poesía de su negritud." *Cuadernos Americanos* 5 (1975): 182–99.

———. "El tema de la liberación en la poesía de Nicomedes Santa Cruz." *Cuadernos Americanos* 4 (1981): 182–94.

———. *Asedios a la poesía de Nicomedes Santa Cruz.* Quito: Editora Andina, 1982.

Salazar Bondy, Sebastián. "Nicomedes ante su enigma." *El Comercio, Dominical Semanario,* 24 May 1964, 8.

Sánchez, Luis Alberto. *Introducción crítica a la literatura peruana.* Lima: P. L. Villanueva, 1974.

Santa Cruz, Nicomedes. "De Senegal y Malambo." *Caretas* 479 (1973): 22–24.

———. "La décima en el Perú." *El Comercio,* 1 October 1961, 2, 11.

———. "Folklore peruano: Cumanana." *Estampa,* 24 May 1964, 5.

———. "Racismo en el Perú." *Estampa,* 24 September 1967, 12.

Thompkins, William David. "The Marinera: A Historical and Analytical Study of the National Dance of Peru." Master's thesis, University of California, Los Angeles, 1973.

Tolmos Marcos, Luis. *Síntesis monográfica de la provincia de Chincha.* Chincha: N.p., 1968.

Valcárcel, Luis. *Ruta cultural del Perú.* 1945. Reprint. Lima: Editorial Universo, 1973.

Valcárcel, Rosina. *Universitarios y prejuicio étnico: un estudio del prejuicio hacia el negro en los universitarios de Lima*. Lima: Escuela de Administración de Negocios, 1974.

Valega, J. M. *Historia general de los peruanos*. 3 vols. Lima: Iberia, 1968.

Vargas Ugarte, Rubén. *Historia general del Perú: la república 1879–1884*. 10 vols. Lima: Milla Batros, 1971.

———. *Vida de San Martín de Porras*. Buenos Aires: Imprenta López, 1963.

———. *El beato Martín de Porras*. Buenos Aires: Editorial Coni, 1949.

Ecuador

Authors

Estupiñán Bass, Nelson. *Canto negro por la luz: poemas para negros y blancos*. Quito: Editorial Rumiñahui, 1954.

———. *Timarán y Cuabú: cuaderno de poesía para el pueblo*. Quito: Casa de Cultura Ecuatoriana, 1956.

———. *Las huellas digitales: poemas*. Quito: Casa de la Cultura Ecuatoriana, 1971.

———. *Las tres carabelas: poesía, relato y teatro*. Portoviejo: Editorial Gregorio, 1973.

———. *El desempate: cuaderno de poesía para el pueblo*. Portoviejo: Editorial Gregorio, 1980.

Ortiz, Adalberto. *Tierra, son y tambor: cantares negros y mulatos*. Mexico: La Cigarra, 1945.

———. *Tierra, son y tambor: cantares negros y mulatos*. 2d ed. Guayaquil: Casa de la Cultura Ecuatoriana, 1953.

———. *Camino y puerto de la angustia: poemas*. Mexico: Isla, 1945.

———. *El animal herido: antología poética*. Quito: Casa de la Cultura Ecuatoriana, 1959.

———. *Fórmulas; El vigilante insepulto; Tierra, son y tambor*. Quito: Casa de la Cultura Ecuatoriana, 1973.

Preciado, Antonio. *Jolgorio: poemas*. Quito: Casa de la Cultura Ecuatoriana, 1961.

———. *Tal como somos*. Quito: Ediciones Siglo 20, 1969.

Other Works Consulted

Acosta Solís, Misael. *Nuevas contribuciones al conocimiento de la provincia de Esmeraldas*. Vol. 1. Quito: Editorial Ecuador, 1944.

Barriga López, Franklin and Leonardo Barriga López. *Diccionario de la literatura ecuatoriana*. Quito: Casa de la Cultura Ecuatoriana, 1973.

Coba Andrade, Carlos. *Literatura popular afro-ecuatoriana*. Otavalo: Instituto Cultural, 1980.

Cornejo, Justino. *Los que tenemos de mandinga*. Guayaquil: Editorial Gregorio Portoviejo, 1974.

Espinosa Tamayo, Alfredo. *Psicología y sociología del pueblo ecuatoriano*. Guayaquil: Imprenta Municipal, 1918.

Estupiñán Bass, Nelson. "Apuntes sobre el negro de Esmeraldas en la literatura ecuatoriana." *Norte* 5 (1967): 101–4.

———. "La Lira Negra." *Colegio Nacional 5 de agosto* (1981): 6–14.

Estupiñán Tello, Julio. *El negro en Esmeraldas: apuntes para su estudio*. Quito: Talleres Gráficos Nacionales, 1967.

Fierro Ruiz, Wistting. *Los ecuatorianos despreciados y humillados*. Cuenca: Publicaciones y Papeles, 1979.

Fuentes Roldán, Alfredo. "San Lorenzo: puerto marítimo de población negra." *Boletín de Informaciones Científicas Nacionales* 88 (1958): 368–91.

García-Barrio, Constance. "Blacks in Ecuadorian Literature." In *Cultural Transformation and Ethnicity in Modern Ecuador*, edited by Norman E. Whitten, 535–62. Urbana: University of Illinois Press, 1981.

Guevara, Dario. "El refranero de Timarán y Cuabú." *Letras del Ecuador* 114 (1959): 18, 21.

Luna, Violeta. *La lírica ecuatoriana actual*. Quito: Casa de la Cultura Ecuatoriana, 1973.

Martán Góngora, Helcías. "Nelson Estupiñán Bass: *el último río.*" *Boletín cultural y bibliográfico* 2 (1967): 356–57.

Newman, Ronna Smith. "Life and Works of Adalberto Ortiz." Ph.D. diss., Northwestern University, 1981.

Paredes Borja, Virigilio. *Tercera época*. Vol. 1 of *Historia de la medicina en el Ecuador*. Quito: Casa de la Cultura Ecuatoriana, 1963.

Peñaherrera de Costales, Piedad, and Alfredo Costales Samaniego. *Coanque, historia cultural y social de los negros del Chota y Salinas*. Quito: Instituto Ecuatoriano de Antropología y Geografía, 1958.

Pesántez Rodas, Rodrigo. *Poesía de un tiempo*. Quito: Casa de la Cultura Ecuatoriana, 1974.

Preston, D. A. "Negro, Mestizo and the Indian in an Andean Environment." *The Geographical Journal* 131, pt. 2 (1965): 220–34.

Ramón y Rivera, Luis Felipe. "Música afro-ecuatoriana." *Folklore Americano* 15 (1967): 70–86.

Unión Panamericana. *Diccionario de la literatura latinoamericana*. Vol. 5. Washington, D.C., 1962.

Walker, Michael Lee. "The Black Social Identity in Selected Novels of Nelson Estupiñán Bass and Adalberto Ortiz." Ph.D. diss., University of California, Riverside, 1977.

Weil, Thomas, et al. *Area Handbook for Ecuador*. Washington, D.C.: U.S. Government Printing Office, 1973.

Whitten, Norman. *Black Frontiersmen*. Cambridge, Mass.: Schenkman, 1974.

Colombia

Authors

Artel, Jorge. *Tambores en la noche: 1931–1934*. Cartagena: Editora Bolivar, 1940.

———. *Poemas con botas y banderas*. Barranquilla: Universidad del Atlántico, 1972.

———. *Antología poética*. Bogotá: Ecoe Ediciones, 1979.

Salazar Valdés, Hugo. *Sal y lluvia*. Cali: Tip. Lutamon, 1948.

———. *Carbones en el alba*. Bogotá: Editorial Iqueima, 1951.

———. *Dimensión de la tierra (1947–1952)*. Popayán: Universidad del Cauca, 1952.

———. *Casi la luz*. Bogotá: Editorial Cosmos, 1954.

———. *La patria convocada*. Bogotá: Litografía Villegas, 1955.

———. *El héroe cantado*. Bogotá: Editorial ABC, 1956.

———. *Toda la voz*. Bogotá: Imprenta Nacional, 1958.

———. *Pleamar: poemas*. Cali: Departamento del Valle, 1975.

———. *Rostro iluminado del Chocó*. Cali: Impresión Feriva, 1980.

Zapata Olivella, Juan. *Albedrío total: poemas*. Guatemala: José de Pineda Ibarra, 1970.

———. *Amor en azul transparente*. Guatemala: José de Pineda Ibarra, 1971.

———. *Bullanguero: poesía popular*. Bogotá: Ediciones Tercer Mundo, 1974.

———. *Panacea: poesía liberada*. Cartagena: Editora Bolívar, 1976.

———. *La hamaca soñadora*. Cartagena: Heliógrafo Moderno, 1979.

Other Works Consulted

Arrazola, Roberto. *Palenque, primer pueblo libre de América: historia de las sublevaciones de los esclavos de Cartagena.* Cartagena: Ediciones Hernández, 1970.

Escalante, Aquiles. *El negro en Colombia.* Bogotá: Universidad Nacional de Colombia, 1964.

Gutiérrez Azopardo, Ildefonso. *Historia del negro en Colombia: ¿sumisión o rebeldía?* Bogotá: Editorial Nueva América, 1980.

Holguín, Andrés, ed. *Antología crítica de la poesía colombiana.* 2 vols. Bogotá: Biblioteca del Centenario del Banco de Colombia, 1974.

Humphry, Norman D. "Race, Caste and Class in Colombia." *Phylon* 2 (1952): 161–66.

Lannoy, Juan Luis de, and Gustavo Pérez. *Estructuras demográficas y sociales de Colombia.* Bogotá: Centro de Investigaciones Sociales, 1961.

Mejía Duque, Jaime. "El Chocó en la nueva poesía americana." *Bolívar* 34 (1954): 734–37.

Morales, Guillermo Abadía. *La música folklórica colombiana.* Bogotá: Universidad Nacional de Bogotá, 1973.

Orjuela, Héctor H. *Bibliografía de la poesía colombiana.* Bogotá: Instituto Caro y Cuervo, 1971.

Pardo Tovar, Andrés. *La poesía popular colombiana y sus orígenes españoles.* Bogotá: Ediciones Tercer Mundo, 1966.

Pujol, Nicole. "La raza negra en el Chocó: antropología física." *Revista Colombiana de Antropología* 15 (1970–1971): 257–92.

Sánchez López, Luis María. *Diccionario de escritores colombianos.* Barcelona: Plaza y Janés, 1978.

Sanders, Thomas G. "The Blacks of Colombia's Chocó." *American Universities Field Staff: Field Staff Reports* (January 1970): 1–7.

Sayers, William C. "Racial Mixture and Cultural Variation in a Rural Colombian Community." *América Indígena* 3 (1956): 221–30.

Velásquez, Rogerio. "Leyendas y cuentos de la raza negra: leyendas del Alto y Bajo Chocó." *Revista Colombiana de Folclor* 4 (1960): 71–120.

———. "Adivinanzas del Alto y Bajo Chocó." *Revista Colombiana de Folclor* 5 (1960): 103–29.

West, Robert Cooper. *The Pacific Lowlands of Colombia: A Negroid Area of the American Tropics.* Baton Rouge: Louisiana State University Press, 1957.

Zapata Olivella, Delia. "La Cumbia: síntesis musical de la nación colombiana." *Revista Colombiana de Folclor* 7 (1962): 188–204.

Zapata Olivella, Manuel. *El hombre colombiano.* Bogotá: Canal Ramírez-Antares, 1974.

Index